A Guide to
NAMIBIAN
GAME PARKS

WILLIE & SANDRA OLIVIER

Longman
Namibia

Longman Namibia (Pty) Ltd
Eros Shopping Centre, Cnr Omuramba and Klein Windhoek Roads,
PO Box 9251, Windhoek

Associated companies, branches and representatives throughout
the world

© Longman Namibia 1993

First published 1993

ISBN 99916 1 005 7

Design concept by Etienne van Dyker
Cover photographs:
    Sand-dune at Sossusvlei © Tony Pupkewitz
    Elephants at an Etosha waterhole © Mark van Aardt
Cover design by Janine Poezyn
Textual photographs:
    © Willie and Sandra Olivier, © Mark van Aardt and © Jonathan Wright
Maps by Anne Westoby
Line illustrations by Anne Westoby and Hélène Marshall

Set in 9/10 pt Stone Serif
Typesetting and reproduction by Peter Green & Associates, Cape Town
Printed by CTP Book Printers, Cape Town

Acknowledgements

The publishers and authors wish to thank the following for
permission to reproduce material in this Guide:

The Council for Scientific and Industrial Research (CSIR) in Pretoria
for the LANDSAT MSS image of the Kuiseb River which was received
and processed by the Satellite Applications Centre, MIKOMTEK.

The National Archives of Namibia for the photographs on pages 171,
182 and 221.

The Ministry of Wildlife, Conservation and Tourism of Namibia for
the adaptation of E. Joubert's diagram on page 172.

Although we have made every effort to trace all copyright holders,
we should like to apologise for any infringement of copyright and
will be happy to make the appropriate arrangements at the first
opportunity.

CONTENTS

LIST OF MAPS

The circled numbers below refer to the game parks shown on the map of Namibia on page viii.

KEY TO MAPS

Major road

Proclaimed road

Road route number ── B1

Four-wheel drive track

Road under construction

Railway line

Park boundary

International border

Border post ⌐

International airport ✈

Regional airport ✈

Capital ◼

Town ●

Small settlement ·

Perennial river

Seasonal river

Omuramba

Open waterhole ○ or 🫘

Closed waterhole ◉

Waterfall or rapids

Grassland

Marsh

Permanent sand-dunes

Canyon

Camp site ▲

Rest camp 🏠

Hiking or walking trail 🚶 ●●▶●

Hiking trail hut 🏠

Picnic site ⅢⅠ

Caravan park 🚐

Place of interest ★

Viewpoint ⤜

Hot mineral spring ♈

Hide ⊞

Lighthouse ⎕

Castle ♜

Shipwreck ⚓

Grave or graveyard †

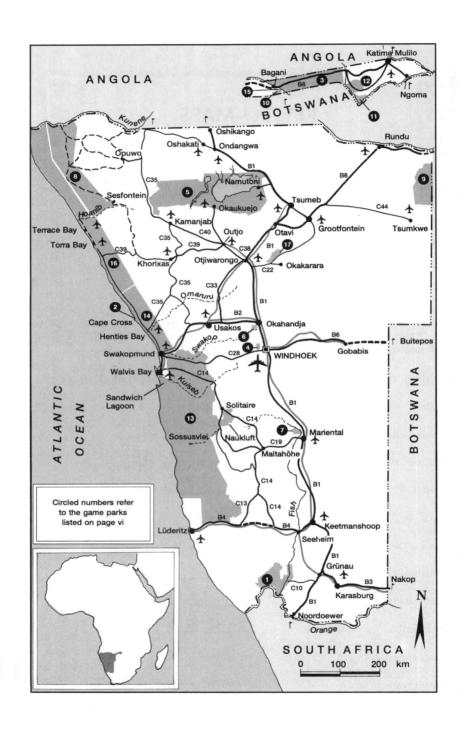

INTRODUCTION

Namibia has established itself as one of Africa's leading nations as far as conservation is concerned, and each year thousands of tourists visit the country in order to explore its unique wildlife heritage.

Already 20 game reserves and resorts, covering nearly 15 per cent of the country's surface, have been set aside. Among these are the renowned Etosha National Park and the Namib-Naukluft Park, which is the fourth-largest conservation area in the world. Accommodation facilities range from basic camp sites and rustic thatched-roofed huts to comfortable rest houses and the historic Fort Namutoni in the Etosha National Park.

There are a number of areas which have not yet been officially proclaimed as natural parks, but are currently being considered. It is hoped that they will be set aside in the near future. A summary of these areas and some of the resorts not covered in detail has been included at the end of the guide.

With the exception of the Etosha National Park and the Namib Desert, information on the country's game parks and resorts is not readily available and this guide has been prepared so that your visit is more rewarding. All possible care has been taken to ensure that the information is correct, but visitors should bear in mind that changes might take place, especially in respect of regional and colonial place names.

To ensure consistency the following reference works have been used throughout: *Roberts' Birds of Southern Africa*, *The Mammals of the Southern African Subregion* by Skinner and Smithers and *The National List of Indigenous Trees*. The numbers that appear after bird and tree names in the text refer to these works. Although some of the tree, shrub and bird names are not descriptive of their distribution within Namibia we have nevertheless used them so as to avoid contributing to the confusion caused by colloquial names.

The secret of an enjoyable visit to a game park is to be well prepared. By paying attention to the information arranged at the beginning of each chapter you will avoid unnecessary frustrations. **In the sections headed "When to visit", references to specific months refer to the *best***

months for a particular activity, but other months are not excluded unless specified.

This book is based on our own experiences in Namibia's conservation areas during the past six years, but it would have been impossible if we had not enjoyed the generous co-operation of conservation officials and many others. Although we are not archaeologists, botanists, geologists or zoologists, many individuals have happily shared their knowledge with us over a long period of time. We would especially like to thank the following: Dr Hugh Berry, Peter Bridgeford, Dr Chris Brown, Treigue Cooper, Brian Jones, Dr Eugene Joubert, Jill Kinahan, Dr John Kinahan, Achim Lensin, Dr Malan Lindeque, Dr Mike Muller, John Olszweski, Dr Mary Seely, Dr Rob Simmons, Peter Tarr, Dr John Ward and Dr Tony Williams.

We would also like to thank Graham van der Vyver of Longman Namibia for his enthusiasm in taking on this project, Eben Maasdorp, editor Tracey Whitelaw, illustrator and cartographer Anne Westoby, illustrator Hélène Marshall and all the Longman staff members who were involved in publishing this guide.

NAMIBIA – AN OVERVIEW

Namibia has been variously referred to as "Africa's Harsh Paradise", "The Ageless Land" and "A Thirstland Wilderness". It is a land of contrasts with scenery that ranges from the orange dunes of the Namib Desert to the papyrus-lined channels of the Linyanti Swamp.

Bounded in the west by the cold Atlantic Ocean and in the east the sprawling Kalahari, the country's northern border consists of the Kunene and Zambezi rivers, while the Orange River forms the southern border.

Geology and geomorphology

Over countless aeons fire, ice, extreme temperatures, rain and wind have combined to fashion one of the most fascinating landscapes in the world. The awesome Fish River Canyon in the south of the country, moon landscapes, columns pointing skywards, table-top mountains and isolated *inselbergen* all provide a testimony to these Herculean forces.

The floor of the country was laid down some 2 000 million years ago when sediments were deposited on ocean beds and in lakes, while vast quantities of lava poured from the bowels of the earth. These formed rocks which were subsequently intruded by granite and other igneous rocks to form the basement on which all younger rocks were deposited.

The next important event in Namibia's geological history took place about 800 million years ago when basins were formed over almost all the northern half of the country, as well as in the south-eastern corner. Initially, sediments were deposited in these basins and then, some 200 to 300 million years later, during the final phase of the Damara Epoch, the rocks were intensely thrusted and folded. As a result of the accompanying heat the shales were metamorphosed to schist, sandstone changed to quartzite and, in areas where the metamorphisis was even more intense, the schists and quartzites were further transformed to granite.

At about this time ice sheets planed the mountainous area south of Rehoboth into a level surface which was later flooded to form a vast, shallow sea. Most of the mountains formed in the central and northern parts of the country during the Damara Epoch were similarly eroded almost to sea level, leaving only the Windhoek and Otavi highlands elevated.

Another cold period prevailed 280 million years ago, covering the entire sub-continent with ice-sheets and glaciers. These icy conditions prevailed for almost 60 million years before the climate again became warmer. The melting ice gave rise to reed-fringed swamps and freshwater lakes which became the habitat of dinosaurs. Arid conditions set in and eventually the swamps and lakes were smothered by windblown sands.

During the final stages of the Karoo Era, 190 million years ago, the earth's crust became unstable and vast amounts of lava were forced to the surface. Although the volcanoes have long since been eroded, the granite which intruded the volcanoes provides evidence of this era.

The youngest intrusions took place 80 million years ago, giving rise to Brukkaros in the south of the country. During the past 80 million years the coastline of Namibia was pushed up and down several times, and since then the erosion of the ancient Namibian landscape has continued unabated.

Weather

First and foremost, Namibia is a land of sunshine. Well over 90 per cent of the habitable land receives three-quarters of its possible hours of sunshine as direct sunlight. This, coupled with the general height above sea level of most of the country, means that particularly pale and tender skins will be at risk from the ultra-violet rays, if protective clothing and barrier creams are ignored.

The ever-present sunshine has a direct bearing on the generally mild to warm winter temperatures and the warm to very hot summer temperatures which are regularly experienced. Although, during winter nights, frost (sometimes severe) can be experienced over most of the habitable parts of the country, the number of days when the temperature does not reach 20 °C during the daylight hours are few and far between. Most winter days are noteworthy for their clear blue skies and many hours of sunshine: at least $10\frac{1}{2}$ hours a day. On such days, the temperature will be approaching the 20 °C mark by 11:00 in the late morning and will only start to fall again between 16:00 and 17:00 in the afternoon. Those who expect to be out of doors on a winter evening are well-advised to have at least a warm jersey close by.

Summer is, in rainless conditions, never colder than mild. Minimum temperatures, usually between dawn and sunrise, rarely drop below 15 °C. From eight in the morning, temperatures will pass the 20 °C mark, 25 °C will be reached before 11:00, 30 °C before 13:00, and the eventual maximum will depend on the height above sea level of the place in question. The upper limit of summer temperatures lies between 35 °C and 42 °C, and in these torrid conditions a mid-afternoon siesta is recommended. The temperature cools shortly before sunset. Hot nights, those with minima above 25 °C, can occur thirty times in the summer season (November to February).

Although these warm conditions are endemic, the air is usually sufficiently dry to alleviate the sweltering conditions that are normally associated with moist, tropical air. During rainy spells, there is much more moisture in circulation and the rain lowers temperatures sufficiently to prevent unpleasant mugginess.

Inland, wind is normally gentle and gales are hardly ever experienced. Although wind gusts just before a summer thunderstorm are forceful, their duration is no more than a couple of minutes.

Rainfall in Namibia is characterised by its overall scarcity. Wet years do occur when there are abundant summer rains, but dry, sunny spells do intervene – there will be more sunny than rainy days, and it is pleasantly warm throughout. Dry years – or years with only intermittent rains – are, however, the norm.

Winter rain is very scarce over most of the interior and only a small area in the south-western region has most of its rain in the winter. Being virtually rainless in all other seasons, however, this is still a very dry area.

The accepted rainfall season begins during October when a few thunderstorms can develop. The number increases in November and December. January and February usually provide the major rains of the season, while good falls can normally be expected during March and early April. The end of the summer season is the end of April or early May, and any rain which falls after this time will be an extremely rare occurrence.

The coast deserves special attention as it differs in many climatic respects from the interior. The immediate proximity of the cold Benguela Current (mean sea surface temperatures vary between 12 °C and 14 °C) cools off the reasonably dry air to the point of condensation, giving rise to fog banks which regularly penetrate inland. The daytime clearance is rapid from 10:00 onwards on most occasions. However, the further inland one is, the less the chance of foggy mornings. Fog is more prevalent north of the Walvis Bay area, but it can occur anywhere along the coast and in any season. Days on which there are calm or light air conditions or which have a north-westerly breeze will be followed by overnight foggy conditions. The southern parts of the coast are in the tradewind belt, and this persistent wind is often strengthened by the presence of a small low-pressure cell over the northern coast and the reaction of some part of the ever-present high pressure zone over the south-eastern Atlantic. Wind speeds of 50 knots are not impossible and 25 to 40 knots are considered normal in the Lüderitz area. Calmer conditions do occur, but visitors to this area will remember the "South-Easter" at Lüderitz.

The area known as the Namib Desert can be considered together with the coast as it forms a coastal plain along the entire coast. This is an area of extremely scant rainfall, but the cool moist air which penetrates far inland softens the harshness of this desert. Temperatures can often be higher in winter when the central and southern areas experience the berg wind phenomenon. This is actually noted more for its higher temperatures than for the wind itself, but the winds are sufficiently strong to raise dust-storms. Any dust-storm is unpleasant – even those which are not particularly severe.

Namibia's people

Stone Age hunter-gatherers roamed the plains and valleys of the Namibian landscape thousands of years ago, leaving behind mementoes in the form of paintings. Two painted slabs, dating back 26 000 to 28 000 years, have been discovered in the south of the country, and these are not only the oldest known artworks in Africa, but are amongst the oldest in the world. Stone Age artists used the walls of caves and overhangs as a canvas for their magnificent paintings – in the Brandberg about 20 000 individual paintings have been recorded. Others engraved animals, spoor and abstract motifs into rock slabs, creating open-air art galleries such as the one at Twyfelfontein.

Groups of early pastoralists also wandered about the landscape, constantly in search of grazing for their livestock. Numerous stone settlements scattered about the arid western reaches of the country provide some insight into their nomadic existence.

Other groups followed and today Namibia is inhabited by a rich diversity of people. However, few of the country's indigenous people still pursue their traditional way of life. The San people have lost most of their traditional hunting and gathering skills and territories. The traditional hunter, wearing a loin cloth and hunting with bow and arrows, is a legend which lives on only in coffee-table books. In the far north-west of the country, however, the Himba people still continue their traditional way of life, but the age-old lifestyle of these pastoralists is being threatened by their growing contact with western lifestyles.

Flora

Although the name "Namibia" conjures up visions of vast expanses of desert, the country does have an interesting diversity of flora, with some 300 indigenous trees and shrubs and 3 500 flowering plants. The significance of Namibia's botanical heritage does not, however, lie in its diversity, but rather in that the country has some of the most unusual plants in the world.

The vegetation of Namibia has been divided into three major zones: desert, savanna and woodland, within which fifteen main vegetation types have been distinguished.

Desert vegetation covers about 16 per cent of the country's surface and ranges from the almost vegetationless dune seas of the northern Namib to the barren granite plains between the Swakop and Kuiseb rivers. One of the most interesting species of flora to be found here is the strange-looking *Welwitschia* – a primitive species which is not related to either the cone-bearing or to the flowering plants.

Some of the most extensive lichen fields in the world can be seen along the coast of the central Namib and so far more than 100 species have been identified in the area, many of which are found nowhere else in the world! Also known as "stone flowers" and "old man's beard", these small plants are often overlooked by visitors but have attracted the attention of scientists from all parts of the world.

A desert vegetation area which is especially rich in indigenous plant species is the Desert and Succulent Steppe in the south of the country. Amongst the rare species which are only found here and in the adjoining Richtersveld south of the Orange River are the elephant's trunk (649) and the giant quiver tree (30). At least ten other *Aloe* species are confined to this area which also provides a habitat for a large number of species of the *Mesembryanthemacea* family. Also known as "vygies", most species are succulents and range from annual herbs to the stone-like *Lithops* plants.

Although the Etosha Pan is seldom considered to be a desert, the 5 000 km^2 pan is in effect a saline desert, while the vegetation fringing the pan has been classified as dwarf shrub savanna.

Covering about 64 per cent of the country's surface, the savanna vegetation zone has been divided into eight areas, ranging from the mopane landscape of north-western Namibia to the highland savanna of central Namibia and the camel thorn (168) savanna of the east.

Particularly eye-catching in central and western Owambo is the tall real fan palm (24) which lines the banks of seasonal rivers (oshana), while the enormous baobab (467) occurs in the savanna of the east.

In the north-central and north-eastern parts of the country the vegetation is characterised by dense tree savannas and woodlands dominated by Zambezi teak (206), wild seringa (197), copalwood (199) and wild teak (236).

The plantlife in the extreme north-eastern corner of Namibia contrasts sharply with that of the rest of the country. Vast areas are seasonally flooded, creating a world of papyrus-fringed channels, dense reedbeds and quiet side channels carpeted with waterlilies. Here trees, unlike those found elsewhere in Namibia, grace the banks of the perennial rivers to form dense riverine forests in places. They include Lowveld mangosteen (486), water berry (555), jackal-berry (606) and sausage tree (678).

Fauna

A rich variety of mammals, ranging from the elephant to the diminutive Damara dik-dik, is attracted to Namibia's diverse habitats. To date some 136 mammal species (excluding bats and marine mammals) have been recorded within the country. Ten species enjoy the status of specially protected game namely elephant, hippopotamus, black rhinoceros, white rhinoceros, Hartmann's mountain zebra, Burchell's zebra, giraffe, impala, black-faced impala and klipspringer.

The Etosha National Park in the north of the country is rated as one of the finest game sanctuaries in Africa. The wide open expanses of the park are a sanctuary to large herds of typical plains animals – springbok, gemsbok, Burchell's zebra and blue wildebeest. Following close on the heels of the herbivores are the predators, and Etosha is renowned for its large population of lions. The park is also a refuge for rare species such as roan, black-faced impala and black rhino.

Animals typical of the mountainous escarpment zone and the central highlands include Hartmann's mountain zebra, while the woodlands of eastern Namibia provide a habitat for roan and sable. This is also one of the few remaining areas in Namibia where wild dogs still roam freely.

The wetlands of the far north-east of the country are the home of three antelope species which are found nowhere else in Namibia – reedbuck, red lechwe and sitatunga. Elsewhere in southern Africa the latter two species are found only in the Okavango Delta in Botswana.

Visitors and scientists alike have long been fascinated by the desert-dwelling elephant, black rhinoceros and giraffe of the arid north-western reaches of the country. Although they are not a separate species from those occurring in Etosha, they have adapted to survive in this inhospitable area. Elephant and rhino often cover vast distances over rugged terrain between waterholes, while the Kaokoland giraffe have never been observed drinking.

Birdlife, too, is prolific and Namibia boasts an impressive 617 species. The arid western zone provides a habitat for several Namibian "specials". The central Namib coast supports a significant proportion of the world's breeding population of Damara tern (334), while Rüppell's korhaan (236) and Gray's lark (514) are attracted to the gravel plains of the central and northern Namib. The dune lark (503) is confined to the dunes and sandy flats of the southern Namib.

Namibian "specials" to keep an eye out for in the Pro-Namib and the escarpment transition zone include Hartlaub's francolin (197), Rüppell's parrot (365), Monteiro's hornbill (462), barecheeked babbler (564), Herero chat (618), rockrunner (662) and whitetailed shrike (752). Other interesting species you may be lucky enough to spot here include augur buzzard (153) and violet woodhoopoe (453), while Carp's black tit (555) may be found further inland.

Several species reach the southern limit of their distribution in the extreme north of Namibia. Species of interest here are grey kestrel (184), threebanded courser (302), Angola swallow (519) and sharptailed starling (767), while the rufoustailed palm thrush (604) and the cinderella waxbill (849) are confined to the Kunene River.

Although wetlands cover only 5 per cent of the country's surface, Namibia has a surprising variety of wetland habitats, ranging from seasonal pans in the Namib to the extensive wetlands of the Caprivi.

After good rains, the usually dry Etosha Pan becomes a vast inland lake, providing a breeding-ground for up to a million flamingoes and large numbers of pelicans.

Another important wetland is the Bushmanland panveld in the east of the country. Notable species that have been recorded here include slaty egret (70) and wattled crane (207), while great snipe (285) is seen regularly in the Naye-Naye pans area.

The coastal wetlands between the Kunene and Orange rivers support large numbers of Palaearctic migrants. Sandwich and Walvis Bay are two wetlands of international importance, supporting up to 179 000 and 79 000 waders respectively.

In the north-east of the country many of the Okavango "specials" are shared with the Caprivi wetlands. Species of particular interest here are slaty egret, copperytailed coucal (389), whiterumped babbler (562), greater swamp warbler (636), chirping cisticola (676) and swamp boubou (738).

Other species with a limited distribution elsewhere in southern Africa but which may be seen in north-eastern Namibia include rufousbellied heron (75), western banded snake eagle (145), wattled crane, whitecrowned (259) and longtoed (261) plovers, rock pratincole (306), African skimmer (343), mourning dove (353), Bradfield's hornbill (461), Angola swallow (519), blackfaced babbler (561) and brown firefinch (843).

Often overlooked by first-time visitors are the lesser creatures of the Namib Desert. There is, in fact, a fascinating variety of beetles, spiders, lizards and other forms of life and, although many species are elusive, a few hours spent exploring the dunes or the gravel plains will reveal some of the secrets of this seemingly lifeless desert.

Wildlife conservation

The first formal conservation areas in Namibia were set aside in 1907 when three game reserves were proclaimed by the German colonial administration of Governor von Lindequist. Game Reserve No. 1 covered an area north-east of Grootfontein, while Game Reserve No. 2 included the Etosha Pan and the Kaokoveld from the Kunene to the Hoarusib rivers. Game Reserve No. 3 stretched between the Swakop and the Kuiseb rivers.

Early conservation efforts focused mainly on Etosha. When South Africa assumed responsibility for the administration of the territory in 1915, control over Game Reserve No. 2 was entrusted to the South African Police. In 1955, however, the South West African Administration established a game and game reserve section and in the following year a commission of enquiry recommended that Game Reserve No. 3 be enlarged. The Kuiseb Canyon, the Swakop River Valley and the Welwitschia Plains were then incorporated into the enlarged park which was renamed the Namib Desert Park.

In 1958 Etosha was declared a national park and handed over to the South West African Department of Nature Conservation and Tourism. However, that same year saw Game Reserve No. 1 being deproclaimed, leaving the territory with only two formal conservation areas. The deproclamation of large areas of Game Reserve No. 2 in line with the recommendations of the Odendaal Commission (which divided the country into ethnic homelands) brought about a greater conservation awareness and several new areas were proclaimed during the late 1960s and the early 1970s.

Except for the Caprivi Game Park these conservation areas were all established outside communal lands but, in 1983, the first conservation areas in communal lands were set aside by the former Executive Committee of the Kavango Representative Authority. However, plans to establish a 562 000 ha conservation area in Bushmanland in the early 1980s were opposed because of the fear that the San people of the area would lose their land. Negotiations to give conservation status to areas in Damaraland (which had formerly formed part of the Etosha National Park) also failed, partly because of what was regarded as the high-handed attitude of conservation officials. At the same time, the former Damara Second Tier Authority was reluctant to give away nearly a third of its territory, despite the relatively small population and the unsuitability of the area in question for farming. In 1990, two areas in eastern Caprivi were accorded formal conservation area status, following years of negotiations.

At present, Namibia's conservation areas cover approximately 14,8 per cent or 12 212 530 ha of the country's surface.

Namibia's wildlife scientists are held in high esteem internationally, and large numbers of visiting scientists are attracted to the Etosha Ecological Institute each year. The institute was established in 1974 to conduct research into topics as diverse as the vegetation of the park, animal diseases, migration patterns and behavioural studies. In 1987 a Windhoek gynaecologist, Dr Jock Orford, and the former chief biologist of Etosha, Dr Hugh Berry, were awarded a place in the *Rolex Awards for 1987* book for their work on birth control in lions.

The Desert Ecological Research Unit at Gobabeb is renowned internationally for its research into desert ecosystems, and its Director,

Dr Mary Seely, has been acknowledged as being one of the leading experts on deserts and desertification.

Faced with the challenges of large-scale game translocations in the 1960s, Namibia's conservation authorities established a game capturing unit in 1966. Among the notable successes of the unit were the first-ever translocation of a large number of roan under prolonged sedation by aircraft (1970) and the successful translocation of black rhino (1970–72) and black-faced impala (1970–71) from Kaokoland to the Etosha National Park. In 1969 one of the world's largest bird rescue operations was launched to save more than 20 000 young flamingoes from starvation in the Etosha National Park when the water had dried up before the chicks had learnt to fly. More recently, conservation officials took a bold decision to dehorn black rhino in Damaraland in an attempt to deter poachers. Conservationists initially responded with mixed reactions, but the gamble appears to have paid off.

Over the years Namibia's conservation authorities have maintained excellent relations with their counterparts and scientific institutions in other southern African countries. Black rhino from Etosha were reintroduced to the Vaalbos and Augrabies Falls national parks in South Africa, while giraffe were translocated to the Kalahari Gemsbok National Park. In addition, roan from the Waterberg Plateau Park were donated to the Mlilwane Game Sanctuary in Swaziland. In 1987 nine Burchell's zebra from Etosha were made available for a unique programme aimed at recreating the extinct quagga by selective interbreeding.

When poachers turned their attention to the black rhino of the Etosha National Park in 1987, Namibia's conservation authorities responded decisively by establishing a crack anti-poaching unit. As a further measure, black rhino from the Otjovasandu area were resettled elsewhere in the park, while some animals were translocated to parks and reserves elsewhere in Namibia.

Namibia also took the lead by being the first country in southern Africa to introduce severe penalties for the illegal hunting of elephant and rhino. The *Nature Conservation General Amendment Act* of 1990 makes provision for penalties of up to R200 000 or imprisonment for up to 20 years for the illegal hunting of elephant and rhino. At the same time the maximum fines for the hunting of any other specially protected game were increased from R6 000 to R20 000, while maximum jail sentences were increased from five to six years.

Non-governmental conservation bodies have played a significant role in the conservation of wildlife, especially in the Kaokoveld.

Namibia's farming community has also been active in the conservation of Namibia's natural heritage. In 1967 the former Department of Nature Conservation and Tourism of SWA became the first conservation authority in southern Africa to transfer ownership of ordinary game to the landowner on whose property the game occurred. This opened the doors for the commercial exploitation of game on private property and at present game farming is the fourth largest agricultural activity in the country. Namibia is a popular destination for trophy hunters and in 1991 an estimated 2 000 hunters visited the country. Other game farming operations include live capture, night culling and sport and biltong hunting.

What does the future hold for conservation in Namibia? Article 95 (l) of the Namibian Constitution determines that the government shall adopt policies aimed at the "maintenance of ecosystems, essential ecological processes and biological diversity of Namibia and utilisation of natural resources on a sustainable basis for the benefit of all Namibians, both present and future; in particular, the Government shall provide measures against the dumping or recycling of foreign nuclear and toxic waste on Namibian territory." In addition, Article 91 (c) charges the Ombudsman with investigating "complaints concerning the over-utilisation of living natural resources, the irrational exploitation of non-renewable resources, the degradation and destruction of ecosystems and failure to protect the beauty and character of Namibia".

However, constitutional protection alone will not be sufficient to protect the environment in a country where resources are limited and where there is strong pressure for the redistribution of the land. Fortunately, though, Namibia's conservation authorities have gradually come to realise during the past few years that the exclusion of people from natural areas is a luxury Namibia cannot afford. Socio-ecological investigations have been conducted in western Caprivi, Bushmanland, Owambo and eastern Caprivi and the concept of multiple land-use has become firmly established.

Bearing in mind, too, that tourism has been identified by the government as one of the country's highest priorities, the future of conservation in Namibia appears bright.

ESSENTIAL INFORMATION

Reservations

Written reservations for accommodation in the parks can be made up to eighteen months in advance with The Director, Directorate of Tourism, Private Bag 13267, Windhoek, Namibia, but can only be confirmed eleven months before the reservation date.

Telephone and personal reservations are accepted eleven months in advance. The reservations office in Windhoek is situated in the Oude Voorpost Building on the corner of Molkte and John Meinert streets (near the kudu statue), just off Independence Avenue.

When making reservations the following information is required:

* the type of accommodation required. Camping and caravan sites must also be reserved in advance;
* arrival and departure dates as well as alternative dates; and
* the number of adults and the number and ages of children.

Once a reservation has been made, a provisional reservation form will be sent, indicating the amount due and the date on which payment must be effected. If payment is not received by the due date, the reservation will automatically lapse. Reservations made less than 29 days prior to the first day of occupancy must be paid in full immediately.

Telephone numbers:	(061) 36975 (Reservations) (061) 33875 (Information only)
Telegraphic address:	NATSWA Windhoek
Telex number:	0908-3180
Fax number:	(061) 224900
Reservation hours:	Monday to Friday 08:00 – 13:00 and 14:00 – 15:00
Cashier hours:	Monday to Friday 08:00 – 13:00; closed in the afternoons.
Information hours:	Monday to Friday 08:00 – 13:00 and 14:00 – 16:30

Cancellations

Please note that no alterations or cancellations will be accepted less than ten days prior to the first date which appears on the reservation advice.

Cancellations or alterations made more than thirty days and between ten and thirty days prior to the first date of occupancy are subject to handling fees of 10 and 20 per cent respectively. No refund is payable in respect of cancellations or alterations made less than ten days before the first date of occupancy.

Entry permits

In addition to accommodation reservations, entry permits are required for all parks. Permits for the Namib section of the Namib-Naukluft Park can be obtained at the reservations office in Windhoek, the information offices at Lüderitz and Swakopmund, the tourist offices at Hardap and Sesriem and certain service stations at Swakopmund and Walvis Bay. Entry permits for all other parks are issued and paid for when checking in at the rest camp. Confirmed reservation advices are necessary for entry to Naukluft, Terrace Bay and Torra Bay.

Day visitors

Day visitors to Hardap, Daan Viljoen, Gross Barmen and Von Bach must make reservations with the relevant park/resort office prior to entering.

Day visitors are not admitted to the Naukluft section of the Namib-Naukluft Park, Terrace Bay and Torra Bay.

Permits to drive through the Skeleton Coast Park are obtainable from the reservations office in Windhoek and the tourist offices at Swakopmund and Okaukuejo, as well as at the Ugab and Springbokwasser gates.

Accommodation

Accommodation may only be taken up after 12:00 on the day of arrival and must be vacated by 10:00 on the day of departure. Apart from the Kaudom Game Park and Von Bach Recreation Resort, bedding and towels are supplied in all categories of accommodation (except caravan/camp sites).

No crockery, cutlery or cooking utensils are available in any of the accommodation units, except in the flats and luxury flats at Ai-Ais.

During the Namibian school holidays (May, August/September and December/January) visits to the Etosha National Park are restricted to three nights per camp and to ten nights at Ai-Ais, Gross Barmen and Daan Viljoen.

The service hours of restaurants indicated in the sections entitled "Visitor amenities" refer to times during which meals can be ordered and not to opening and closing times. It is advisable to confirm these when checking in.

Money matters

Cash, Visa, Master and Diners Club cards, bank-guaranteed cheques and South African Rand traveller's cheques are accepted in rest camps, but not foreign currency. There are no facilities to exchange foreign currency in any of the rest camps except at Okaukuejo and Namutoni where an agency of a commercial bank operates on Thursdays only.

General regulations

1. All plants, animals, archaeological artefacts, gemstones and other objects are protected in parks and reserves and it is an offence to pick or collect flowers, shrubs, trees or any plants. It is also an offence to disturb, injure or kill any animal or to disfigure or damage any object in a park.
2. Firearms must be declared on arrival and will be sealed by park officials.
3. To prevent the transmission of diseases, pets are not allowed in any of the rest camps or game reserves. Kennels are available at the entrance gates to the following rest camps: Ai-Ais, Hardap, Daan Viljoen and Gross Barmen, as well as at the Andersson and Von Lindequist gates to the Etosha National Park. Visitors must, however, feed their animals themselves.
4. Motor cycles are not permitted in any of the parks or resorts.
5. With the exception of the Etosha National Park, visitors are free to alight from their vehicles in all other state-owned parks and resorts. However, owing to the presence of potentially dangerous animals in the Kaudom, Mahango, Mudumu and Mamili parks, visitors must be especially cautious when exploring these areas on foot. In the Etosha National Park visitors may only alight from their vehicles in rest camps and at designated points. Vehicle doors must be kept closed and, for their own safety, visitors may not stretch further than their shoulders through car windows or sunroofs.
6. Uncontrolled fires can devastate large areas and fires are, consequently, permitted only in designated places in rest camps. Do not make excessively large fires and do not throw burning matches or cigarette butts out of the car window. Also remember that it is an offence to collect firewood in game parks and reserves.

7. Refuse is not only unsightly, but tin cans, glass and plastic bags can injure or even kill animals. Refuse must be placed in the bins provided in all rest camps and when travelling it is a good idea to keep a small refuse bag handy.

8. Anglers should not leave or discard fishing line along the coast. Fishing line can entangle, injure and kill large numbers of sea-birds and other forms of marine life. Discarded fish hooks also pose a threat.

9. Wild animals which are fed by visitors often become a nuisance and can be extremely dangerous. Once they have become a threat to people it is often necessary to put them down. Baboons and monkeys can cause havoc when they raid a camp site or bungalow and should not be fed under any circumstances. **Remember: by feeding animals you could be signing their death warrants**.

10. Motorists must adhere to the speed limits applicable in parks and reserves. Not only does this improve their chances of seeing game, but it also reduces the possibility of an unexpected encounter with an elephant while rounding a corner, or an antelope leaping into the road. The general speed limit in parks is 60 km/h and in camps 20 km/h.

11. The substrate of many areas in Namibia is extremely sensitive to disturbance and motorists must keep to designated roads. Tracks can scar the landscape for decades before they disappear and, in addition, many forms of life which may not be obvious at first glance are destroyed. Roads indicated by no-entry signs are used for park management and do not lead to wildlife havens reserved for park officials. Moreover, should a motorist break down along one of these roads he or she might have to wait for a considerable time before help arrives.

12. One of the most enjoyable aspects of a visit to any game park or reserve is the peace and tranquility which can be enjoyed. Radios and cassette players can be extremely irritating and the volume should be kept down so as not to disturb other visitors. Between 22:00 and 06:00 silence must be observed.

GAME-VIEWING HINTS

The thrill of observing animals and birds in their natural environment is one of the most important reasons for visiting game parks and reserves. All too often, though, visitors complain that they did not see "anything", which usually means that they did not see lion, rhinoceros or elephant. If you keep the following in mind you will substantially increase your chances of successful game-viewing.

Field guides will greatly enhance your understanding and appreciation of nature, and will also keep you occupied while you are waiting at waterholes. *Land Mammals of Southern Africa* by R.H.N. Smithers is the standard field guide on mammals, while *Trees of Southern Africa* by K. Coates Palgrave is recommended for tree identification. *Roberts' Birds of South Africa* is the authoritative reference book on birds, but there are also a number of other excellent field guides. Especially popular are *Newman's Birds of Southern Africa* which is illustrated with paintings and Ian Sinclair's *Field Guide to the Birds of Southern Africa* which is illustrated with colour photographs.

You will also find that a pair of good binoculars is essential for successful game-viewing and bird-watching.

Game-viewing in Namibia is generally most rewarding during the dry winter months when the animals are forced to congregrate in the vicinity of permanent springs and waterholes. During these months the grass is usually short and this, combined with the reduced foliage of deciduous trees, greatly improves visibility and hence game-viewing.

First-time visitors are often impatient, and travel vast distances in their eagerness to see game – more often than not with disappointing results. Early mornings and late afternoons are generally the most rewarding times for game-viewing and photography. You should make a point of setting out at sunrise as soon as the rest camp gates open.

Animals blend incredibly well with their natural surroundings and even lions are often obscured by long grass at close range, while smaller, but nevertheless interesting, animals are easily overlooked. You stand a better chance of seeing something interesting or unusual by driving at a speed of between 20 and 30 km/h. In dense vegetation you might have to slow down even more!

Visitors to the Etosha National Park often record interesting sightings in the visitors' books in the tourist offices. Consult these and talk to other tourists, who are normally only too willing to share their experiences with others. Then plan your route accordingly. Ideally you should travel either west or south during an early-morning game drive while in the afternoon the recommended direction of travel is either north or east to avoid travelling into the sun. Take a flask of coffee or a coolbox with cooldrinks, a packed picnic basket and reading matter and make yourself comfortable at one of the waterholes. If there is little or no activity when you arrive, don't leave straightaway – a waterhole can become a hive of activity within a matter of minutes. Wait at least an hour to see whether the waterhole is "working" before you decide to move on.

A knowledge of the drinking patterns of the various game species is extremely useful. Research in the Etosha National Park has shown that blue wildebeest, springbok and ostrich drink over a twelve-hour daylight period, while kudu, eland and red hartebeest are morning drinkers. Gemsbok, Burchell's zebra and warthog, on the other hand, are mainly afternoon drinkers, while giraffe show no clear preference. Elephant, black rhino, lion and jackal visit waterholes predominantly between six in the evening and midnight, while the spotted hyaena tends to quench its thirst between midnight and six in the morning.

Although a particular animal species is often to be found throughout a park or reserve, a knowledge of the habitat preferences of the various species is useful. Cheetah, for example, favour open country and open woodland, while leopard favour wooded areas, hills and mountains. Springbok and blue wildebeest are typical species of the open plains, whereas the red hartebeest prefers woodlands. Species like reedbuck and waterbuck have specialised habitat requirements and can be found only where there is open water.

Most animals take shelter under the trees during the heat of the day, and these hours are best spent catching up on your reading, writing postcards or at the pool in the rest camp.

Larger animals like elephant, rhinoceros and predators – lion, leopard and cheetah – usually rank high on the list of species that visitors are keen to see. Although there are few events to be seen that are as dramatic as a kill at close range, much pleasure can be derived from watching out for and observing the host of smaller animals which often escape the attention of visitors. Many of these animals are nocturnal and you will have your best chances of spotting them either shortly after sunrise or just before sunset.

Many bird species reach the southernmost limit of their African distribution in Namibia and bird-watching is a very worthwhile pastime, especially between August and April when large numbers of Palaearctic migrants spend the northern winter in Namibia. During the dry winter months you stand a good chance of getting excellent views of raptors at waterholes.

Finally, a word on game-viewing ethics. A car parked alongside the road is often an indication that there is something interesting about – it could be a kill or a rare species. Don't just drive past at high speed, but approach carefully and remain behind the vehicle, taking care not to block the view of the occupants. After all, firstcomers should enjoy priority and latecomers must be prepared to settle for second-best! If there is nothing of interest to you, pass the vehicle slowly, taking care once again not to cause a disturbance. Never stop too close to the car ahead of you, but allow some room for a quick getaway in the event of an emergency.

Few things are as annoying as being disturbed by a noisy group of tourists arriving at a waterhole. All of a sudden the peace and tranquility is disturbed, the animals bolt for cover and "because there's nothing interesting at the waterhole" the group drives off again. When approaching or leaving waterholes, do so quietly to avoid disturbing the animals. Do not start the car unnecessarily and stay well away from your car's hooter!

Similarly, it is important to be absolutely silent at hides such as those in the Waterberg Plateau Park. Some animals are extremely nervous when they drink and an untimely movement or noise could send them scattering.

Game-viewing ethics do not only apply to fellow visitors, but also to animals. Although there have been relatively few incidents with dangerous animals in Namibian game parks, bear in mind that animals always have the right of way, particularly large game like elephant and rhino! Many of the roads in the Etosha National Park were originally built along the age-old routes followed by elephants and it is advisable to keep a safe distance from these large animals when they are encountered on the road. Elephants follow set routes to waterholes, so make sure that you do not block their approach when parking at one of the waterholes. These routes are usually well-defined and easy to identify.

Often it is necessary to get into the right position to get that very special photograph. In doing so, be careful that you do not agitate the animal or block the direction in which it is moving. Be especially wary of elephant and rhino with calves – separating a mother and her calf can have disastrous consequences. Black rhinoceros and breeding herds of elephant can be extremely aggressive and, despite their seemingly bulky appearance, can move at an incredible speed. Make sure that there is sufficient room to either move forward or to reverse, should these animals display any aggressive behaviour.

NATURE PHOTOGRAPHY

Namibia's natural beauty offers photographers a wide choice of subjects, ranging from impressive landscapes to dramatic wildlife shots. Award-winning photographs often feature Namibian scenes. Here are a few suggestions as to how to get the best photographic results when visiting this photogenic country.

Although it is often a case of being in the right place at the right time, good photography requires a sound knowledge of wildlife and lots of patience. Animals often reveal themselves for a few seconds only before taking cover and dramatic sunsets can lose their colour in a matter of minutes, so you will also need quick reflexes and an ample supply of film.

The type of photographic equipment you use will depend on whether you are satisfied with memory shots or want really outstanding photographs. A medium telephoto or zoom lens will generally provide satisfactory wildlife shots, but frequently animals are just out of range of a 200 mm lens and a 250 to 300 mm zoom is more likely to give the desired effect. For action photography a motor drive is absolutely essential.

The Namibian landscape is characterised by wide open spaces, which means that a 28 mm wide-angle lens can be invaluable if you want to emphasise the foreground, such as the ripple pattern on a dune. On the other hand, distant subjects tend to fade into insignificance – so remember that whether or not you use a wide-angle lens will depend largely on what you want to achieve.

Because of the very harsh sunlight, early mornings and late afternoons are usually the best times for photography. At Sossusvlei, for example, the dunes are at their best shortly after sunrise when the jet black shadows contrast sharply with the bright orange slopes facing the sun. The granite *inselbergen* of the Namib also undergo spectacular colour transformations during the early mornings and late afternoons. During these times and at times during the day when there may be sharp contrasts, a useful photographic technique is to bracket your shots by adjusting the aperture one stop up and down.

Much of Namibia is, however, characterised by harsh scenery, and the mirages of the Namib and the dancing heatwaves of the midday sun can be used to good effect to capture the harshness of the landscape. An ultra-violet filter is essential to reduce glare and it will also protect your lens against scratches. Another useful accessory is a lens hood. This is an inexpensive, but handy piece of equipment which prevents light from partly diffusing an image (flaring) when shooting towards the sun.

Dust is an ever-present problem and you are well-advised to keep your equipment stowed away when not in use. A chamois bag for each piece of equipment will serve this purpose well. It is advisable to clean the lenses and the moving parts of the camera regularly. This will not only produce sharper images, but will also eliminate wear and tear on your equipment.

For landscape photography film with an ASA rating of 50 or 64 is recommended, but a tripod or beanbag will be necessary in the early morning and late afternoon to prevent camera shake.

A low ASA rating will provide excellent results for animal photography in good lighting conditions. However, wildlife photography often takes place in poor light and film with an ASA rating of 200 will yield better results during the early mornings and late afternoons. High speed film is also essential for action shots such as a cheetah in hot pursuit of its prey.

Unusual shots often require extremely quick reflexes and your camera should be kept loaded and ready at all times. If there is a likelihood of disturbing an animal, do the necessary settings – aperture, speed and focusing – before approaching the subject.

Keep an eye out for the unusual and avoid pictures of static animals. A giraffe drinking at a waterhole makes an infinitely better photograph than one ambling across the road, while two young springbok rams locked in battle create a far more exciting picture than one staring straight into the lens. Photographs like these are, admittedly, difficult to take, but patience and a fair bit of luck will produce the desired results.

Waterholes are fascinating places and are ideal for wildlife photography. This is where kills often take place, where animals gather to drink and where you can observe their social behaviour. Most large animals drink regularly and, instead of driving endless kilometres in search of them, you can wait for them at a waterhole. This also has the advantage that you can select a vantage point which has the correct backdrop and lighting.

When photographing animals and seascapes, ensure that the horizon remains level!

Birds and smaller mammals like tree squirrels that frequent rest camps are usually quite tame and provide excellent photographic opportunities. However, you must ensure that you have a natural background or foreground.

Do not risk the chance of spoiling your photographs by leaving a loaded camera or film on the car seat or in the cubby hole. Your camera is best stowed in a cool place, while film should be kept in a coolbox – a small polystyrene cooler packed with icebricks wrapped in newspaper will suffice.

GLOSSARY

Environmental terms

aquatic   living in or on water

arboreal   living in trees

biome   the living part of a geographical region

browser   an animal that feeds on the leaves and shoots of shrubs and trees

carnivore   flesh eating animals, although not necessarily restricted to an exclusively meat diet

diurnal   active mainly during the day

dune street   interdune plain or valley separating parallel dunes

ecology   study of the interactions and relationships between living organisms and their non-living environment

ecosystem   any area, large or small, that encompasses all interactions between living (animals and plants) and non-living (soil, water, sun) components

endemic   a plant or animal found in a particular area only

fauna   all animal life

floodplain   grass or reed-covered fringe alongside a river or estuary which is seasonally inundated

flora   all plant life

gallery forest   forest occurring in narrow strips along river banks or river valleys. Also known as riverine forest

genus   a group of closely related animals or plants, e.g. all zebras are grouped in the genus *Equus*

grazer   an animal that feeds on grass

gregarious   living in groups or flocks

guano   nitrogen and phosphate rich droppings of sea-birds; highly valued as fertilizer

habitat	the surroundings in which an animal or plant lives
herbivore	a plant-eating animal
indigenous	occurring naturally in a particular area, but not necessarily restricted to that area
intra-African migrant	birds that migrate regularly within Africa
lagoon	stretch of water partly or completely separated from the sea by a sand-spit or sandbar
migrant	animals that move seasonally
lichen	a primitive plant consisting of a fungus and an algae co-existing in symbiosis (a mutually beneficial partnership)
nocturnal	active mainly during the night
Palaearctic migrant	birds that migrate from the northern hemisphere
perennial	a plant living for more than two years. Alternatively, a stream or river containing water throughout the year
predator	an animal that kills and feeds on other animals
Pro-Namib	arid zone between the coastal desert and the escarpment mountains to the east. Also referred to as the inner Namib
raptor	diurnal bird of prey, i.e. one that hunts and feeds on other animals
riparian	of or on a riverbank, e.g. riparian forests
sand sea	a dune field extending over an area of 100 km^2 or more
savanna	grassland containing scattered shrubs, trees and scrub vegetation
scree	loose fragments of rock covering a slope
species	the most basic unit of classification. Members of the same species are identical in structure and are capable of reproducing within the group
talus slope	slope consisting of loose rock fragments (scree) caused by the weathering of a cliff face
terrestrial	living on land
tufa	calcium deposits formed when carbon dioxide is extracted by moss from flowing calcium-rich water. Usually associated with waterfalls

wader	collective name for nine families of the sub-order *Charadrii*, including plovers and sandpipers. However, the term is often used very generally when referring to all wading birds, i.e. birds which wade in search of food
wetland	an area which is permanently flooded or seasonally inundated, i.e. lakes, estuaries, lagoons, pans and flood-plains
woodland	vegetation type characterised by trees with a well-developed, but not completely closed, canopy
xerophytic	a plant that grows in arid conditions

Local words

Acacia	trees of the genus *Acacia* which is represented by 44 indigenous species in southern Africa; characterised by straight spines or recurved thorns
baai	bay
berg	mountain
bergveld	mountainous landscape covered in woodlands or grass-veld
bos	bush
drift	a ford; usually natural, but could be artificial
fontein	fountain or spring
gat	hole
gemsbok	southern African antelope also known as *Oryx gazella*
gramadoelas	rough, desolate country
inselberg	isolated mountain rising above the surrounding plains (German)
kassaias	side channels of main rivers in north-eastern Namibia
klip	stone or rock
kloof	a narrow defile, ravine or gorge
koppie	hillock
kraal	cluster of huts occupied by indigenous people
krans	cliff
mond	river mouth
mulapo	Kavango name for a seasonally inundated primary flood-plain (plural: melapo); this term is also used in Botswana
nek	saddle or col

omuramba	seasonal fossil drainage line in north-eastern Namibia; not necessarily inundated along its entire course (plural: omiramba)
oshana	seasonally flooded river-courses in northern Namibia
pan	seasonally flooded natural depression
poort	narrow passage through a mountain range or range of hills
rant	ridge
rinderpest	highly infectious disease affecting ruminant animals; characterised by inflammation of mucous membranes, fever and dysentery
rug	ridge
sandveld	area characterised by light, sandy soil
sloot	ditch or furrow
spoor	tracks of animals; including droppings, scent and urine
spruit	a stream that is usually almost dry
stroom	stream
tafel	table; used to refer to flat-topped mountains
trek	a journey or migration
veld	open country with natural vegetation
vlakte	plain
vlei	a low-lying area into which water drains during the rainy season; usually smaller than a lake

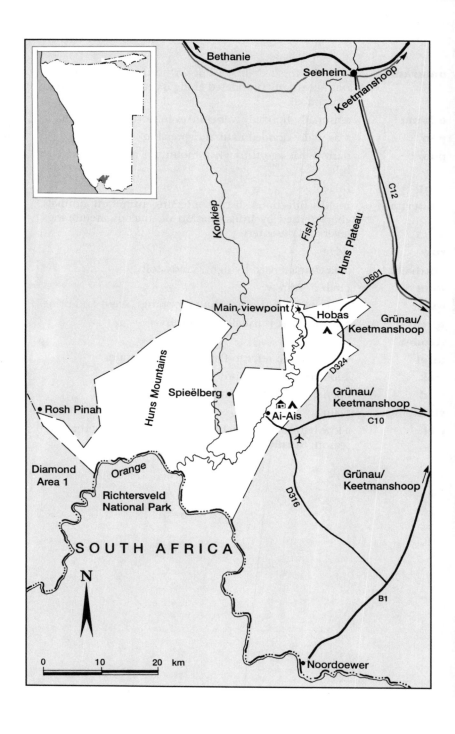

AI-AIS HOT SPRINGS
AND THE FISH RIVER CANYON
Size: 346 117 ha   Proclaimed: 1965

Location

Southern Namibia.

What to do and see

Sightseeing, thermal springs, backpacking, angling.

Climate

The average daily maximum temperatures during mid-summer range between 36 °C and 38 °C, while they fluctuate during the cooler winter months between 20 °C and 25 °C. However, temperatures in excess of 40 °C are not uncommon at midday in the canyon. Average daily minimum temperatures during July, the coldest month, range between 7 °C and 8 °C.

The annual rainfall varies between 50 and 100 mm per year, but is highly variable and erratic.

When to visit

Due to excessive summer temperatures, the resort at Ai-Ais is closed from 1 November to the second Friday in March. Overnight visitors with reserved accommodation may enter at any time, but may not leave the rest camp between 23:00 and 06:00.

Day visitors are admitted from sunrise to sunset, but must leave the rest camp before 23:00.

The Hobas camp site near the main viewpoint is open throughout the year. Day visitors wishing to view the canyon are restricted to the hours between sunrise and 22:00, but visitors camping at Hobas may gain access to the canyon at any time.

BACKPACKING: 1 May to 31 August.

Where to stay

AI-AIS: The resort at Ai-Ais offers visitors a variety of accommodation. The luxury flats each have one double and two single beds, a kitchen fitted out with a fridge, kettle and a hot plate and a bathroom containing a wash basin, bath, shower and toilet. The balcony overlooking the Fish River has a built-in fireplace.

Each of the ordinary flats contain four single beds, a kitchen equipped with a fridge, kettle and hot plate, and there is also a shower, wash basin and toilet.

The huts near the entrance to the resort are each fitted out with four single beds and a kitchen with fridge, kettle and hot plate, as well as an outside fireplace. Visitors share ablution facilities.

Bedding, towels and soap are provided irrespective of the type of accommodation, but crockery, cutlery and cooking utensils are only provided in the luxury flats.

There is also a camp site at Ai-Ais with communal ablution facilities and field kitchens.

HOBAS CAMP SITE: Hobas caters only for campers, and overnight facilities are limited to twelve beautifully shaded camp sites with fireplaces, a field kitchen and ablutions.

Visitor amenities

Amenities at Ai-Ais include a shop, restaurant, filling station, spa complex, outdoor swimming pool and tennis courts.

SERVICE HOURS:
Office: 07:00 — 13:00 and 14:00 — 18:30

Shop: 09:00 — 12:00 and 15:00 — 18:00 (Monday to Saturday)
09:00 — 12:00 and 15:00 — 17:00 (Sunday)

Restaurant:
Breakfast: 07:00 — 08:30
Lunch: 12:00 — 13:30
Dinner: 18:00 — 20:30

Amenities at Hobas include a kiosk and a swimming pool, which is especially appreciated during the hot summer months. There is, however, no filling station or restaurant.

Where to book

See page 13.

How to get there

Approaching from the south, the turnoff to Ai-Ais is signposted about 40 km north of Noordoewer. Continue for about 73 km along the D316 until it joins the C10. Turn left here to reach Ai-Ais 10 km further on.

Visitors travelling via Keetmanshoop have a choice of approaching the resort either via Grünau or via Seeheim.

Motorists approaching the reserve via Grünau can either continue along the B1 for a further 31 km before turning onto the C10 to reach Ai-Ais after 74 km or, alternatively, they can approach Ai-Ais via the viewpoints. Should you decide on the latter, you should turn onto the C12 at Grünau and continue for about 51 km to the junction with route D601. Turn left here and you will reach the turnoff to the viewpoints 30 km further on. Hobas gate is about 2,5 km beyond the signposted turnoff, while the main viewpoint is about 11,5 km further. Apart from the B1 all approach routes are gravel, but they are usually in a reasonable condition.

The route via Seeheim and Holoog is not only the shortest (228 km), but it also provides convenient *en route* access to Hobas and the viewpoints. On the negative side, all but the first 36 km are gravel.

Due to the inaccessible terrain, travel in the reserve is restricted to the proclaimed road and the roads leading to the various viewpoints that overlook the canyon.

A landing strip 11 km from Ai-Ais is available to visitors flying to the resort. Landings and transport to Ai-Ais must be arranged with resort officials in advance. No aviation fuel is available.

What you should know

☐ Although the roads to Ai-Ais are usually in a fair condition, motorists unfamiliar with driving on gravel roads should exercise caution. Be especially cautious when approaching sharp curves in the road or dry river beds, which tend to have sandy patches.

Ai-Ais is an oasis in an otherwise barren, harsh and desolate landscape. The focal point of the reserve is the awe-inspiring canyon and the arid landscape, although the well-appointed resort with its thermal spring and tranquillity is naturally an attraction.

Ai-Ais

Origin of the name

Ai-Ais is a Khoikhoi word meaning "scalding hot – an apt reference to the hot spring around which the resort is centred.

Hot mineral springs

Fractures which occurred millions of years ago in the underlying rocks in the area allowed subterranean water to emerge as a spring.

The eye of the spring is near the outdoor swimming pool and is worth visiting on cool mornings and evenings when steam rises from the water. With an average temperature of 60 °C, it is rich in fluorides, sulphates and chlorides and is reputed to have a therapeutic effect on ailments such as rheumatism. Higher up in the canyon further fractures in the rock gave rise to the Sulphur Spring, a well-known landmark for backpackers on the Fish River Canyon trail.

Fish River Canyon

Although the canyon stretches for 160 km, the most spectacular section is 56 km long, starting a few kilometres upstream of the northernmost viewpoint and ending at the southernmost lookout.

Viewpoints

Several viewpoints along the western rim of the canyon afford visitors splendid vistas of the dramatic canyon. These are particularly attractive early in the morning and at sunset, when the steep cliffs are awash with colour. The two most popular vantage points, the main viewpoint and the northernmost lookout, reveal dramatic views of Hell's Corner, while the Sulphur Spring viewpoint, about 10 km south of the main viewpoint, and the southernmost viewpoint, another 12 km further on, offer visitors a different perspective of the canyon.

Downstream from Hell's Corner, a few kilometres upstream of the northernmost viewpoint, the river meanders so violently that a straight-line distance of 32 km is more than doubled by the river-course. These meanders were probably incised by the mature Fish River which once flowed over the broad, level plain which today forms the floor of the upper canyon.

From these viewpoints visitors can gain a clear insight into the forces which shaped the canyon.

Geological origin of the canyon

One of the fascinating features of the canyon is the way in which the river has carved a tortuous, winding route in its middle reaches – a phenomenon known in geomorphological terms as meandering.

The dark slopes leading up from the canyon floor at an angle of about 45° originally consisted of sandstone, shales and lavas deposited some 1 800 million years ago. Later, between 1 300 and 1 000 million years ago these deposits were folded and metamorphosed into gneisses and granites. These rocks were, in turn, intruded some 800 million years ago by dolerite dykes which were up to twenty metres wide.

A long period of active erosion followed and the strata were eroded to form the floor of the shallow sea which inundated the southern part of Namibia between 750 and 650 million years ago.

The vertical Nama sediments that cap the Namaqua Metamorphic Complex were washed into the shallow sea from the surrounding highlands. The layer of small pebble conglomerate at the base, the Kanies Member, is only a few metres thick. It is covered by a 150 to 200 metre thick layer of carbonates, grits, sandstone, and quartzites of the Kuibis Subgroup and is topped by a ten metre band of limestone which forms the base of the Schwarzkalk Series. West of the canyon the limestone band is succeeded by sandstones and shales, but elsewhere they have been eroded away.

About 500 million years ago a system of fractures on a north-south axis facilitated the formation of the early Fish River Valley, which was then deepened by southward-moving glaciers during the Gondwana Ice Age, some 200 million years later.

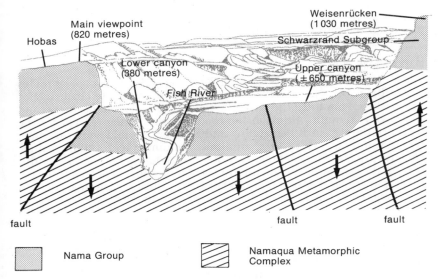

The geomorphology of the Fish River Canyon

Canyon within a canyon

An interesting feature of this natural wonder is that it consists of a canyon within a canyon. The upper canyon originated when the lower plateau was left behind during major crustal movements which created a wide trough. The lower canyon was formed by the incision of the Fish River into the underlying strata. The erosion of the lower canyon was further accelerated by extreme temperatures which caused the decomposition of the basement rocks and the disintegration of the Nama sandstones.

Legendary origin

The early inhabitants of the region attributed the spectacular meanders of the canyon to the supernatural. According to a San legend the canyon originated when the serpent, Kouteign Kooru, retreated into the desert to escape the hunters who were pursuing him and carved deep scars into the earth here.

Day walks

Day walks into the canyon can be undertaken from the northernmost and the Sulphur Spring viewpoints, provided one is fit. The descent takes between 45 and 90 minutes and an early start is advisable. Remember to take a daypack, swimming costume, snacks, a full water-bottle, sun-hat and sunscreen cream.

Another excursion is to hike to the crest of the hills that overlook the resort at Ai-Ais. The rather strenuous ascent takes about 45 minutes, but the bird's-eye view of the rest camp, Spieëlberg to the west and the lower reaches of the canyon makes the effort worthwhile.

Backpacking trail

The Fish River Canyon Backpacking Trail is one of the most popular routes in southern Africa and is revered by many as the ultimate challenge for backpackers. Be warned though – the trail is unsuitable for beginners and those who are unfit! Although the route is basically flat (except for the descent), the terrain is demanding and even during mid-winter daytime temperatures can soar to 40 °C. Ironically, minimum temperatures can be equally extreme, while light rain is not unusual during the winter months.

From the start at the northernmost viewpoint, the trail descends steeply to the canyon floor, losing some 500 metres in altitude. The large boulders and stretches of fine loose sand encountered on the first two days exact a heavy toll and many backpackers have been forced to abandon their hike at the Sulphur Spring, where there is an emergency exit. For the weary backpacker the first view of the palm trees growing at the spring is always a welcome sight. Here tired feet and aching limbs can be soothed in the thermal waters of the spring.

Beyond the Sulphur Spring, the canyon begins to widen and the boulders and loose sand give way to hard gravel plains on the inside of

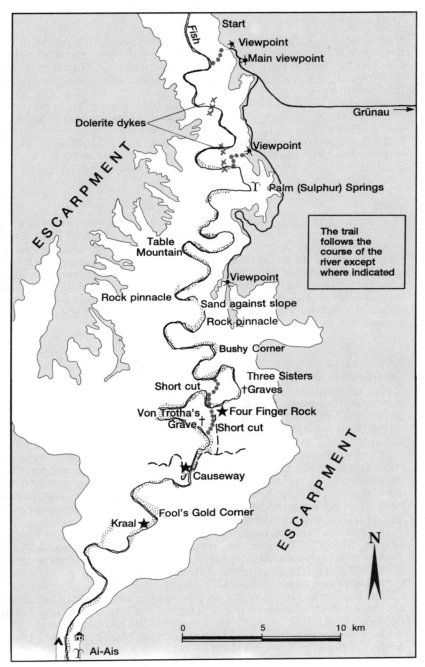

Fish River Canyon Backpacking Trail

river bends and long stretches of pebbles. The meandering course of the river necessitates frequent river crossings and by the time Ai-Ais is reached the river has been crossed no less than twenty times. Depending on the level of the river, crossings can be either knee-deep or simply involve boulder-hopping.

No facilities are provided on the trail and, consequently, there are no set overnight stops. Depending on the fitness of the group, the 80 km long trail is usually hiked in four to five days.

Groups must consist of at least three people and a medical certificate on a prescribed form must be handed in prior to commencing the trail. A maximum of forty people are permitted to start the trail each day.

Game

Opportunities for game-viewing are limited, but springbok and steenbok are sometimes encountered on the plains at Hobas. Although Hartmann's mountain zebra are fairly common they favour the rugged ravines and are seldom seen, while kudu inhabit the densely-vegetated lower reaches of the canyon above Ai-Ais. The boulder-strewn slopes are the habitat of klipspringer and troops of chacma baboon, while leopard also occur in the area. Smaller mammals that might be seen are Cape ground squirrel, rock dassie and dassie rat. Herds of gemsbok occur west of the Fish River Canyon.

Birds

Compared to its barren surroundings which is poor in birdlife, the Fish River Canyon attracts an interesting variety of birds. Species with a limited distribution in southern Namibia, such as the olive thrush (577) and the Cape robin (601), use the river as a flyway to penetrate as far north as the Hardap Dam, while the African black duck (105) has extended its range as far north as the Naukluft Mountains.

Open water species include dabchick (8), darter (60), Egyptian goose (102) and knobbilled duck (115), while grey heron (62), hamerkop (81), threebanded plover (249) and Cape wagtail (713) are attracted to the shallow water, mudbanks and rocks. The reedbeds bordering some of the permanent pools are the habitat of purple gallinule (223), moorhen (226) and African marsh warbler (631).

The riverine bush is, however, the habitat favoured by most species. Species likely to be seen here are whitebacked mousebird (425), swallowtailed bee-eater (445), redeyed bulbul (567), blackchested prinia (685) and Cape white-eye (796). African fish eagle (148) are occasional visitors and may sometimes be seen perched in trees near large pools.

The scree slopes attract mountain (586) and familiar (589) chats, as well as Cape bunting (885), while the cliffs provide nesting sites for grey heron, hamerkop, rock pigeon (349), Alpine swift (418) and rock martin (529). Birds of prey to watch out for in this habitat are black eagle (131), lanner falcon (172) and rock kestrel (181).

The rocky outcrops and plains east of the river valley are the habitat of ostrich (1), Karoo korhaan (235), Burchell's (299) and doublebanded (301) coursers, longbilled lark (500), tractrac (590) and Karoo (592) chats, as well as scalyfeathered finch (806).

Angling

Angling is permitted, provided a permit has been obtained from the resort office. The permanent pools abound with smallmouth yellowfish (*Barbus aeneus*), largemouth yellowfish (*Barbus kimberleyensis*), sharptooth catfish (*Clarias gariepinus*), common carp (*Cyprinus carpio*) and Mozambique tilapia (*Oreochromis mossambicus*). Angling can be a rewarding pastime during good flood years. During dry years, however, many of the permanent pools in the lower reaches of the river dry up completely, ruling out any possibility of angling. For details of freshwater angling regulations see the box on page 98.

Water monitor or leguaan

The pools are also the habitat of water monitor (*Varanus niloticus*), commonly known as the leguaan.

The lower reaches of the river are the habitat of the Namaqua barb (*Barbus hospes*), a species which is otherwise restricted to the Orange River below the Augrabies Falls. This silvery-white fish attains a length of approximately 65 mm and favours fairly deep flowing water. It is classified in the *South African Red Data Book on Fishes* as rare, but is possibly not endangered.

Vegetation

Characteristic trees of the sparsely-vegetated plains east of the Fish River Canyon include quiver trees (29), shepherd's tree (122) and wild green-hair tree (214), while clumps of *Euphorbia gregaria* are a common sight. Camel thorn (168) and ebony (598) trees occur along some of the larger drainage lines on the plateau.

As a result of the scouring action of the flood waters in the relatively narrow upper reaches of the canyon, the vegetation is confined to the rocky slopes. Species found here include quiver tree, Namaqua fig (51) and *Euphorbia virosa*. South of the Sulphur Spring, however, the canyon begins to widen, leaving sufficient room for camel thorn, wild tamarisk (487) and ebony trees, while dense stands of sweet thorn (172) grow on the inside of river bends, especially in the lower reaches of the canyon. Other species to be seen are ringwood (136) and wild green-hair trees, as well as buffalo-thorn (447).

Amongst the unusual species of flora found in the rugged Huns Mountains to the west of the canyon is the elephant's trunk (649), which derives its Afrikaans name, *halfmens* (half human), from the Nama belief that the trees are transformed human beings. The area is also the habitat of several aloe species which are confined to the winter-rainfall region of southern Namibia and the Richtersveld, including the giant quiver tree (30) which reaches heights of up to ten metres.

History

In an otherwise inhospitable area, the canyon with its permanent waterpools, plentiful fish, and relative abundance of game, gamebirds and waterfowl provided a refuge for the early inhabitants of the region.

During an archaeological survey conducted between the northernmost viewpoint and Ai-Ais, six Early and three Middle Stone Age sites were located, while the remains of eighteen settlements associated with pre-colonial herders were also recorded.

More recently, at the beginning of this century, the lower reaches of the canyon witnessed bitter clashes between the German *Schutztruppe* and the Bondelswarts, the most southerly Nama group. Evidence of this clash can be seen at Gochasdrift, about 25 km upstream from Ai-Ais, where the grave of Lieutenant Thilo von Trotha guards the desolate landscape. While Von Trotha was negotiating for peace, thirty cavalrymen under Lieutenant von Rosenthal entered the Fish River through the Auchoba Valley in order to recover cattle stolen from the German post at Kanibes. In the shoot-out which ensued one of the Bondelswarts shot Von Trotha from behind after suspecting him of trying to distract the Bondelswarts' attention from the German attack. The lonely grave is a familiar landmark along the Fish River Canyon Backpacking Trail.

Proclamation

The need to conserve the Fish River Canyon was realised as long ago as 1962 when the canyon was accorded the status of a national monument.

Ai-Ais was declared a game park in 1965 and four years later the boundaries of the park were amended to incorporate the Fish River Canyon, thus increasing its size to 46 117 ha.

The rugged Huns Mountain area west of the canyon was incorporated into the Ai-Ais conservation area in 1989 increasing its size to 346 117 ha. However, because of its inaccessibility and a lack of facilities, it has not yet been opened to the public.

Covering some 300 000 ha, the chief attraction of this area lies in its incomparable mountain scenery which is reminiscent of a lunar landscape, as well as its wealth of rare and endangered xerophytic flora.

Geologically and botanically the area has much in common with the Richtersveld National Park south of the Orange River, and the two conservation areas lend themselves to the management of a future trans-frontier park.

References

Broekhuizen, G.J. & M.G. and Winterbottom, J.M. & M.G. (1966) 'Birds recorded from Ai-Ais, Fish River, South West Africa'. *The South African Avifauna Series of the Percy Fitzpatrick Institute of African Ornithology*, 42.

Kinahan, J. (1987) 'Archaeological sites in the Fish River Canyon, southern SWA/Namibia'. *Madoqua*, 15 (1): 17 – 19.

Olivier, W.A. & Olivier, S.W. *Fish River Canyon Backpacking Trail Map*. (Windhoek: Directorate of Nature Conservation and Recreational Resorts, undated).

Simpson, E.S.W. & Hywel Davies, D. (1957) 'Observations on the Fish River Canyon in South West Africa'. *Transactions of the Royal Society of South Africa*, 35 (2): 97 – 108.

Skelton, P.H. (1987) *South African Red Data Book – Fishes*. South African National Scientific Programmes Report, 137: 81 – 83. Pretoria: CSIR.

Van Huyssteen, C.N.L. (1981) *The Lonely Grave in the Fish River Canyon*. Roodepoort: CUM Books.

Winterbottom, J.M. (1967) 'Report on the Percy Fitzpatrick Institute of African Ornithology Expedition to Namaqualand, April 1966'. *The Ostrich*, 38 (2): 116 – 122.

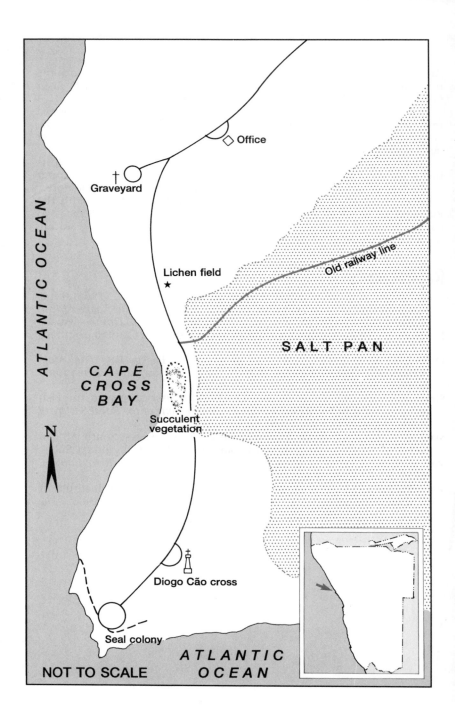

CAPE CROSS SEAL RESERVE

Size: 6 000 ha   Proclaimed: 1969

Location

Central Namibian coast.

What to do and see

Sightseeing.

Climate

See the National West Coast Recreation Area, page 199.

When to visit

Open daily, except Friday, from 10:00 to 17:00.

Where to stay

No accommodation is available, but the reserve is easily accessible from Swakopmund, Henties Bay and camp sites in the National West Coast Recreation Area. It is *en route* to the Skeleton Coast Park.

Visitor amenities

Amenities are limited to toilets and drinking water.

Where to book

Entry permits are obtainable at the reserve gate.

How to get there

The turnoff to the reserve is signposted on the C34, 120 km north of Swakopmund. The entrance gate is 3 km beyond the turnoff and the reception office is 1 km further.

What you should know

☐ Angling is not permitted in the reserve.

The seal colony at Cape Cross is undoubtedly the main attraction for most visitors, but the promontory has had an interesting and varied history – it was here that the first Europeans set foot on Namibian soil more than 500 years ago. To enable visitors to appreciate the reserve more fully, a self-guided drive incorporating six points of interest in the reserve has been planned.

Graveyard

A short way beyond the reserve office, you pass the turnoff to a graveyard. Between 1899 and mid–1903, 124 people died at Cape Cross, and the wooden crosses and mounds of stone are grim reminders of the days when Cape Cross was a bustling little port.

Variety of lichens

Continuing along the main access route, the road passes among a number of seemingly uninteresting rocks. Stop here and alight from your vehicle to have a closer look at the variety of lichens clinging to the rocks.

Relics of the guano industry

About 600 metres on there is another reminder of the heyday of Cape Cross. During the closing years of the previous century and the early 1900s, vast quantities of guano were collected from the islands in the huge salt pan system south of the Cape Cross reserve office. In the first year of operation 5 400 tonnes of guano were collected.

Left: Backpackers descending into the Fish River Canyon (see page 27)

Below: *Hoodia* spp. is typically found in Namibia's arid areas

Bottom: Seals at the Cape Cross Seal Reserve (see page 39)

Above: Dusk falling over the Kavango River, which forms the western boundary of the Caprivi Game Park (see page 45)

Below: The focal point of the Daan Viljoen Game Park is the Augeigas Dam (see page 53)

Above: Fort Namutoni, Etosha National Park (see page 61)

Below: Burchell's zebra at a waterhole, Etosha National Park

Above: The Moringa Forest, Etosha National Park — this is the only place where such a dense concentration of these trees occurs on a plain (see page 79)

Below: A lioness takes refuge from the heat, Etosha National Park

A 16 km long narrow-gauge railway line, the first in Namibia, was built across the salt pan to transport the guano to the harbour which had sprung up at Cape Cross. The coco-pans were drawn by a steam locomotive and donkeys. The remains of the railway line can still be seen where the road skirts the edge of the saltpan.

Dune hummock vegetation

A short way further on the road passes a patch of dune hummock vegetation, which is characteristic of river washes and the coast.

Replica of Diogo Cão padrão

The site where the Portuguese navigator Diogo Cão erected a cross in 1486 is about 2,5 km beyond the reserve office. The area was landscaped in 1974 and a number of interlinking terraces depicting the Southern Cross – symbolic of the direction in which Cão sailed – were built.

Two groups of rocks form a natural entrance at the first circle, and the Cão family crest or *padrão* has been engraved on an oval-shaped rock. At the second terrace the wording of Cão's *padrão* has been engraved in Afrikaans, German and Portuguese on a long, flat rock, while the third terrace contains an English version of the Latin and Portuguese texts on the *padrão*.

On level four there is a dolerite replica which was unveiled on 11 October 1980, at the exact spot where Cão erected his limestone cross during his second expedition along the west coast of Africa. The replica was commissioned by the National Monuments Council as the German replacement (on level five) was not a true replica of the original.

The cross on the highest level was erected in 1894 by order of Kaiser Wilhelm II, after the original *padrão* had been shipped to the German Academy of Science in Berlin in January 1893. The cross bears the German coat of arms and an inscription in German which reads:

> Erected at the command of the German Kaiser and King of Prussia Wilhelm II in 1894 on the site of the original which was weathered by the years.

The stones at the base of the cross depict a star and symbolise the importance that early navigators attached to stars.

Seal colony

The seal colony at Cape Cross is one of 24 breeding colonies of the Cape fur seal along the coast of Namibia and South Africa. Although they generally prefer small, rocky islands as breeding sites, there are six mainland sites along the Namibian coast, as well as ten offshore colonies, with an estimated total population of 650 000. About 480 000 of the Namibian seal population occur along the southern half of the coastline, while the number of seals at Cape Cross fluctuates between 80 000 and 110 000.

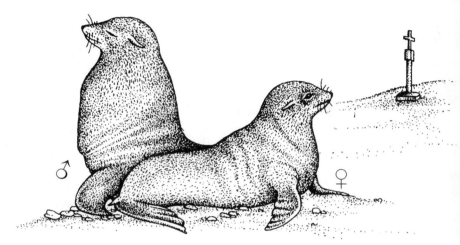

Cape fur seals at Cape Cross

Breeding

Towards the middle of October the bulls start arriving at the colony ahead of the pregnant cows and demarcate their territories, which are then vigorously defended. Within a day or two of their arrival the cows give birth to a single pup weighing about 5 kg. About seven days later they come on heat and mate with the nearest bull and then return to the sea to feed for a few days, leaving the pups to fend for themselves. During this period the pups are particularly vulnerable to predation by black-backed jackal and brown hyaena, which accounts for a mortality rate of up to 25 per cent. Drownings, trampling by adults, premature birth and other natural causes account for a further 8 per cent mortality rate. When they return from the sea, the cows locate their pups by a combination of scent and call and then suckle them for a few days before returning to the sea to feed. The pups are weaned at about eight to ten months.

Diet

Calls for the reduction of southern Africa's seal population are often based on the misconception that vast quantities of commercial fish are consumed by the seals. However, research on the diet of seals off the coast of Namibia has shown that 52 per cent of their diet consists of non-commercial goby, 23 per cent horse mackerel and less than 5 per cent snoek. Based on these figures, one can see that most of their total annual consumption of 1,3 million tonnes of fish is non-commercial.

Pelt industry

The seals at Cape Cross have been exploited for almost a century. Sealing began in 1895 when 2 500 skins were exported. Although the industry has had mixed fortunes, it has continued to this day. Demand reached a peak between the early 1970s and the early 1980s, but in 1983 the industry crashed as a result of the anti-sealing lobby. However, controlled harvesting has continued at some colonies. In 1990 the total quota for all colonies in Namibia was set at 17 500 pups and 1 500 bulls, while 23 400 pups and 2 000 bulls were harvested in 1991, despite pressure by international animal rights and environmental groups.

References

Krynauw, D.W. (1969) 'Kaap Kruis'. *Historical Monuments Commission of South West Africa, Publication No. 4.* Windhoek: Historical Monuments Commission of South West Africa.

Minie, J.H. (1980) 'Cape Cross'. *National Monuments Council, Publication 4A.* Windhoek: National Monuments Council.

Nature Conservation, SWA. *The Seals of Cape Cross.* (Windhoek, undated).

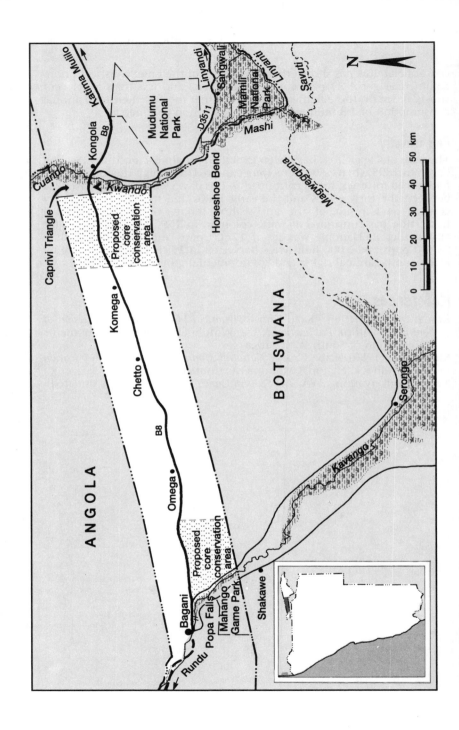

CAPRIVI GAME PARK

Size: 600 000 ha   Proclaimed: 1963

Location

North-eastern Namibia.

What to do and see

Game-viewing, bird-watching.

Climate

Maximum daily temperatures are usually above 30 °C in all but four months (May, June, July and August). Combined with a humidity of up to 70 per cent, summer days can therefore be uncomfortably hot. The winter months, on the other hand, are pleasant with average maximum temperatures ranging between 26 °C and 28 °C. Evenings and early mornings are usually refreshingly cool with daily variations of up to 20 °.

The area has an annual rainfall of about 530 mm, 80 per cent of which falls between December and March.

When to visit

The park is open throughout the year.

Although visitors are not permitted off the B8 road that links Rundu and Katima Mulilo, there are no restrictions on the use of this road. Limited access, however, is allowed in the triangle bordering the Kwando River.

Where to stay

At present there is no accommodation or other tourist facilities in the park. However, a camp site in the Kwando triangle adjoining the park in the east is available to visitors. Facilities at Nambwe, situated 12 km south of the B8, are limited to a number of basic camp sites.

Where to book

The necessary entry and camping permits must be obtained in advance from the Chief Conservation Officer at Katima Mulilo, telephone (067352) 27.

How to get there

Approaching from Rundu along the B8, the park is entered at Bagani Bridge, 199 km east of Rundu. After travelling for 190 km through western Caprivi, you leave the park at the Kwando River crossing near Kongola Bridge, 120 km west of Katima Mulilo. Visitors planning to explore or camp in the Kwando triangle must report at the Susuwe office. The turnoff to the office, which is situated a few kilometres north of the B8, is signposted about 3 km west of the Kongola veterinary checkpoint.

What you should know

- ☐ On account of the sandy nature of the tracks in the area, access is limited to four-wheel drive vehicles.
- ☐ A map indicating routes which are open to tourists is available from the Chief Conservation Officer at Katima Mulilo.
- ☐ Visitors must be self-sufficient in respect of their food and fuel requirements.
- ☐ Travellers may not leave the main road (B8) while passing through the park.
- ☐ The Caprivi lies within an endemic malaria region, so remember to take the necessary precautions when visiting the area.
- ☐ After heavy rains the road is often in a poor condition. Motorists are therefore advised to exercise extreme caution.

Stretching for about 180 km from west to east and with a width of 32 km, the Caprivi Game Park is bounded by the Kavango River in the west and the Kwando River in the east, while the Angolan border forms the northern boundary.

Game

The park is a sanctuary to 35 large and numerous small mammal species, but visitors travelling along the B8 are unlikely to see much in the way of game. This is because motorists are not allowed to leave the main road while passing through the park, and the dense woodlands fringing the road make game-viewing difficult. The restrictions on travel in the park are mainly due to the extremely sandy terrain (which can only be negotiated by four-wheel drive vehicles), the lack of facilities for tourists and because the future status of the park is still being considered.

Although the Kwando triangle has not yet (March 1993) been incorporated into the park, the area is open to tourists and there are several delightful drives along the Kwando River and through the woodlands. The game tends to be skittish, but game-viewing can, nevertheless, be rewarding, especially during the dry winter months when the animals congregate in the vicinity of the Kwando River.

Elephant, roan and kudu occur throughout the area, while buffalo favour the western part of the park. Until the mid–1980s the park was also a refuge for a small black rhino population, but these animals have unfortunately fallen prey to the guns of poachers.

As there is no permanent surface water in the central areas, most species tend to congregate mainly along the Kavango River in the west, the Kwando River in the east and the Malombe and Ndwasa pans in the north-east. These species include Burchell's zebra, impala, blue wildebeest, Chobe bushbuck and giraffe.

Sitatunga

Red lechwe are fairly common on the extensive floodplains of the Kavango and Kwando rivers while reedbuck are abundant. The less commonly-seen waterbuck occurs mainly along the Kwando River. Although the shy sitatunga has been seen, sightings are rare as this species prefers the papyrus reedbeds. Hippos and crocodiles occur in both the Kavango and the Kwando rivers. The wide floodplain between the Popa Falls and the eastern bank of the Kavango River is an important grazing area for hippo and as many as 100 animals have been counted here.

Lion, leopard, cheetah, spotted and brown hyaena, as well as several smaller predators are known to occur in the park.

The park is also a sanctuary for a wide variety of smaller mammals such as common duiker, oribi, steenbok, vervet monkey, chacma baboon, porcupine and badger.

Depending on the season, game numbers fluctuate considerably and during the summer months when the seasonally-inundated pans and omiramba have water, the animals disperse more widely. Some species like elephant and buffalo leave the park altogether, migrating either north-wards to Angola or southwards to the Okavango Delta system.

Birds

As compensation for the often poor game sightings when passing through the park, bird-watchers are usually amply rewarded. To date 339 bird species have been recorded in the area, while a further 71 species have been confirmed as being present in the adjacent regions of Kavango and eastern Caprivi and may be found in the park. Interestingly, the only species recorded in western Caprivi, but not in either of the adjacent regions, is the redthroated twinspot (839).

Saddlebilled storks

The wetlands are the habitat which attracts the largest variety of birds. Here 88 species have been recorded with woollynecked (86) and saddlebilled (88) storks, wattled crane (207), African skimmer (343) and swamp boubou (738) being interesting possibilities for bird-watchers.

However, until the park is developed for tourists, opportunities for bird-watching along the rivers are limited to where the road crosses the Kavango and Kwando rivers. Nevertheless, similar species can be seen along the Kavango River at Popa Falls and the Mahango Game Park.

Riparian woodlands (the forests and woodlands fringing the perennial rivers) are the second most important habitat. Pel's fishing owl (403), Narina trogon (427), longtailed starling (763) and brown firefinch (843) are among the 24 species recorded here.

Indications are that 70 per cent of this habitat, which constitutes less than 0,01 per cent of all habitat types in Namibia, has already been destroyed and its conservation is a priority. During a survey conducted in 1990 it was found that 13 of the 24 species occurring in the riparian woodland habitat of the western Caprivi Strip are Namibian Red Data species.

Species that you might see alongside the road are whitebacked vulture (123), gabar goshawk (161), kori bustard (230), Meyer's parrot (364) and ground hornbill (463), while yellowbilled kite (126) can be spotted during the summer months.

Vegetation

The park lies at an altitude of nearly 1 000 metres and, although the landscape is generally flat, 30 to 60 metre high linear east to west-trending dunes are scattered throughout the area. However, since they are well-vegetated, the dunes are not very obvious.

The vegetation of the area is dominated by short and tall deciduous woodlands, in which characteristic species are wild seringa (197), copal-wood (199), Zambezi teak (206) and wild teak (236), as well as several wild raisin (*Grewia*) and bushwillow (*Combretum*) species.

History

Caprivi, a finger-like projection in the north-east of Namibia, has an intriguing colonial history. It was named after Count Leo von Caprivi, who succeeded Bismarck as German Imperial Chancellor in 1890. In the same year Britain ceded the Caprivi Zipfel to Germany in exchange for Heligoland and the island of Zanzibar. However, the Zipfel did not become an integral part of the German empire until 1908, when an administrative headquarters for eastern Caprivi was established at Schuckmannsburg. At the outbreak of World War I the Caprivi Zipfel was seized by troops from what was then known as Southern Rhodesia. It was subsequently administered through the British High Commissioner as part of Bechuanaland (now Botswana), until the South West African Protectorate authorities assumed responsibility for its administration in 1930. However, because of its inaccessibility from Windhoek, the South African Government took over the administration of the eastern Caprivi in 1939 in order to rule it from Pretoria.

Almost the entire western Caprivi was proclaimed a game park in 1963, but very little attention was paid to aspects such as the migration patterns of game and other ecological considerations. Because of its strategic military importance during South Africa's administration of Namibia, the entire area became a military zone in the late 1960s and for over twenty years only transit travel was permitted and the park could not be developed for tourism.

The Ministry of Wildlife, Conservation and Tourism regained control of the game park when the South African Defence Force withdrew from Namibia prior to Independence, and in April 1990 a socio-ecological survey of the western Caprivi was carried out in conjunction with other government and non-governmental bodies. The survey placed particular emphasis on the needs of the people who had been resettled within the park during the civil war in Angola. The refugees were mainly Khwe people, a sub-group of the Cape San, whose traditional area stretches from north-western Botswana through eastern Kavango and Caprivi into south-eastern Angola. A large settlement developed around Bagani at the western end of the park, while several thousand people also lived in military bases which had been established by the South African Defence Force in the Caprivi Strip.

Oribi

In terms of the recommendations of the Ministry of Wildlife, Conservation and Tourism two core conservation areas were identified: an area of approximately 50 000 ha on the Kavango River opposite the Mahango Game Reserve and an area of about 90 000 ha adjoining the Kwando River in the eastern section of the park. Another recommendation was that a small triangular piece of land on the Kwando River, which had originally not been proclaimed, be incorporated into the eastern core conservation area.

It was also recommended that the north-western section of the park be set aside as a development area, with Bagani as the main centre for the Western Caprivi Resettlement Programme of the Ministry of Lands, Resettlement and Rehabilitation. Another recommendation was for the remainder of the park to be zoned as a multiple land-use area, but not to be deproclaimed. This would enable the inhabitants to go about their daily activities – collecting veld food and grass for thatching – undisturbed.

The Caprivi Game Park and the adjoining Luiana Game Park in neighbouring Angola have been included in the World Conservation Union (IUCN) global list of border parks and there is a possibility that these two areas could be administered as a trans-border conservation area in the future. This conservation area could then be further enlarged by incorporating the Siona-Ngwezi and West Zambezi area in Zambia, which has also been identified as a possible trans-frontier park.

References

Brown, C.J. (1990) 'Birds of the West Caprivi Strip, Namibia'. *Lanioturdus* 25 (1/2): 22 – 37.

Venootskap Francois Marais (1984) *Ondersoek na die Boesmanbevolking in SWA*. Cape Town: Venootskap Francois Marais.

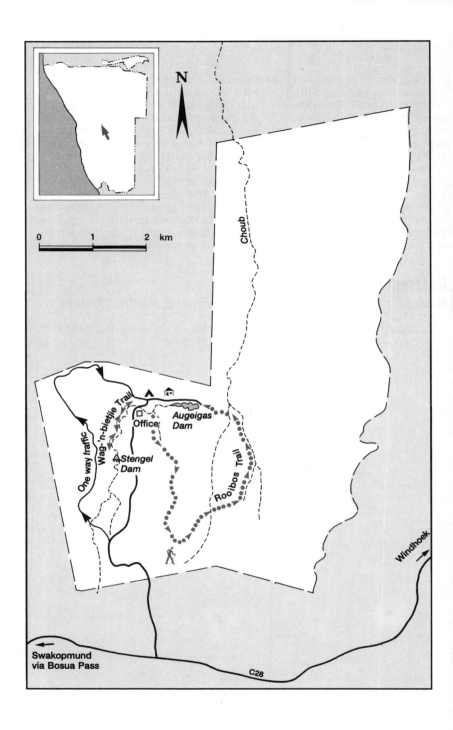

DAAN VILJOEN GAME PARK

Size: 3 953 ha   Proclaimed: 1962

Location

Central Namibia.

What to do and see

Game-viewing, bird-watching, day walks.

Climate

During winter the early morning and evening temperatures in the Central Highlands are generally cold, and temperatures of 5 °C and below are quite common. Winter days are, however, pleasant with temperatures rising to the mid–20s.

Average maximum summer temperatures range from 27,2 °C in March to 30,7 °C in December while minimum temperatures are 12 to 15 degrees lower.

The rainy season usually begins in October and lasts until April, although isolated thundershowers continue into May. Nearly two-thirds of the area's annual rainfall of 365 mm is recorded between January and March. Dense masses of clouds begin to form by mid-morning, and by late afternoon to early evening the highlands are lashed by heavy thunderstorms.

When to visit

The park is open throughout the year.

Overnight visitors with reserved accommodation may enter the park until 24:00.

Day visitors are not permitted unless the necessary reservation has been made in advance at the park office — telephone (061) 226806. The necessary fees must be paid before sunset and day visitors are required to leave the park before 18:00.

Where to stay

Accommodation consists of two-bedded bungalows equipped with a fridge, kettle, hot plate and wash basin, as well as an outside fireplace. Field kitchens with gas cookers and a scullery, as well as ablution facilities, are shared.

Camp sites with communal ablutions are available for those who prefer to get down to the basics.

Visitor amenities

Amenities include a restaurant, kiosk and swimming pool. For day visitors there are picnic sites along the edge of the dam, while two open-air entertainment areas are popular with groups.

There is no filling station or shop in the park.

SERVICE HOURS:
Office: 07:00 − 13:00 and 14:00 to sunset

Restaurant:
Breakfast: 07:30 − 08:30
Lunch: 12:00 − 13:00
Dinner: 19:00 − 20:30

Where to book

See page 13.

How to get there

Turn west from Independence Avenue in the centre of Windhoek into Curt von Francois Street and pass through three sets of traffic lights to the intersection of Gammams and TV More streets. Follow Gammams Road for about 3 km, passing under the Western Bypass and continuing along the C28 until you reach the turnoff to the park after 12,5 km. The entrance gate is 1,5 km further while the park office is another 2,5 km.

What you should know

☐ The picnic areas and swimming pool are usually well patronised by Windhoekers over weekends, but during the week the surroundings are more tranquil.

☐ Swimming is prohibited in all the dams in the park.

Situated amongst the rolling hills of the Khomas Hochland, the Daan Viljoen Game Park is a sanctuary for game typical of Namibia's highland region. Because of its proximity to Windhoek and its tranquil setting, it is a popular overnight stop for visitors who wish to avoid the hustle and bustle of the capital. At weekends it is also popular with Windhoekers.

Although small, the park supports a healthy game population and is also a good spot for bird-watching. In addition to the tarred access road, there is a 6,4 km gravel-surface circular drive which facilitates game-viewing.

However, the best way to get a closer look at the plants and animals of the park is on foot, and as there are no large predators, visitors are encouraged to explore the environment on foot.

Day walks

Wag-'n-bietjie Trail

The 3 km Wag-'n-bietjie Trail along the Augeigas River is an undemanding route, ideally suited to families with small children. The trail takes its name from the Afrikaans common name for the buffalo-thorn (447), *wag-'n-bietjie*, which is translated as "wait a while". As the name suggests, your progress is halted when you are caught up in the sharp, recurved thorns of this species and it can take quite a while before you manage to untangle yourself.

The start of the trail is reached by walking along the tarred road from the office to its junction with the circular game drive where you turn right. The turnoff to the trail is marked by a white post a few metres further. Tall trees are generally confined to the river banks and kloofs but among the trees occurring along the walk are camel thorn (168), sweet thorn (172) and candle thorn (170) (which grows as a dense, tangled bush), as well as karree (386).

After following the course of the river upstream for about 1,5 km, the trail ends with high cliffs that overlook the Stengel Dam. Although the dam is often dry after poor summer rains, the cliffs offer an excellent vantage point for observing a variety of birds when the dam holds water. Species you might see here include dabchick (8), hamerkop (81), knobbilled duck (115) and blackwinged stilt (295), to mention but a few. Provided you approach quietly and the wind is favourable, you are also likely to get good close-up views of game quenching their thirst. The same route is followed back to the office.

Rooibos Trail

The 9 km Rooibos Trail takes its name from the red bushwillow (532), a dominant tree of the highland savanna. The Afrikaans vernacular name, *rooibos*, means "red bush" – a reference to the reddish-brown colour of the mature fruit and the autumn colours of the leaves. In Namibia this species is also known as the *koedoebos* (kudu bush).

The trail starts at the swimming pool from where it winds up through the highland savanna vegetation of the Khomas Hochland to a beacon marking the highest point on the trail (1 763 metres). From here trailists are afforded magnificent views of the surrounding hills and Windhoek in the distance.

During the dry winter months the hills are covered with waving yellow grass, but towards the end of the dry season they are often almost barren, revealing the sharp mica ridges and quartz outcrops which are characteristic of the Khomas Hochland. However, the grasslands are most attractive after the summer rains when they take on a deep green sheen.

The bungalows at Daan Viljoen Game Park

Trees dominating the landscape are blue thorn (164), mountain thorn (171) and red umbrella thorn (181), while worm-bark false thorn (150), weeping candle thorn (170.1), Namibian resin tree (369), bitter karree (389.2), common wild pear (471), small-leaved guarri (601.1) and wild camphor bush (733) are scattered throughout the grasslands. Character-istic shrubs include trumpet thorn (*Catophractes alexandri*), which is very obvious in summer with its conspicuous white trumpet-shaped flowers, brosdoring (brittle thorn, *Phaeoptilum spinosum*) and several honey-thorn bush (*Lycium*) species.

From the beacon the trail descends to a tributary of the Choub River before winding back to the restaurant. The route is fairly demanding, so pack a few trail snacks and a full two litre water bottle in a day pack and remember to take precautions against the sun.

Game

Although small the park supports healthy populations of Hartmann's mountain zebra, blue wildebeest and springbok, as well as smaller numbers of gemsbok, red hartebeest and impala. Kudu favour the more densely vegetated kloofs, while eland are often seen on the perimeter of the camp or drinking at the dam.

Smaller antelope include klipspringer and steenbok, while chacma baboon and rock dassie inhabit the rocky areas.

Klipspringer

Birds

Of the more than 200 bird species recorded in the park, the Namibian "specials", which reach the southernmost limit of their distribution in central Namibia, are likely to be the most interesting to bird-watchers. Keep an eye out for Rüppell's parrot (365), Monteiro's hornbill (462), Carp's black tit (555), rockrunner (662) and whitetailed shrike (752). Also of interest is the violet woodhoopoe (453) which reaches its southernmost limit in the Khomas Hochland, although it also occurs in East Africa.

Other species with a fairly limited distribution in southern Africa are redbilled francolin (194) and redbilled buffalo weaver (798).

An uncommon intra-African summer visitor is the dusky lark (505), while the chestnut weaver (812), another intra-African migrant, is only present after good summer rains, when its untidy nests can be seen in camel thorn trees. Between September and March you might also spot the European bee-eater (438), a Palaearctic migrant.

The colourful swallowtailed bee-eater (445) can be seen throughout the year, as can the whitebrowed sparrowweaver (799), which builds untidy-looking nests and, being highly vocal, is likely to attract your attention. Violeteared (845) and blackcheeked (847) waxbills are two small but colourful birds which are usually very active in thickets.

Bird-watching is especially rewarding in the vicinity of the artificial impoundments, where dabchick, South African shelduck (103), knob-billed duck, Maccao duck (117) and moorhen (226) can be spotted. Although the greenbacked heron (74) is generally restricted in Namibia to suitable habitats in the far north of the country, it has been recorded at Daan Viljoen and at Hardap Dam.

Guidebook

You will find the guide, *Birds of Daan Viljoen Game Park*, an invaluable aid to the identification of species likely to be seen in the park. In addition to a checklist of 194 species and a description of the six habitat types of the park, the guide also contains a short description and photographs or illustrations of sixty species. According to the introduction in the guide, the average visitor should be able to identify sixty species in the summer time.

Geology and history

Situated at an altitude of about 1 700 metres, the park lies within the Khomas Hochland – a landscape dominated by an endless succession of rolling hills which are deeply etched by river valleys. The Khomas Hochland is underlain by mica schists of the Kuiseb Formation, which is rich in mica, biotite and quartz. Some 650 to 750 million years ago layers of mud accumulated at the bottom of the shallow sea which covered large areas of southern Namibia. Towards the end of the sedimentation cycle, 600 to 650 million years ago, the layers were metamorphosed to form schists during the Damara Orogenic phase which gave rise to well-known features like the Auas Mountains, the Khomas Hochland and the Otavi Highlands. During this period the schists were folded and tilted, and most of the folded mountains, except the Windhoek and Otavi highlands, were subsequently extensively eroded.

Earlier inhabitants

Prior to the proclamation of the park in 1962, the area was inhabited by Damara people who had been allocated land on the farms "Fürstenwalde" and "Aukeigas" by the German Colonial Administration before 1914. By

1932 the Aukeigas Reserve covered 13 837 ha but, because of overgrazing, newcomers were prohibited from settling at Aukeigas after 1947. In June 1956 the reserve was deproclaimed and 254 families, totalling 1 500 people, together with 1 780 head of large stock and 15 820 small stock units were resettled in the north-west of the country. The reserve was subdivided into two farms of 5 000 ha each, 2 000 ha were added to the Aukeigas farm school and 1 000 ha was set aside for the Daan Viljoen Game Park, which was subsequently enlarged to its present size.

Origin of the name
The park was named after Daan Viljoen, who was then the South African Administrator of South West Africa. He had played a major role in having the area proclaimed as a game park. It has, however, been suggested that the park should be renamed after Alpheus Haraseb, the chief of the Damara people who had inhabited the area until the deproclamation of the Aukeigas Reserve.

References

Clinning, C.F. & Jensen, R.A.C. (undated) *Birds of Daan Viljoen Game Park.* Windhoek: Division of Nature Conservation and Tourism, SWA Administration.

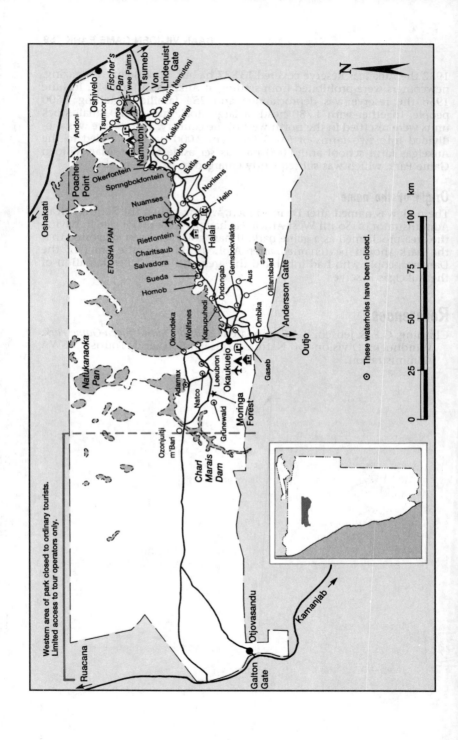

Western area of park closed to ordinary tourists.
Limited access to tour operators only.

⊙ These waterholes have been closed.

N

km

0   25   50   75   100

ETOSHA NATIONAL PARK

Size: 2 227 000 ha   Proclaimed: 1907

Location

Northern Namibia.

What to do and see

Game-viewing, bird-watching, photography.

Climate

The average annual maximum temperature at Okaukuejo is 31 °C, while the average minimum temperature is 13,7 °C. October, November and December are the hottest months with average maximum temperatures of 32 °C and higher. Early mornings and evenings are generally cold between May and August, when minimum temperatures are usually below 10 °C. In July, the coldest month, the average minimum temperature is 6 °C. During the winter months the average maximum temperatures are below 30 °C and the days are pleasant.

Okaukuejo has an average rainfall of 358 mm which occurs as convectional summer thunderstorms. The wettest period is from January to March when nearly 70 per cent of the area's rainfall is recorded. In contrast, the period July to September is extremely dry with no rainfall whatsoever.

When to visit

The park is open between sunrise and sunset throughout the year.

GAME-VIEWING: May to September.
BIRD-WATCHING: November to March.

Where to stay

Both Okaukuejo and Halali rest camps provide accommodation ranging from camp sites to tents, bungalows and tourisettes. Communal ablutions and field kitchens are available for those who wish to camp or hire tents. At Namutoni rooms in the fort, mobile homes, tourisettes and camp sites are available.

Bedding and bath towels are supplied with all overnight accommodation (except camp sites) but no eating or cooking utensils are available. All bungalows and mobile homes are equipped with electric kettles, fridges and hot plates (except for the one-room bungalows at Halali).

Visitor amenities

Each of the three rest camps is serviced by its own filling station, shop, kiosk and restaurant. The swimming pools at all three rest camps are particularly popular during the hot summer months. Picnic sites and field kitchens are available to day visitors.

It is well worth visiting the interesting display on various aspects of Etosha at the Information Centre at Okaukuejo. The Centre is staffed between 07:30 – 13:00 and 14:00 – 16:30 on weekdays only, but the display can be viewed outside these hours.

SERVICE HOURS:
Office: Sunrise to 13:00 and 14:00 to sunset

Shop: 07:30 – 09:00; 11:30 – 14:00 and 17:30 – 19:30 (Monday to Saturday)
08:00 – 09:00; 12:00 – 14:00 and 18:00 – 19:00 (Sunday and public holidays)

Restaurant:
Breakfast: 07:00 – 08:30
Lunch: 12:00 – 13:30
Dinner: 18:00 – 20:30

Post Office: 08:30 – 13:00 and 14:00 – 16:30 (Monday to Friday)
(Namutoni and Okaukuejo rest camps only)

Where to book

See page 13.

How to get there

Both entrance gates to the park, Andersson Gate in the south and Von Lindequist Gate in the east, are accessible from Windhoek by fully-tarred roads.

Travelling from Windhoek, Okaukuejo is reached by taking the B1 to Otjiwarongo where you turn onto the C38. Andersson Gate is 96 km beyond Outjo, with Okaukuejo Rest Camp a further 18 km on.

Namutoni Rest Camp is reached by turning off the B1 onto the C38, 74 km north-west of Tsumeb. The Von Lindequist Gate is a further 24 km on while Namutoni is another 12 km past the gate.

What you should know

☐ Etosha falls within an endemic malaria area and it is advisable to take anti-malarial precautions, especially during the summer months. Also remember to take along mosquito repellant.

☐ As there may be predators nearby, do not alight from your vehicle other than at clearly designated areas.

☐ Although the network of gravel roads in Etosha is well-maintained, careful driving and adherance to the speed limit is advisable. During 1991 an average of one car accident per month was recorded. By driving irresponsibly you could be endangering not only the lives of other tourists but also the animals.

☐ For much of the time you will travel on white surface gravel roads. An acute glare can strain your eyes, so remember to take sunglasses.

Etosha – the great white place – is one of Africa's finest conservation areas. Covering 22 270 km², the Etosha National Park in northern Namibia is a refuge for large herds of plains' animals, several rare and endangered species, and richly diverse birdlife.

The park is the home of no less than 114 mammal species, 340 bird species, 110 reptile species, 16 amphibian species and, surprisingly, one fish species.

Visitors to the park are, however, unlikely to see more than about 30 mammal species, as nearly three-quarters of the total number of species are smaller mammals (rodents, bats, etc.) which are easily overlooked.

Several large animal species occurring in conservation areas elsewhere in southern Africa do not occur in Etosha, including white rhinoceros, hippopotamus, buffalo, sable and crocodile.

Game

The animals of Etosha are typical of the southern savanna plains of Africa, and large herds of springbok, Burchell's zebra, gemsbok, blue wildebeest, giraffe and elephant roam the plains.

The numbers of animals can vary considerably depending on factors such as migration patterns, the condition of the veld and the availability of water. The following are averages based on counts conducted in the late 1980s and early 1990s.

Numbers of larger game species in the Etosha National Park	
Elephant	1 500
Black rhinoceros	300
Giraffe	1 500 - 2 000
Gemsbok	4 000 - 6 000
Eland	250 - 300
Blue wildebeest	2 600 - 3 000
Burchell's zebra	5 000 - 6 000
Hartmann's zebra	600 - 700
Kudu	1 000 - 2 000
Springbok	15 000 - 20 000
Red hartebeest	600
Black-faced impala	700 - 1 000
Lion	300
Cheetah	Unknown
Leopard	Unknown
Ostrich	1 500

Migration

After the first summer rain has fallen there is an abundance of veld water and large herds of springbok, gemsbok, blue wildebeest and Burchell's zebra are attracted to the sweet-grassveld of the Okondeka plains along the western and north-western edge of the pan and Grootvlakte. As the rainwater pools begin to dry up and the pastures to fail, the large herds split up into smaller groups. These groups are drawn to the permanent waterholes around Okaukuejo before trekking further east to their winter-grazing area around Gemsbokvlakte. A few days after the summer rains have stopped, the animals migrate back to the grasslands north and west of Okaukuejo where they remain until about April before starting the next migration cycle.

Elephant

Although the park fences have restricted the age-old migration routes of the animals, elephants still follow an annual migration pattern and their numbers consequently fluctuate from 1 500 in the dry winter months to less than 750 during the rainy season. During the dry winter, however, there is an influx of elephants from the adjoining Kaokoveld and the Owambo region, and large herds congregrate around the permanent waterholes in the central areas of the park. During the rainy season the elephants disperse to the south and north of the park.

Black rhinoceros

With a black rhinoceros population of nearly 300, Etosha is a safe home for one of the largest such populations in Africa. They are found mainly in the west of the park, but you also stand a chance of spotting them in the vicinities of Okaukuejo and Halali. Being browsers, they favour densely-vegetated areas and, as they lie up during the heat of the day, you are most likely to see them during the early morning or late afternoon hours. They usually quench their thirst at night, and so the Okaukuejo waterhole is one of the easiest places to observe black rhino if you are prepared to wait late into the night.

Black rhinoceros

Lion

Etosha is world-renowned for its lions, which number about 300. Twenty per cent of these are nomads while the remainder make up an average of twenty prides, each of which dominates the area around a particular waterhole. The number of lions in Etosha increased from 200 to 500 between 1926 and 1981, and the lion-prey relationship became totally disproportionate when compared with the other conservation areas in Africa.

Lion population explosion

The lion population explosion was the result of human interference in the park's natural systems. Fences halted the natural migration routes of hoofed animals. Artificial water holes also discouraged seasonal migration, and encouraged the lions to settle permanently in one place, which in turn reduced cub mortality. Gravel pits created during the building of roads were a third contributing factor. During the rainy season they filled with water, and anthrax bacteria thrived there, killing hundreds of animals. Wildebeest and Burchell's zebra were particularly affected and provided an easy source of food for the lions.

Birth control

It became apparent that the park management would have to control the number of lions in the park. As an alternative to culling, a Windhoek gynaecologist, Dr Jock Orford, suggested trying birth control on the lions. Assisted by Etosha's Chief Biologist at the time, Dr Hugh Berry, and other park staff, Dr Orford implanted a slow-releasing hormonal contraceptive capsule in the necks of ten lionesses. None of the lionesses became pregnant while the capsules remained implanted, but became pregnant soon after the implants were removed. The lionesses were closely monitored, and no behavioural differences were noticed between the treated and the control lionesses.

The decision not to cull Etosha's lions proved to be a fortunate one as the population declined from 500 in 1981 to 250 in 1985. This dramatic population crash can be attributed not only to the shooting of significant numbers which had strayed onto adjoining farms but also to natural causes.

Effects of increased lion population

The numbers of other larger predators which compete with lions for prey were severely affected by the unnatural increase in the lion population. Between 1926 and 1982 the numbers of hyaena and wild dog decreased from an estimated 4 000 and 2 200 to 400 and 20 respectively, while the park's cheetah population crashed from 900 to an estimated 50. For at least the past decade wild dogs have not been seen in Etosha and, because they are often considered problem animals, they have been eradicated by farmers on surrounding land, despite being considered an endangered species.

Wild dog — experimental re-introduction fails

Attempts were made in 1988 to re-introduce wild dog into the park after five animals had been obtained from the De Wildt breeding station and another five from a farmer. This attempt failed but a second attempt was made in mid–1990 when nine cubs and four adults were obtained from a game dealer close to Windhoek. Unfortunately two of the wild dogs escaped while *en route* to the park, and the remaining eleven were initially kept in a camp some 140 km north-west of Okaukuejo. After a few weeks they were released in the vicinity of the Moringa Forest but it soon became evident that hand-rearing had caused them to lose their hunting and survival instincts. Within a relatively short period seven of the wild dogs had been killed after they had approached lions without due respect. The four survivors were re-captured and kept in an enclosure close to Ombika, but they were also doomed, and they died after contracting rabies.

Cheetah

Although Namibia boasts one of the world's largest populations of free roaming cheetah, the relatively small number of cheetah to be found in Etosha is surprising, especially if the ideal habitat of the large open plains is considered. As they are diurnal, there is always the possibility of seeing cheetah on a game drive, and most sightings are recorded in the vicinity of Namutoni, Charitsaub and Ombika. Springbok, steenbok, ostrich and hares are the most common prey of cheetah, although young Burchell's zebra, blue wildebeest and red hartebeest are also occasionally taken.

Leopard

Leopards, with their rosette-like spots, are nocturnal and unlikely to be seen during the day. However, on a late afternoon or early morning drive you could be lucky, especially in the vicinity of Kalkheuwel, Klein Namutoni, Ngobib and Rietfontein.

Antelope

The park is also the habitat of three uncommon antelope species:

Black-faced impala

The first group of black-faced impala was translocated to the park from northern Kaokoland in 1970, while a second group of 114 animals was released in Etosha the following year. As the name suggests, the most striking feature of this antelope is its distinctive purplish-black facial blaze. Roughly half of the park's total black-faced impala population lives in the Namutoni area, while smaller numbers can be seen in the Halali and Ombika areas.

Damara dik-dik

In the Namutoni area you are likely to spot the diminutive Damara dik-dik. Standing 40 cm tall and with a weight of only 5 kg, it is Namibia's smallest antelope. In southern Africa this species is confined to wooded areas in central and northern Namibia, and north-western Botswana, extending into south-western Angola. They occur either singly, in pairs, or in small family groups and your best chances of seeing members of this species are either during the early morning or late afternoon.

Roan

Another uncommon antelope species you might see in the western parts of the park is roan. These beautiful antelope were first introduced into the park in 1970 from Kaudom in the east of the country. A Hercules cargo aircraft was used to transport the sedated animals in what is said to be the first airlift of a large number of antelope over such a long distance.

Sable — re-introduction attempts fail

Attempts to re-introduce sable into the park from western Caprivi in the early 1970s were not very successful and this species is today confined to the Caprivi, Kaudom and Mahango game parks, and the Waterberg Plateau Park.

Blue wildebeest

Blue wildebeest

Until the mid–1950s the sweet grasslands of the park attracted large migratory herds of blue wildebeest during the summer months. However, the erection of game-proof fences during the 1960s and the fencing of the park in the 1970s prevented the animals from following their traditional migration routes, and by 1973 their numbers had fallen from an estimated 25 000 to 4 000.

A research project conducted between 1974 and 1978 showed that the wildebeest population had been influenced by three human factors: the erection of fences, the creation of artificial water points, and the excavation of gravel pits during road construction.

The creation of artificial water points in the park enabled predators, especially lions and hyaenas, to permanently extend their range over the entire grassland area, while the gravel pits created ideal incubator areas for anthrax bacteria. The research showed that anthrax was responsible for up to 76 per cent of wildebeest mortalities during the rainy season and, as the park's carnivores were apparently not susceptible to anthrax, the carcasses provided an easy source of food. The study proposed that the park's boundaries be modified to incorporate the grasslands north of Etosha and recommended that artificial water points should be created with caution. It also recommended the control of anthrax and indirect control of predators by, for example, closing some of the artificial waterholes.

Game-viewing drives

Each of the 30-odd springs and waterholes in the tourist area east of the Charl Marais Dam has a distinctive character. This section looks at the various game drives from each camp and the waterholes which can be visited.

Okaukuejo area

Okaukuejo waterhole

Within easy walking distance is the Okaukuejo waterhole on the perimeter of the rest camp. During the dry season this is one of the best waterholes in the park for game-viewing. The waterhole is floodlit at night and the chances of seeing black rhinoceros and lion are good. During the day, elephant, springbok, Burchell's zebra and giraffe are common visitors.

Okaukuejo-Ombika-Gemsbokvlakte-Okaukuejo

This circular route covers about 60 km and is an ideal afternoon drive requiring about three hours. From Okaukuejo, follow the tarred road towards Andersson Gate for 11 km before turning onto the western Ombika detour and following this for about 6 km to the waterhole. **Ombika** is visited by a variety of game, including lion, black-faced impala, blue wildebeest, Burchell's zebra and giraffe. Although the waterhole is quite far from the parking area, animals often pass close by. From Ombika the route continues for 4,4 km along the eastern detour, passing through mopane woodland to the junction with **Gaseb** waterhole which has been closed. **Gemsbokvlakte** waterhole is about 18 km further on. The waterhole is situated in open grassveld and attracts large numbers of springbok, gemsbok and blue wildebeest, as well as herds of elephant, especially during the dry season. From here the drive is about 20 km back to Okaukuejo.

Okaukuejo-Aus-Okaukuejo

From Okaukuejo head towards Halali and take the Gemsbokvlakte turnoff a few kilometres east of Okaukuejo to reach **Gemsbokvlakte** (see above) 17 km further on. From here the road winds for 8 km through mopane woodland to **Olifantsbad**. As the name suggests, this drinking place is favoured by large herds of elephant, and they are often encountered on the road which follows their age-old path. Kudu, Burchell's zebra, springbok, gemsbok, black-faced impala and red hartebeest, all quench their thirst at this waterhole. There is also a possibility of spotting black rhinoceros in the area. **Aus** is 10 km further on and attracts the same species as Olifantsbad, but the waterhole frequently dries up during the dry winter months. From here the road heads north-west and intersects the pan road after 15 km. Turn right here and then left about 400 metres on to get to **Ondongab** on the edge of the pan. Springbok, blue wildebeest and gemsbok are attracted to this spring which is, however, often dry. Return to the main road and head for Okaukuejo, stopping off at **Kapupuhedi**, which is also often dry. Both these springs are ideal for photographing typical plains' animals against a background of the stark white pan. From here it is a 19 km drive back to Okaukuejo.

Okaukuejo-Moringa Forest-Okondeka-Okaukuejo

This 100 km round trip is ideally suited for a morning or afternoon drive. Take the Leeubron turnoff 2,7 km north-west of Okaukuejo and continue for about 12 km before turning onto the Sprokieswoud (Moringa Forest) road to join the Sprokieswoud/Okondeka road 2 km on. Turn left here to reach the **Moringa Forest** 22 km on. Toilets have been provided close to the **Grünewald** turnoff and from here it is possible to continue to the **Ozonjuitji m' Bari** waterhole. This is, however, a 39 km detour. From Moringa Forest retrace your tracks, ignoring the turnoff to **Natco** and **Adamax**, both of which have been closed. Continue past **Leeubron**, which has also been closed, to reach **Okondeka** waterhole 11 km further on. The stark white pan forms a dramatic backdrop to this spring on its western edge. In addition to large numbers of blue wildebeest, springbok, gemsbok, and giraffe, you might also be fortunate enough to encounter the Okondeka lion pride here. The turnoff to **Wolfsnes** is reached 6 km south of Okondeka, but this spring on the edge of the pan is not as popular as Okondeka. Okaukuejo Rest Camp is about 17 km south.

Okaukuejo to Halali

From Okaukuejo the main road to Halali Rest Camp runs fairly close to the pan edge. **Kapupuhedi** and **Ondongab** springs, 19 and 24 km east of Okaukuejo, attract typical plains' animals, but are often dry. About 13 km beyond Ondongab you will reach the turnoff to **Homob** waterhole. In addition to springbok, gemsbok and blue wildebeest, elephant also visit this scenic spring, and there is a possibility of encountering lion. Toilets are provided about 2 km beyond the Homob turnoff. After another 2,5 km you will reach the Sueda/Charitsaub/Salvadora detour branching off to the left. The Sueda/Charitsaub/Salvadora triangle is renowned for its lions, while cheetah may also be seen in the vicinity. Species likely to be encountered at these waterholes include large numbers of springbok, blue wildebeest and Burchell's zebra. **Sueda**, a spring on the edge of the pan, takes its name from the salt-loving *Sueda* plant which is characteristic of the pan fringe. Some 300 metres after rejoining the detour, the turnoff to

Charitsaub is reached, and a detour could be rewarding. The nearby **Salvadora** spring on the edge of the pan takes its name from the mustard tree (*Salvadora persica*), a shrub with greenish-yellow leathery leaves, which grows in the vicinity. The parking area looks down onto the spring and affords excellent photographic opportunities, especially in the afternoon. About 3 km beyond Salvadora the main road is once again rejoined and after another 4,5 km the turnoff to **Rietfontein** is reached. Situated in mopane and combretum woodland, this scenic spot takes its Afrikaans name from the clump of reeds dominating the waterhole. It is frequented by a large variety of game, including lion, leopard and elephant, and also offers excellent opportunities for bird-watching. Halali Rest Camp is reached some 20 km on.

Springbok at a waterhole in Etosha National Park

Halali area

Halali waterhole

Tsumasa Koppie forms a natural viewpoint onto this waterhole, which was constructed in March 1992 by Venturers of the first Raleigh International expedition to visit Namibia. Unlike Okaukuejo, this drinking place is situated a fair distance from the accommodation units and, therefore, has a much more peaceful atmosphere. Species likely to be seen here include elephant, black rhinoceros, black-faced impala, Burchell's zebra and lion.

Halali circular drive

The first stop after leaving Halali is **Helio**, a small waterhole on the north-western side of the twin dolomite hills named Tweekoppies (two hills). Elephant and a variety of other game can be seen at this small waterhole.

From Helio follow the road along the base of the Tweekoppies hills to join the **Nuamses** road after 15 km, the waterhole being another 12 km further. The Halali/Okaukuejo road is reached after 5 km and a detour to the **Etosha viewpoint** is well worth the effort. The final 1,5 km of the route traverses the clay pan which is otherwise inaccessible, giving visitors a rare opportunity to enjoy close-up views of the sun-baked pan. Return to the main road and continue towards Namutoni. Further along, expansive views of the pan can be enjoyed from the road and 11 km beyond the Etosha viewpoint turnoff there is a picnic spot which suggests itself as a good brunch stop. Since the area is unfenced, visitors are advised to check that there are no dangerous animals around before alighting from their vehicles. Facilities include a large, thatched eating area and toilets with running water. Starting 5 km east of the picnic spot, a 6 km detour links up with the Goas/Noniams route. **Goas** is a scenic waterhole with parking areas that overlook the fairly large expanse of water from two directions. Game likely to be seen here are elephant, Burchell's zebra, blue wildebeest and black-faced impala, as well as lion. This is also a good waterhole for seeing red hartebeest, a species which is relatively uncommon in Etosha. **Noniams**, a small waterhole some 3 km further south, attracts species similar to those of Goas. From Noniams one can either return to Halali via Rhino Drive (29 km) or take the slightly shorter (23 km) route via Helio.

Halali to Namutoni via Eland Drive

This route follows Rhino Drive before joining Eland Drive 21 km out of Halali. The road winds through dense mopane woodlands with tall trees. Although **Kamaseb** is the only waterhole along the 32 km loop, the scenery is pleasant and there is always a chance of an encounter with the unexpected. A toilet in a fenced enclosure is passed shortly before the end of this loop.

Batia, a short detour from the main road, appears to be fairly uninteresting at first glance, but it attracts large herds of elephant, springbok and blue wildebeest.

Situated alongside the road 1,7 km after the drive has rejoined the main road, **Springbokfontein** is easily overlooked. It attracts mainly gemsbok, blue wildebeest and, as the name suggests, springbok.

If you have the time, take the **Okerfontein** detour by turning to the left shortly after you have passed Springbokfontein. The spring on the edge of the pan is reached after about 14,6 km and, although it could be expected to attract game similar to that of Springbokfontein, it is often deserted. The expansive views of the pan make the detour worthwhile, even if there are no animals about. Continuing along the detour, a toilet is passed less than 3 km further and the main road is rejoined 9,2 km later.

Here you have the option of taking a 19,5 km circular drive to **Ngobib**. This waterhole is somewhat obscured by dense growth, but leopard are known to roam the area, while the open vegetation along stretches of the circular drive is ideally suited to cheetah.

Back on the main road again, it is usually worthwhile taking the turnoff 3,5 km on to **Kalkheuwel**, 4 km off the main road. This is undoubtedly one of the best waterholes in the park, affording good close-up views of a variety of game. Species you can expect to see include black- faced impala, Burchell's zebra, kudu, giraffe and elephant, while leopard and lion are other possibilities.

The first turnoff to **Chudop**, another good waterhole, is 11,5 km futher on and only 5,5 km from Namutoni. The well-positioned parking area at this artesian spring allows for good views of game such as giraffe, eland, Burchell's zebra and blue wildebeest.

From Chudop there is an alternative route of about 4 km back to the main road, and a short distance after turning right, the turnoff to **Koinachas** is reached. This is also an artesian spring and, as it is very close to the main road, it is always worth checking out. From Koinachas it is less than 2 km until you pass through the gates into Namutoni Rest Camp.

Damara dik-dik

Namutoni area

Dik-dik Drive

From Namutoni there are various interesting possibilities. The Dik-dik Drive is recommended as an early morning drive. **Klein Namutoni** waterhole is passed 2,2 km out of the rest camp and, although it is unsuitable for morning photography, it is especially popular with giraffe, and a variety of other species. This makes a stop here worthwhile. Once you have rejoined the road it is a further 2,5 km to the start of Dik-dik Drive. This short drive (5,3 km) nearly always results in good sightings of Namibia's smallest antelope, the Damara dik-dik. In addition, there is a good possibility of spotting leopard.

Fischer's Pan circuit

This is an ideal early morning or late afternoon drive. Shortly after leaving Namutoni, the road crosses Fischer's Pan which is normally flooded for several months after good summer rains. The pan attracts a variety of birds, including marabou stork (89), greater (96) and lesser (97) flamingoes, and a variety of Palaearctic waders. A variety of game is attracted to **Aroe** waterhole, which is reached 16 km after turning onto the circular drive. The real fan palm (24) trees at the appropriately named **Twee Palms** (Two Palms) waterhole, silhouetted against an orange African sunset, is a favourite with photographers. Care should be taken, though, not to lose track of time as it is a 12 km drive back to the camp from Twee Palms.

Klein/Groot Okevi drive

With **Klein** and **Groot Okevi** being only 5 and 7 km respectively out of Namutoni Rest Camp, both are good options for pre-breakfast drives, especially if you are in search of cheetah or leopard. Both waterholes are situated below the parking area, and both offer good views. As an alternative, return along the detour which follows the edge of the pan.

Namutoni to Andoni Plains

Although the almost 100 km round trip to the Andoni waterhole might seem to be rather out of the way when there are so many attractive waterholes near Namutoni, a drive to Andoni is definitely worth the effort if you have the time. **Tsumcor**, which is passed *en route* is often a rewarding detour. This artificial waterhole is especially popular with elephants and is good for afternoon photography. For most of the way, the road passes through impressive woodlands and at times it seems unnecessarily straight, but this adds to the enjoyment as one tries to identify animals crossing in the distance.

Shortly before reaching the Andoni Plains, the woodlands give way to expansive grasslands. Game-viewing is especially rewarding at **Andoni** waterhole during the dry winter months and, in addition to the more commonly seen species, you might also see black rhinoceros. Another attraction of this waterhole is the continual activity of a variety of birds at the water's edge and amongst the grass.

For a change, take the 19 km **Stinkwater** detour on your return journey. This route commences just south of the toilet enclosure which is 5 km south of Andoni waterhole. About 7 km past the Tsumcor turnoff there is an 8 km deviation which skirts the edge of the pan. Along this section you might have almost surreal views of giraffe, gemsbok and ostrich making their way across the shimmering pan.

Birds

To date about 340 bird species have been recorded in five broadly defined habitat types: the pans and waterholes, grassveld, mopane veld, eastern

Etosha woodland and the dolomite hills. Since nearly a third of these species are migrants, bird-watching is usually most rewarding during the summer months.

Greater (left) and lesser (right) flamingoes

Flamingoes

Etosha is one of the most important breeding grounds of southern Africa's greater and lesser flamingo populations. After the summer rains, tens of thousands of flamingoes are attracted to the shallow water masses of Fischer's Pan and the Ekuma River mouth. However, good rains lead to large areas of the Etosha Pan being flooded and as a result up to a million flamingoes may congregrate on the pan.

Disaster threatened in 1969 when the pan dried up before the young flamingoes were able to fly. With no water to retreat to, the adult birds were forced to leave and a colony of 100 000 chicks were trapped on the parched, sun-baked pan. One of the world's largest bird rescue operations, Operation Flamingo, was launched and approximately 20 000 chicks were rescued and then released at Fischer's Pan where there was still sufficient water. Thousands of stronger young birds managed to get to other waterholes in the park, but thousands more had dispersed onto the pan where the rescue teams could not reach them, and they died of thirst and exhaustion.

In 1971 the waters again receded earlier than usual and in late July about 30 000 flamingo chicks trekked from the nesting colonies near Okerfontein to Poacher's Point 30 km north-west. By August the water at Poacher's Point had dried up and the chicks set off on the second leg of their incredible trek to the Ekuma River mouth – 50 km to the west. During their arduous journey the young chicks were fed by the adult birds that were feeding at the Ekuma River mouth.

In May 1989 765 greater flamingo chicks faced death when they were trapped on the dry pan at the Okerfontein nesting site. Various zoological gardens and bird parks were asked if they would like flamingo chicks and, as the response was overwhelming, it was decided to rescue the birds rather than abandon them to their fate. Most of the birds were donated to zoological gardens and bird parks in South Africa, while 40 were ringed and released in the park as part of a project to study their migration patterns.

Pelicans

During favourable years the pan also attracts large numbers of pelicans. After two attempts to breed had failed first at Lake Oponono outside the park, and near Okerfontein in 1971, several thousand white pelicans (49) established a breeding colony at Poacher's Point, despite the fact that the water was drying up rapidly. When it became clear that the chicks were threatened by large-scale mortality, a rescue operation was launched and 1 040 chicks were released at the Ekuma River. Sadly, most of the chicks died, either because of a lack of fish or because they were unable to feed themselves. A further 2 000 birds died in the vicinity of the Poacher's Point nesting site, while 2 000 chicks fledged successfully and retreated to Lake Oponono.

Palaearctic waders

Etosha is also used as a stopover by large numbers of Palaearctic waders at the beginning and the end of summer. Species include ringed plover (245), Caspian plover (252), grey plover (254), marsh sandpiper (269) and sanderling (281).

Short grassveld species

The short grassveld along the southern and south-western edge of the pan is the habitat of such species as black korhaan (239), crowned plover (255), doublebanded courser (301), Namaqua sandgrouse (344) and some larks, while the tall grassveld of the Andoni Plains attracts clapper lark (495). Blue crane (208) are common in the grassland bordering the pan, while crowned crane (209) have been recorded at Andoni and at Fischer's Pan.

Mopane woodlands species

Species typical of the mopane woodlands include redbilled hornbill (458), goldentailed woodpecker (483) and violet woodhoopoe (453), while redcrested korhaan (237), monotonous lark (493) and Kalahari robin (615) are widespread in scrub mopane veld.

A species worth keeping an eye out for in the woodlands of eastern Etosha is the blackfaced babbler (561), which in southern Africa is confined to northern Namibia and north-western Botswana. The woodlands also attract Swainson's francolin (199), emeraldspotted dove (358), pied babbler (563) and blue waxbill (844).

Tweekoppies and Tsumasa hills

A number of species which are otherwise restricted to the eastern half of the park occur further westwards at isolated dolomite hills such as Tweekoppies and Tsumasa in the Halali area. Tsumasa lies within Halali Rest Camp and a species found there which is likely to be of particular interest to bird-watchers is the barecheeked babbler (564) which occurs only in northern Namibia and Angola. Other species you could spot during a ramble about the koppie include Swainson's francolin, Meyer's parrot (364), blackfaced babbler and shorttoed rock thrush (583).

Swainson's francolin

Birds of prey

Because there is such an abundance of prey animals and carrion, raptors are well-represented and so far 35 species have been recorded. Of the six vulture species recorded in the park, the whitebacked vulture (123) is the most common and most widely distributed, while the lappetfaced vulture (124) is also common. The hooded vulture (121) is confined to the eastern half of the park and is infrequently sighted, while the Egyptian vulture (120) occurs as a vagrant. Records of this species accepted by the Rarities Committee of the Southern African Ornithological Society include an immature bird sighted at Ombika waterhole in 1988 and two adults and an immature bird at Otjovasandu in August 1987. Another rare record from Etosha is that of a sooty falcon (175), which was sighted about 20 km north of Okaukuejo in 1985. The only other Namibian record of this extremely rare vagrant is that of a bird sighted in Windhoek in 1982.

Species seen infrequently

Notable species which are infrequently recorded in Etosha include slaty egret (70) and dwarf bittern (79) – an intra-African migrant occurring between October and April. Among the rare vagrants recorded are blacktailed godwit (287), Mongolian plover (250) and one of only three Namibian sightings of lesser blackbacked gull (313) recorded.

Vegetation

The vegetation of Etosha can be divided into three broad sub-types – tree savanna in the east, shrub and thornbush savanna in the west and the pan with its dwarf shrub savanna fringe. However, of the 21 vegetation types which have been identified in the park, the Etosha Pan itself makes up the largest single vegetation type. The pan has in fact been classified as a saline desert and is largely devoid of vegetation, except for patches of the salt-loving *Sporobolus salsus* which grows during wet years.

The dwarf shrub savanna along the perimeter of the pan, is replaced by grasslands, in which four distinct sub-types have been identified. Along the southern perimeter of the central pan is a relatively narrow band of sweet-grass on lime, while the western margin of the pan has been classified as the Okondeka duneveld. The grassland along the Ekuma River takes its name from the water course, while the Andoni grassland is an important winter grazing area.

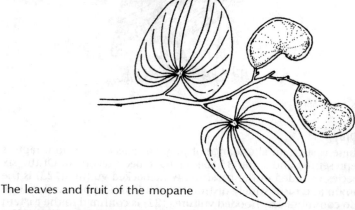

The leaves and fruit of the mopane

You will not fail to notice that the mopane (198) is the most dominant tree in Etosha, constituting more than 80 per cent of the trees in the park. It occurs either as tall trees forming dense woodlands, as can be seen in the Halali area, or extensive shrublands such as those west of the Moringa Forest.

Towards the east of the park the mopane is replaced by dense woodlands. South of Namutoni these woodlands are dominated by tamboti (341) and Lowveld cluster-leaf (550), while several *Acacia* species and sickle-bush (190) also occur. Characteristic trees and shrubs of the north-eastern sandveld north of Namutoni include Kalahari apple-leaf (239), Lowveld cluster-leaf, and rough-leafed croton (*Croton menyhartii*).

In the vicinity of Halali the flat mopane-dominated landscape is broken by a few dolomite outcrops. Here you have the opportunity to take a closer look at the koppie within the perimeter of the camp. You might be able to identify a scraggly bush at the base of the hill – it is the white raisin (458) bush. After the summer rains it produces a hairy, orange-brown berry which is a traditional veld food. Although these berries are not very fleshy, they have a refreshing sweet-sour taste.

A well-defined path will lead you to the top of Tsumasa Koppie where you will be rewarded with a commanding view. The moringa (137) trees growing amongst the black dolomite slabs create perfect silhouettes for interesting sunset photographs.

These trees usually grow amongst rocky outcrops, but an unusually dense stand of moringas can be seen at the Moringa Forest west of Okaukuejo – the only place where such a dense concentration occurs on a plain. According to the early inhabitants of the area, the Heikum San, these weird-looking trees with their distorted trunks were flung from Heaven by Thora (the divine being in which they believed) because he was angered by their ugliness. Here they landed upside down and continued to grow as they landed.

A conspicious tree that you are unlikely to miss in the Namutoni area is the tall real fan palm which can be seen in the rest camp and at the appropriately-named Twee Palms waterhole. The real fan palm occurs in northern Namibia and Botswana, as well as along the Limpopo River. In rural areas frequented by tourists, carvings are made on the small, white kernels of the seeds which resemble the vegetable ivory of South America. An alcoholic beverage is brewed from the sap drained from the crown of the trunk.

History

Early inhabitants

In earlier times small bands of Heikum San inhabited the area surrounding Etosha, and the pan also played an important role in the economy and religious beliefs of the Owambo. Not only was salt an important bartering commodity, but the salt pan excursion to collect salt was one of the most important religious ritual practices of the Ndonga, Kwambi and Ngandjera kingdoms. The excursion was preceded by the salt pan ritual which was associated with rain-making and agricultural production. However, by the mid–1930s, the practice had ceased.

Explorers' impressions

The first Europeans to set eyes on the Etosha Pan were the Swedish explorer Charles John Andersson and his British companion Francis

Galton who passed by in 1851. Andersson recorded the following description of the pan:

> In the course of the first day's journey, we traversed an immense hollow, called Etosha, covered with saline incrustations and having wooded and well-defined borders ... In some rainy seasons, the Owambo informed us, the locality was flooded, and had all the appearance of a lake; but now it was quite dry, and the soil strongly impregnated with salt.

Others followed in their footsteps, including the hunter Axel Eriksson, the missionary Hugo Hahn and the American trader Gerald McKiernan.

Thirstland Trekkers

Between 1874 and 1877 several groups of "trekkers" emigrated from the Transvaal to Angola in search of a Calvinist state independent from British domination. The hardships that these pioneers endured when they travelled through the waterless Kalahari gave rise to the name "Dorslandtrek" (Thirstland journey). The Thirstland Trekkers stayed at Namutoni and Rietfontein in 1876 before continuing further north to Angola. The solitary grave of the wife of trek leader Gert Alberts is at the Rietfontein waterhole. In 1885 a number of Thirstland Trekkers stayed at the two springs after their return from Angola.

Control posts and forts

Following the outbreak of the rinderpest epidemic in 1896 disease control posts were established at Namutoni, Rietfontein and Okaukuejo and, in an effort to extend German control over the Owambo kingdoms of the area, the posts were converted into police posts. In 1901 a limestone fort was built at Okaukuejo and towards the end of 1903 a six-roomed fort was completed at Namutoni.

While the German forces were suppressing the Nama uprising in the south and the Herero uprising in the central parts of the country, King Nehale of the eastern Ndonga kingdom decided to join the fight against the Germans. Several hundred Ndonga warriors attacked Fort Namutoni on 28 January 1904. The fort was defended by four German colonial non-commissioned military officers and three ex-servicemen who farmed near Namutoni. Since the warriors were unable to withstand the German rifle fire, they retreated to a thorn enclosure where they took cover. With their ammunition virtually depleted the Seven Defenders of the Fort, as they became known, escaped under cover of darkness and the following day the fort was razed to the ground.

In December 1904 Namutoni was once again occupied by a small contingent of troops and in February the following year work commenced on a new fort. The new fort, an irregular quadrangle measuring approximately 60 metres by 68 metres, was completed in 1906 but, following the proclamation of Game Reserve No 2 in 1907 and the so-called protection treaties signed in May/June 1908, the military significance of Namutoni declined and on 1 April 1912 the fort was closed.

Two years later World War I broke out and Namutoni was once again occupied by a contingent of 190 German officers and troops. To prevent the German forces from retreating further north the South African First Mounted Brigade under the command of General Coen Britz advanced on Namutoni via Ombika and Rietfontein and on 6 July 1915 the German commander of Namutoni offered to surrender.

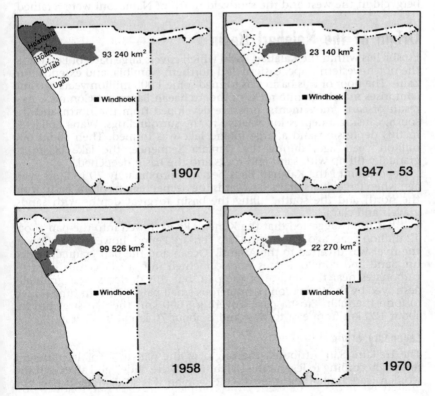

Etosha National Park's boundary changes over the years

Extent of the park

Over the years the boundaries of the park have changed several times. In 1947 the park was reduced from its original size of 93 240 km^2 to a mere 23 140 km^2 when the Kaokoland portion of the reserve was demarcated for occupation by Herero-speaking people. In the same year the south-eastern corner was also deproclaimed and divided into commercial farms. On the recommendation of the Elephant Commission of 1956 the size of the park was increased to 99 526 km^2 by incorporating State Land between the Hoanib and the Ugab rivers.

In 1962 the Odendaal Commission was appointed to investigate the possibility of creating a homeland system similar to that of South Africa. Since the area between the Ugab and Hoanib rivers fell within the proposed Damaraland homeland, the Commission proposed deproclaiming this section and by 1970 Etosha had shrunk to a mere 21 365 km^2. A further 905 km^2 was subsequently added when a number of farms were acquired in the Otjovasandu area to the south-west of the park, while the bergveld in the west and the sandveld north of Namutoni were retained.

Origin of the Kalahari Basin

Etosha lies within the Kalahari Basin which covers large parts of Botswana, the north-western Cape, eastern and northern Namibia, and extends into Zaire. The floor of this basin was formed some 1 000 million years ago and comprises mainly granite rocks of the Archaean Basement Complex. As a result of earth movements, pressure developed from the north and the south, causing a depression relative to the surroundings. Water collected in this depression and a large inland lake was formed. Then about 600 million years ago, during the Damara Sequence, the lake began to gradually fill up with sand and rocks and the basin deepened.

Deposition of the Kalahari Beds began approximately 70 million years ago when large rivers drained towards the deeper regions of the basin from the north and the south, filling the basin to great depths with sands, gravels and clays.

It has been suggested that the Kunene River flowed into the pan about 12 million years ago. During the late Tertiary Period, however, the flow of the river was diverted to the Atlantic Ocean and the pan gradually dried up. Sand and conglomerates were cemented into a calcicerous crust by carbonates near the surface of the pan, but this duricrust was gradually destroyed by the formation of numerous small pans which in time joined to form the main Etosha pan. Covering 5 000 km^2 the pan stretches for about 120 km from east to west and is about 70 km at its widest.

Legendary origin

The Heikum San attributed the origin of the pan to a totally different reason. According to legend the Heikum San were raided and all except the women were brutally murdered. One woman was so distraught over the savage death of her child that her tears formed an enormous lake. With evaporation the lake dried up, leaving the salt pan.

References

Andersson, C.J. (1987) *Lake Ngami or Explorations and Discovery During Four Years of Wanderings in the Wilds of South-Western Africa*. Reprint from 1967; first edition 1856. Cape Town: Struik, 1987.

Archibald, T.J. (1991) 'Etosha flamingoes and the rescue operation in 1989'. *Lanioturdus* 26 (1): 36 – 39.

Berry, C. (undated) *Trees and Shrubs of the Etosha National Park*. Windhoek: Directorate of Nature Conservation and Recreation Resorts.

Berry, H.H. (1972) 'The great flamingo trek'. *African Wildlife* 26 (2): 58 – 60.

Berry, H.H. (1972) 'Pelicans air-freight their fish 100 kilometres'. *African Wildlife* 26 (3): 120 – 124.

Berry, H.H. (1982) 'The wildebeest problem in the Etosha National Park: a synthesis'. *Madoqua* 13 (2): 151 – 157.

Berry, H.H. (1983) 'First catch your lion'. *Rössing Magazine*: April: 1 – 7.

Berry, H.H. (1983) 'The blue wildebeest problem at Etosha National Park'. *African Wildlife* 37 (5): 192 – 197.

Clinning, C.F. & Jensen, R.A.C. (1977) 'Additions to the bird checklist of Etosha National Park'. *Madoqua* 10 (2): 143 – 148.

Davis, S. (1970) 'Operation Flamingo'. *SWA Annual*: 25 – 33.

De La Bat, B. (1982) 'Etosha 75 years'. *SWA Annual*: 11 – 22.

Du Preez, J. (undated) *Animals of Etosha*. Windhoek: Shell Oil.

Giess, W. (1970) 'Ein Beitrag zur Flora des Etoscha Nationalparks'. *Dinteria* 5.

Jensen, R.A.C. & Clinning, C.F. (1983) *Birds of the Etosha National Park*. Windhoek: Directorate of Nature Conservation and Recreation Resorts.

Nature Conservation, SWA (1982) *Etosha 1907–1982*. Windhoek: Directorate of Nature Conservation.

Nature Conservation, SWA (1984) *The History of Namutoni*. Windhoek: Directorate of Nature Conservation.

Nordenstam, B. (1970) 'Notes on the flora and vegetation of the Etosha Pan, South West Africa'. *Dinteria* 5.

Orford, R. (1988) 'Culling lions is not the answer. Contraception: A real alternative'. *African Wildlife* 42 (2): 61 – 65.

Williams, A.J. (1990) 'Crowned cranes and other wetland birds of the Ekuma River and Etosha National Park'. *Lanioturdus* 25 (1&2): 61 – 63.

Williams, F-N. (1991) *Precolonial Communities of Southwestern Africa: A History of Owambo Kingdoms 1600–1920*, 111 – 112 & 148 – 150.

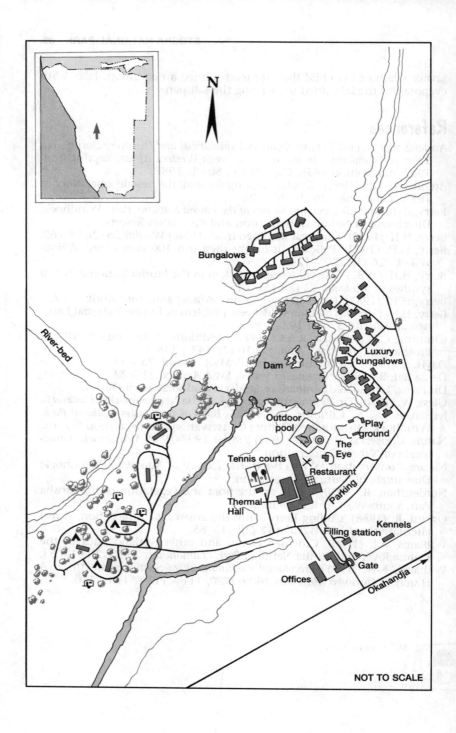

NOT TO SCALE

GROSS BARMEN
HOT SPRINGS RESORT
Size: 100 ha   Proclaimed: 1966

Location

Central Namibia.

What to do and see

Thermal springs, rambling.

Climate

Winter days are usually pleasant (23 °C average in June and July), while nights are cold with temperatures dropping to below 10 °C between May and September.

With an average maximum temperature of 34 °C, December is the hottest month. Summer evenings are generally pleasant, but at times they can be uncomfortably warm.

The area has an average rainfall of 366 mm – 70 per cent of which is recorded between January and March.

When to visit

The resort is open throughout the year.

Overnight visitors with reserved accommodation may enter at any time, but may not leave the resort between 23:00 and 07:00.

Day visitors are admitted from sunrise to sunset, but must leave the resort before 23:00. They are required to make prior reservations with the resort office, telephone (06221) 2091.

Where to stay

Accommodation ranges from luxury air-conditioned units sleeping five to two-bedded bungalows and rooms, while camping and caravan sites with communal ablutions and field kitchens are also available.

All accommodation units are equipped with fridges, kettles and hot plates, as well as with wash basins, toilets and showers, while the luxury bungalows also have baths. Each unit has its own outside fireplace. The two-bed bungalows are not equipped with cooking equipment and a field kitchen is available for visitors booked into them. Bedding and towels are supplied, but not crockery, cutlery or cooking utensils.

Visitor amenities

The chief attractions of the resort are the open-air swimming pool and the indoor thermal bath. Other amenities include tennis courts and a childrens' playground. There is a restaurant, a shop which sells souvenirs, groceries and liquor, and a filling station.

SERVICE HOURS:
Office: Sunrise to sunset.

Shop: 09:00 – 12:00 and 15:00 – 18:00
            09:00 – 12:00 and 16:00 – 18:00 (Sunday)

Restaurant:
Breakfast: 07:00 – 08:30
Lunch: 12:00 – 13:30
Dinner: 18:00 – 20:30

Where to book

See page 13.

How to get there

The turnoff to the resort is signposted a short distance beyond the southern entrance to Okahandja on the B2. Follow the signposted road (Route 87) to reach the turnoff to the resort 25 km further on.

What you should know

☐ The dam attracts mosquitoes all year round, so remember to pack mosquito repellant.

☐ The hot water and high humidity of the indoor thermal pool could have an adverse effect on people suffering from heart or kidney complaints and the pool should be used in moderation.

Gross Barmen nestles on the banks of a tributary of the Swakop River in unsurpassed surroundings, and is a delightful stopover for travellers making their way to the coast or further north. The beautiful setting of the spring was described most aptly by Charles Andersson when he visited the springs in 1850:

> *Towards the west, and immediately behind the station, rise irregular masses of low, broken rocks, ending abruptly on one side in a bluff, about one thousand feet high...To the eastward, it faces the Swakop, the course of which is conspicuously marked by the handsome black-stemmed mimosa. Beyond this, the view is limited by a noble range of picturesque mountains, rising between six and seven thousand feet above the level of the sea.*

Hot mineral spring

The focal point of the resort is the thermal spring which supplies water to the indoor thermal hall and the outdoor swimming pool.

The fountain or "eye" which feeds the two pools has been walled in and is covered with a metal dome symbolising the bubbling spring which has a flow of about 6 700 litres per hour. The concentration of fluoride and sulphate is lower than that of Ai-Ais and, with a temperature of about 65 °C, the water is about 5 °C warmer. Other elements include sodium phosphate, sodium, chloride, silicate and potash.

The clusters of lamps in the thermal hall are also symbolic of the bubbling spring. A novel feature of the indoor thermal hall, which is enclosed on one side with glass, is a sunken bath with an artificial waterfall where bathers can soothe their muscles. The water in the thermal hall is cooled to about 40 °C.

The water temperature of the open-air swimming pool is influenced by the air temperature, but is usually between 25 and 29 °C during daytime, while the water in the children's splash pool is lukewarm.

Birds

The dam, with its reedbeds and the surrounding hillsides, offers good opportunities for bird-watching and to date 150 species have been recorded. A path has been cut through the dense reedbeds which provide an ideal habitat for several warbler species while benches on the edge of the dam provide excellent vantage points for bird-watching. Among the species you are likely to see are whitebacked duck (101), a species which reaches its southernmost limit here, Cape teal (106), lesser moorhen (227) and redknobbed coot (228). Purple gallinule (223) are present too and, provided you are patient and approach quietly, there is a good chance of getting close-up photographs of this usually elusive species.

Worthwhile species to watch out for in the surrounding hills are Monteiro's hornbill (462), Carp's black tit (555), shorttoed rock thrush (583) and rockrunner (662). The colourful lilacbreasted roller (447) and the striking crimsonbreasted shrike (739) with its distinctive black and crimson colours are unlikely to escape your attention.

Rambling

Although no trails have been laid out, the more energetic can explore the rocky outcrops where there is a possibility of chancing upon kudu, warthog or a troop of baboons. Another alternative is to wander along the river-bed immediately to the west of the camping area.

History

Origin of the name

To the pastoral Herero people of the area, the spring was known as *Otjikango* – a name translated as "a spring flowing weakly through rocky ground". The Rhenish missionaries who settled here almost 150 years ago originally named the settlement Neu Barmen in honour of the Rhenish Missionary Society headquarters in Barmen, Germany, but it later became known as Gross Barmen.

Mission station

Work on the mission house began soon after missionaries Hugo Hahn and Heinrich Kleinschmidt arrived at Otjikango at the end of October 1844. Stone was used for the original dwelling, while limestone bricks were used for the subsequent additions. They also set about building a dam which was linked to the nearby garden by an aquaduct, while another garden was established in the bed of the Swakop River.

The first church was built in 1846–7, and the school had 128 pupils by 1851. After a large number of impoverished Herero had been resettled at Gross Barmen in 1869, the church became too small and a new church was consecrated on 28 June 1871.

The mission station was abandoned on several occasions during the seven-year war between the Herero and the Oorlam Afrikaners and other Nama-speaking groups in the 1860s. Gross Barmen became a branch of the RMS mission at Okahandja in 1889 after which missionaries were no longer stationed there.

Military fort

Gross Barmen did not only serve as a mission station. During the closing years of the 1800s it also assumed a military significance. In 1894 a double-storey fort with a quadrangular watch tower was built on a small rise which had a commanding view of the surrounding countryside. The fort was enlarged in 1902, but was abandoned two years later. In 1908–9 the fort was converted into a police station, but not long afterwards the station closed down and the building fell into decay.

Despite its interesting history hardly anything of this period has remained and the only evidence that this historic mission ever existed is the ruins of the old mission house, the site of which is marked by a solitary palm tree.

References

Andersson, C J. (1987) *Lake Ngami or Explorations and Discovery During Four Years of Wanderings in the Wilds of South-Western Africa.* Reprint from 1967; first edition 1856. Cape Town: Struik, 99 – 100.

Mossolow, N. (undated) *Otjikango or Gross Barmen – The History of the First Herero Mission in South West Africa, 1844–1904.* Windhoek: Mossolow.

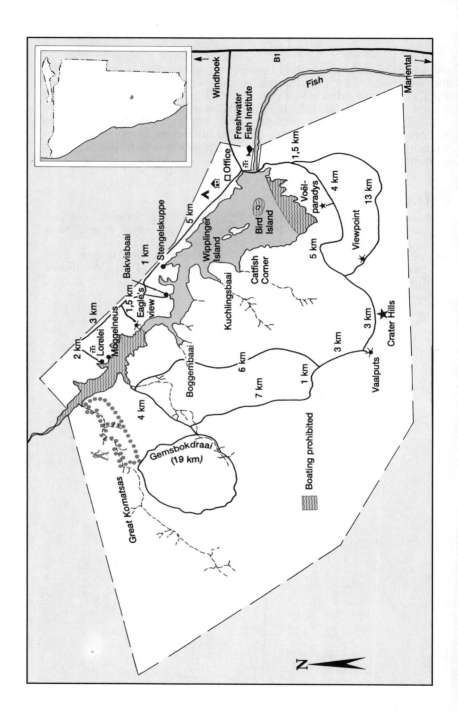

HARDAP DAM RECREATION RESORT AND GAME PARK

Size: 25 177 ha   Proclaimed: 1964

Location

Northern edge of the southern region.

What to do and see

Water sports, freshwater angling, game-viewing, bird-watching, day walks, freshwater aquarium.

Climate

Extremely hot days with temperatures averaging 35 °C are usually experienced during summer. The average summer minimum temperature is 17 °C indicating that nights are often uncomfortably hot. Daytime winter temperatures are pleasant, with the average maximum temperature for June and July being 22,6 °C. However, be prepared for near-freezing temperatures after sunset in mid-winter. The average annual rainfall is 215 mm, with January, February and March being the wettest months.

When to visit

The resort is open throughout the year.

Overnight visitors with reserved accommodation may enter the resort at any time, but may not depart between 23:00 and 06:00.

Day visitors are admitted from sunrise to sunset, but must leave the resort before 23:00. Prior reservations for day visitors are essential and may be made at the resort office, telephone (0661) 381.

The game park is open from sunrise to sunset throughout the year.

Where to stay

For caravaners and campers there are grassed sites with ablution blocks and field kitchens, while groups can hire ten-bed dormitories with communal facilities and field kitchens. There are also two-bed bungalows equipped with a kettle, fridge, shower and toilet, as well as two-roomed bungalows sleeping five which, in addition to the facilities of the two-bedded bungalows, each have a hot plate. Each bungalow has its own outside fireplace but no cooking or eating utensils are supplied. Bedding and bath towels are supplied to guests in the dormitories and bungalows.

Visitor amenities

Facilities include a licensed restaurant, shop, kiosk, filling station, outdoor swimming pool and tennis courts, as well as a playground for children.

SERVICE HOURS:
Office: Sunrise to 13:00 and 14:00 to sunset
Shop: 09:00 − 12:00 and 14:00 − 18:00

Restaurant:
Breakfast: 07:00 − 08:30
Lunch: 12:00 − 13:30
Dinner: 18:00 − 20:30

Picnic sites along the banks of the river below the dam wall are provided for day visitors, while facilities consisting of cement tables and chairs under cover are provided at a number of the popular angling spots along the northern shore of the dam.

Where to book

See page 13.

How to get there

A signpost on the B1 15 km north of Mariental indicates the turnoff to Hardap. From the turnoff it is 6 km to the entrance gate, with the resort office being a further 2,5 km on.

What you should know

☐ Anglers require a permit which is obtainable from the resort office or from any magistrate's office. Fishing is permitted only along certain areas of the shore, while boating is restricted to the central area of the dam. Obtain a map from the resort office to

ensure that you do not fish in restricted areas.
- ☐ Watch out for black rhino whenever you alight from your vehicle in the park.
- ☐ Mosquitoes can be a nuisance, especially during the summer months, so remember to pack a mosquito repellant.

Often regarded as no more than a convenient overnight stop, this resort and its game park warrant at least a two-night stay if they are to be fully appreciated. Obviously the dam is the main attraction for the majority of visitors, but tourists often arrive late in the afternoon and leave early the following morning without exploring the game park.

Perched on the edge of the cliffs along the northern banks of the dam, most of the bungalows overlook the huge artificial lake, while there is also a magnificent view over the water mass from the restaurant. To ensure that the resort blends in with its surroundings, stone from the area was not only incorporated in the face-brick exterior of the bungalows, but was also used extensively for terracing and stone walls.

Origin of the name

The landscape varies from undulating hills and valleys to wide open plains interspersed with conical-shaped hills capped with dolerite crowns. To the early inhabitants of the area one of these formations so closely resembled a female breast in profile that they called it *Hardap*, a Khoikhoi word meaning "nipple" or "wart".

Vegetation

The vegetation of the park consists of the dwarf shrub savanna type, with typical tree species such as shepherd's tree (122), stink-bush (124) and wild green-hair tree (214), especially along drainage lines. Shrubs include trumpet thorn (*Catophractes alexandri*), wool bush (*Leucosphaera bainesii*), brosdoring (brittle thorn, *Phaeoptilum spinosum*) and skilpadbossie (tortoise bush, *Zygophyllum pubescens*). Species to be seen along the more densely vegetated river-courses include camel thorn (168), sweet thorn (172) and buffalo-thorn (447), while Namaqua (51) and laurel (53) figs favour cliffs.

Game

Covering 25 177 ha, the game park is divided by the dam into two sections. Adjacent to the resort is a small area of 1 848 ha along the northern shore of the dam, while the larger 23 329 ha southern section is reached by following the road that runs along the 865 metre long dam wall. The largest game concentrations are found in the southern section and there is a choice of several routes along which visitors can explore the park by car.

Crater Hills picnic spot

An interesting stop and an ideal opportunity for a leg stretch on a game drive is at Crater Hills. Although a volcano did not erupt here, the rocks are naturally arranged in a circle, thus giving rise to the name. A reed canopy has been erected at the parking area to provide shade for picnickers.

Red hartebeest

Antelope

The area was farmland when the park was proclaimed in 1968 and game that had previously occurred naturally in the area had to be re-introduced. On a game drive your chances of seeing kudu, gemsbok, springbok and Hartmann's mountain zebra are fairly good, while red hartebeest and eland also occur. During an early morning or late afternoon drive you might also see steenbok.

Black rhinoceros

In an effort to establish more widely distributed populations of black rhinoceros in Namibia, two bulls and two cows were translocated from Damaraland in 1990, while a third cow was subsequently introduced. This is the southernmost population of black rhino in Namibia.

Following their re-introduction, the rhinoceros settled in the north-west of the park, while one crossed the upper reaches of the dam and wandered into the northern corner of the park. Keep an eye out for tell-tale signs of their presence – the distinctive four-toed spoor and large balls of dung – and you might just be fortunate enough to see them!

Leopard and cheetah

Leopard occur in the vicinity of the Great Komatsas River, while cheetah used to occur naturally. The cheetah were removed from the park because of their rapidly increasing numbers and the damage they were causing to stock on neighbouring farms.

Birds

A wide variety of birds is attracted by the diverse habitats which range from the open dam and the reedbeds below the dam wall to the dwarf shrub savanna and *Acacia* thickets in the river-courses. To date some 260 species have been recorded – 197 of which have been included in a checklist obtainable from the resort office.

Water-birds

Water-birds represent about 20 per cent of the total number of species and research has shown that they consume about 285 tonnes of fish a year at Hardap. The dam is the habitat of one of Namibia's three largest colonies of white pelicans (49). Their numbers fluctuate with the water level of the dam and the availability of water elsewhere, but at times they number up to 800. Even from the rest camp the pelicans may be seen, although only as white specks, bobbing on the water. Pinkbacked pelican (50) and greater flamingo (96) also occur, as do breeding colonies of whitebreasted (55) and reed (58) cormorants, darter (60) and African spoonbill (95), amongst others. Dead trees in the upper reaches of the dam provide a convenient perch for African fish eagle (148) and between October and April you might be fortunate enough to spot osprey (170).

Voëlparadys (Bird Paradise)

Despite its alluring name, Voëlparadys (Bird Paradise) is likely to be disappointing unless the dam is filled to capacity. The site near the southern tip of the dam was given the name when large numbers of whitebreasted cormorants nested in the camel thorn trees which died when the dam filled up in 1963. However, when the water receded the trees lost their appeal and the birds abandoned their nesting sites.

Birds below the dam wall

The well-established stand of sweet and camel thorn trees below the dam wall attracts a wide variety of birds, including burntnecked eremomela (656), barred warbler (658) and scarletchested sunbird (791). The reedbeds below the dam wall are a haven for numerous birds, including squacco (72) and greenbacked herons (74), while dwarf bittern (79) visits between October and April.

Birds along the game drives

Species you might spot on a game drive include ostrich (1), kori bustard (230), Namaqua sandgrouse (344) and Stark's lark (511), and, if you are fortunate, you might also see Sclater's lark (510) which is confined to the north-western Cape and southern Namibia. Mountain (586), familiar (589), sicklewinged (591) and anteating (595) chats have all been recorded, while capped wheatear (587) can be spotted between November and June. The cliffs are the habitat of rosyfaced lovebird (367), and there is also the possibility of seeing Bradfield's swift (413) here.

Day walk

Nature-lovers who are keen to get a closer look at the environment on foot can follow a circular day walk in the north-western corner of the park. It takes about four-and-a-half hours to walk the 15 km route, but there is also a shorter 9 km route which takes about three hours. The route offers trailists an opportunity to identify some of the characteristic plants of the south of the country. Several tree, shrub and plant species, as well as places of interest have been numbered along the route and can be identified by referring to the corresponding number in an information brochure which is obtainable at the office.

Places of interest along the route include the ruins of the country's first school for whites on the banks of the Great Komatsas River. Shortly after passing the school you will reach a spring surrounded by tall shady trees. It is worthwhile planning to take a breakfast or lunch break here. On the homeward-bound stretch of the route, a deposit of Iceland spar is passed. A characteristic of this optically pure variety of calcite is the strong double refraction – if a piece of clear Iceland spar is placed on ruled paper two lines will appear.

Trailists are warned to be on the lookout for black rhino along the trail. Although much of the route passes through short scrub vegetation, be especially alert when passing through dense vegetation.

History

The possibility of harnessing the water of the Fish River for irrigation was first raised in 1897 by a German geologist, Dr Theodor Rehbock. In 1903 another survey was conducted by Alexander Kuhn who reported that a most suitable site for a dam had been identified on the farm Hardap. After further investigations, the *Landesrat* approved plans for a dam at Komatsas North, 8 km upstream of the present site, during 1912–13. However, the dam did not materialise and interest in the scheme was only revived in 1941. Following intensive surveys between 1949 and 1959, the present site was selected as being the most favourable option, and construction began in 1960. The project was completed three years later at an estimated cost of 3,6 million rands. With a capacity of 323 million m^3 and a surface area of 25 km^2, Hardap is Namibia's largest dam. At the time of its completion it was the third largest dam in southern Africa.

Water from the dam is supplied to the Hardap scheme where wheat, maize, lucerne, cotton, grapes and vegetables are cultivated under irrigation on about forty smallholdings. It had originally been estimated that approximately 6 000 ha of land could be placed under irrigation, but this was later reduced to 2 500 ha. The dam is also the main water supply for Mariental and plays an important role in the control of floods. An amazing 5 500 m^3 can be discharged every second through the four radial gates in the spillway.

Angling

Hardap is considered to be the mecca of freshwater anglers in Namibia, and the well-stocked dam is consequently a popular choice for angling competitions. Species to be found there include smallmouth yellowfish (*Barbus aeneus*), Mozambique tilapia (*Oreochromis mossambicus*), common carp (*Cyprinus carpio*), mud mullet (*Labeo umbratus*), Orange River labeo (*Labeo capensis*) and sharptooth catfish (*Clarias gariepinus*), as well as a mudfish hybrid known as "onderbek".

Yellowfish (left) and catfish (right)

Freshwater Fish Institute

The Freshwater Fish Institute at the entrance of the resort is not open to the public, but visitors can obtain close-up views of some of the freshwater species to be found in Namibia by visiting the aquarium adjacent to the tourist office.

Angling regulations

Angling from the shore is restricted to the hours between sunrise and sunset along the northern shore of the dam where angling sites have been set aside. The sites are within 15 km of the rest camp and are accessible by sedan car. Boating, and hence angling from boats, is prohibited upstream of Eagles' View, around Bird Island and in the south-eastern corner of the dam.

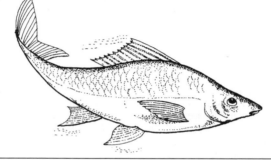

Mudfish

Freshwater angling regulations

The following regulations currently apply in respect of angling in dams and inland rivers in Namibia.

- Anglers fishing outside state conservation areas must be in possession of a valid angling licence which is obtainable from any magistrate's office.
- Anglers fishing in any of the state-owned game parks or resorts must obtain a licence, available at Ai-Ais, Hardap, Von Bach and Popa Falls rest camps or at the reservations office in Windhoek.
- There is a daily bag limit of ten fish in respect of the following species: yellowfish, kurper (bream), catfish (barbel), carp and bass.
- The following minimum sizes of fish are applicable: kurper (bream) 20 cm, carp and bass 25 cm, yellowfish 30 cm and catfish (barbel) 35 cm.
- These regulations are not applicable in the rivers in the north of Namibia, namely the Kwando/Linyanti/Chobe, Kavango, Kunene and Zambezi rivers. Uniform regulations for the entire country are in preparation (1993).

Water sports

The dam is also popular with water sports enthusiasts and yachting, powerboating, water-skiing, windsurfing and canoeing are all enjoyed there. A triathlon is held at the resort in November each year.

References

Anonymous (1990) *Hardap: Hiking Trail, Bird List.* Windhoek: Ministry of Wildlife, Conservation and Tourism.

Stern, C. & Lau, B. (1990) *Namibian Water Resources and Their Management: A Preliminary History.* Windhoek: National Archives of Namibia.

Wipplinger, O. (1961) 'Hardap Dam to be third biggest in southern Africa'. *SWA Annual*: 23 – 27.

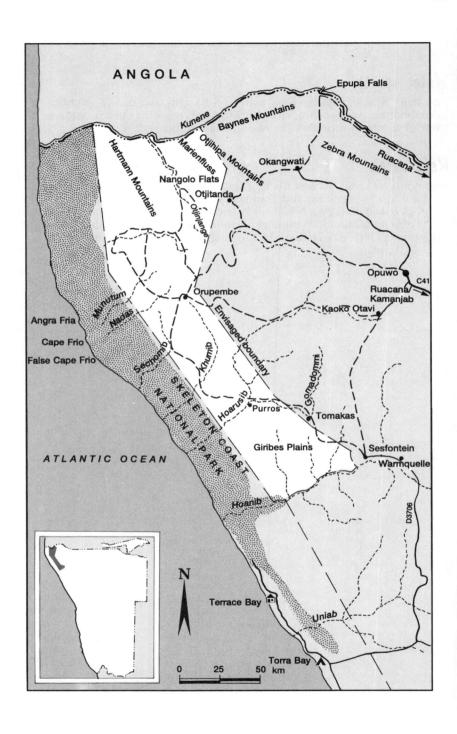

KAOKOLAND
CONSERVATION AREA
Still to be proclaimed

Location

North-western Namibia.

What to do and see

Sightseeing, game-viewing, photography.

Climate

During the summer months temperatures in excess of 35 °C can be expected during the day, especially in the river valleys. Winter days are pleasant with daily maximum temperatures of about 26 °C in June. With an average minimum temperature of 6 °C in mid-winter, evenings tend to be cold and frost is not uncommon in June, July and August.

Situated in the Pro-Namib, the area has an average rainfall of between 30 and 100 mm. The main rainy season starts in January, and reaches a peak in March. Rain usually occurs as heavy thunderstorms in the late afternoon, but the rainfall is, however, highly variable.

When to visit

Open throughout the year, but as summer temperatures are excessive and there is a danger of flash floods, the area is best visited during the cooler winter months.

Where to stay

At present there are no restrictions on where visitors may camp, but this could change once the area has been afforded official conservation status.

There are three privately-run camps in the vicinity of the Kunene River. Synchro camp, operated by Kaokohimba Safaris, is situated in the Marienfluss and consists of a number of wooden huts, a dining area and ablution facilities. The huts are not equipped and visitors must supply their own bedding, stretchers or foam rubber mattresses. Synchro camp is available for do-it-yourself tourists provided it is not occupied by the safari operator.

The two other camps are used exclusively by the safari operators, and are therefore *not available for casual tourists*. Sierra Cafema camp, named after the mountains of that name across the Kunene River in Angola, belongs to Desert Adventure Safaris, while Skeleton Coast Fly-in Safaris has a camp to the west of the Hartmann Mountains along the Kunene River.

Visitor amenities

Other than the amenities offered by Synchro camp, there are no tourist facilities whatsoever in the area.

Travellers should note that fuel is only available at Palmwag south of Sesfontein and at Opuwo, but *not* at Sesfontein.

Where to book

No permits are required at present, but once the area has been officially proclaimed it will be necessary to obtain a permit. Prior to setting off, check with the Ministry of Wildlife, Conservation and Tourism, telephone (061) 63131 and the Local Conservator at Opuwo, telephone (06562) 3.

Synchro camp: Kaokohimba Safaris, P O Box 30828, Pioneers Park, Windhoek, telephone (061) 226779; fax (061) 223540.

How to get there

The area is accessible via either Ruacana in the north, Opuwo in the centre or Sesfontein in the south.

What you should know

☐ Since there are no shops in the area other than at Opuwo and Sesfontein, where a fairly limited range of foodstuffs and beverages are available, visitors must be totally self-sufficient for the duration of their visit.

☐ This remote area is accessible by four-wheel drive vehicle only and groups should travel in at least two vehicles.

☐   Although proclaimed roads are indicated on the Namibian Department of Transport road map, do not be misled. After leaving Sesfontein, Opuwo or Ruacana these roads are no more than tracks and it is necessary both to have a good sense of direction and to be able to refer to the topographical maps of the area.

☐   The 1:500 000 topographical map number 1711: Opuwo is useful for orientation, while the 1:250 000 maps (1712: Swartbooisdrif, 1714: Oshakati, 1812: Opuwo and 1814: Etosha West) are necessary for navigation. They are obtainable from the Surveyor General, Private Bag 13306, Windhoek, telephone (061) 220241 extension 347.

☐   The substrate of the area is extremely sensitive to disturbance, and existing tracks should be followed at all times.

☐   After good summer rains, tall grass growing on the centre ridge of the tracks tends to collect under the vehicle's protection plate and around the driving shaft. This is a potential fire hazard and it is essential that it is removed regularly.

☐   Visitors should not travel along the east to west-running river valleys, as they are used as natural migration routes by game. In most cases the slopes are too steep for the animals to escape approaching vehicles, resulting in exhaustion, serious injury or even death. In addition, flash floods pose a threat during the summer months.

☐   The springs in the area are vital sources of water for game which has to travel up to 30 km between waterholes. Visitors should camp at least a kilometre from waterholes or springs, and should not use the water for washing.

☐   When breaking up camp, ensure that all refuse has been collected and that fires have been properly extinguished. Refuse must not be buried, but must be taken with you.

☐   Camping in river-beds is dangerous during the summer months when rains in the interior cause flash floods, often with little if any warning.

☐   Owing to the presence of crocodiles in the Kunene River, it is inadvisable to swim in the river, although the pools alongside the rapids at Epupa Falls are said to be relatively safe.

☐   It is of the utmost importance to respect the customs and traditions of the Himba people living in the area. As they are nomadic their kraals often appear to be abandoned, and household utensils and other possessions should not be removed under any circumstances. Do not enter a kraal uninvited and *never* walk between the main hut and the holy fire. When taking photographs, first obtain permission and offer

money or food such as maize meal and especially sugar, or tobacco, as payment.
☐ The Kunene River lies within a malaria epidemic area and it is advisable to take the necessary precautions throughout the year, but especially during summer. Also remember to take a mosquito repellant and wear long-sleeved shirts and trousers.

Kaokoland is one of the last remaining wilderness areas in southern Africa. It is a world of incredible mountain scenery, a refuge for the rare desert-dwelling elephant, black rhinoceros and giraffe and the home of the Himba.

The area north of the Hoarusib River originally formed part of Game Reserve No 2, but was deproclaimed when Kaokoland was demarcated for occupation by Herero-speaking people in 1947. Several subsequent attempts to afford the area formal conservation status have met with little success, and during the late 1970s and early 1980s much of the game which occurred in the area was wiped out by poachers.

Extent of proposed conservation area

Proposals to set aside a conservation area have, however, been submitted to the Minister of Wildlife, Conservation and Tourism, and are currently (1993) under consideration. The proposed area will cover approximately 1 500 000 ha, stretching from the Hoanib River in the south to the Kunene River in the north. The eastern boundary will coincide more or less with the escarpment mountains, while the park will border on the Skeleton Coast Park in the west.

Rugged beauty

One of the main attractions of this area is the starkly beautiful scenery. Although it is harsh and offers little respite at midday, the rugged landscape is especially attractive during the early morning and late afternoon when it is transformed into softly glowing pastel shades.

The topography in the south of the area is characterised by rugged mountains which are dissected by numerous watercourses, but north of the Hoarusib the scenery is dominated by table-top koppies. Still further north, the koppies give way to extensive gravel plains and sand flats. In the extreme north, the Otjihipa Mountains rise abruptly above the Pro-Namib floor to form the eastern boundary of the Marienfluss, while the west of the valley is defined by the Hartmann Mountains.

Left: Redknobbed coot – one of several waterbirds which can be seen on the dam at Gross Barmen Hot Springs Resort (see page 87)

Below: A view of the bungalows at Gross Barmen Hot Springs Resort, from across the dam (see page 85)

W & S Olivier

W & S Olivier

Above: The restaurant at Hardap Dam presents visitors with stunning views of the dam (see page 91)

Below: A view of Hartmann Valley in the north of the proposed Kaokoland conservation area (see page 101)

Above: The proposed Kaokoland conservation area is bounded in the north by the Kunene River (see page 101)

Left: The Kaudom Game Park can only be explored in four-wheel drive vehicles as most tracks are very sandy (see page 111)

This satellite photograph of the central Namib clearly shows that the Kuiseb River serves an important ecological role in preventing the encroachment of the sand-dunes of the south on the gravel plains of the north. The Desert Ecological Research Unit at Gobabeb is therefore strategically placed at the convergence of three major ecosystems of the Namib – the sand sea, the Kuiseb River and the gravel plains (see pages 159 and 160).

KEY

1	Walvis Bay	6	Khomas Hochland Mountains
2	Swakopmund	7	Sandwich Lagoon
3	Khan River	8	Kuiseb River
4	Welwitschia Plains	9	Desert Ecological Research Unit, Gobabeb
5	Swakop River		

Game

Elephant

The possibility of obtaining a glimpse, however brief, of a herd of desert-dwelling elephants moving across the lunar landscape of Kaokoland is to many visitors the main attraction of the area. Bear in mind, though, that animal movements are determined by the availability of food and water and there can never be a guarantee that game will be seen in a particular area.

Between 1977 and 1982 a crippling drought gripped the area and wiped out large numbers of game. However, the biggest threat came from poachers, and between 1970 and 1983 the number of desert-dwelling elephants in the Kaokoveld declined from an estimated 300 to 70.

Air-borne conservation officials observing desert elephant in the Kaokoveld

Although the desert-dwelling elephants are not a separate sub-species, they have adapted to their extremely harsh environment – the only other place in Africa where elephants live in such harsh conditions is in Mali on the edge of the Sahara Desert. The secret of their survival in the arid wastelands of the Kaokoveld is an intimate knowledge of their limited food and water resources. During dry periods they will even dig deep holes to obtain water and in this way also provide other animals with water. In the desert margin zone of Kaokoland the elephants mainly occur in the Hoanib, Hoarusib and Khumib rivers where they have been recorded as moving up to 70 km per day between feeding areas and waterholes. Unlike other elephants which drink daily, these ones have been observed going without water for up to four days.

Black rhino

The black rhino of the Kaokoveld suffered a fate similar to that of the elephants and by 1983 the population in the east had been exterminated, while only a few individuals survived in the extreme western parts of Kaokoland. Tourists are unlikely to see rhino, however, as they inhabit only the most remote and inaccessible areas.

Zebra, giraffe, gemsbok and springbok

Age-old zebra tracks criss-crossing the rocky escarpment mountains provide evidence of the presence of Hartmann's mountain zebra, while gemsbok and springbok are fairly common. Giraffe are most likely to be seen in the river valleys and there is a good chance of sighting them in the Hoanib, Khumib and Hoarusib rivers.

Conservation projects

Had it not been for the concern of a group of Namibian conservationists, business people, and non-governmental organisations, the wildlife heritage of Kaokoland would in all probability have been poached to extinction.

In the early 1980s the Endangered Wildlife Trust (EWT) and the South African Nature Foundation became involved in conservation projects in Kaokoland after the dramatic decline in the rhino and elephant populations had become apparent. Early in 1982 the Namibia Wildlife Trust was formed and, realising that the only way to bring poaching under control was to gain the support of the local people, an extensive conservation education and extension programme was launched. By the middle of the following year an auxiliary game guard system had been initiated in southern and western Kaokoland with the co-operation and assistance of the Herero and Himba headmen in the area, and poaching was effectively brought under control.

The work of the Namibia Wildlife Trust was subsequently continued by the Save the Rhino Trust while the Integrated Rural Development and Nature Conservation Project funded by the EWT is enjoying considerable success.

In an effort to restock the area with game, 29 gemsbok and ten giraffe from the Etosha National Park were released at Purros by the Ministry of Wildlife, Conservation and Tourism during the second half of 1990.

Birds

Despite its aridity, Kaokoland is an interesting bird-watching area. Two Namibian specials that inhabit the gravel plains and are likely to be of particular interest to bird-watchers are Rüppell's korhaan (236) and Gray's lark (514), while Ludwig's bustard (232) and Stark's lark (511) are two more typical Namib species that you might see here. Among the more common species likely to be seen are ostrich (1), Sabota lark (498), longbilled lark (500), greybacked finchlark (516), shorttoed rock thrush (583) and Karoo chat (592).

The escarpment, which forms the eastern boundary of the proposed park, is the habitat of several other Namibian specials – namely Rüppell's parrot (365), Monteiro's hornbill (462), barecheeked babbler (564), Herero chat (618), rockrunner (662) and whitetailed shrike (752).

Along the Kunene bird-watchers might see two species which occur nowhere else in southern Africa – the rufoustailed palm thrush (604) and Cinderella waxbill (849). The Cinderella waxbill is endemic to southern Angola, while the rufoustailed palm thrush occurs from the Kunene River northwards to Gabon.

The Kunene River forms a corridor that enables species typical of the south-eastern region of the sub-continent to penetrate Namibia, and bird-watchers might well see several species here which are not usually associated with this arid region.

A species that has a limited distribution elsewhere in southern Africa, but which may be seen here, is the mourning dove (353) which has been spotted in the riverine woodlands of the upper Hoarusib.

Inhabitants – the Herero and Himba

Another fascinating aspect of the area is the history of the people who live here. It is only relatively recently that both Herero and Himba have settled permanently in the Pro-Namib. Prior to about 1980 they inhabited the more vegetated areas to the east of the escarpment, but periodically migrated through the area with their stock when grazing was favourable.

Partially complete Himba (left) and Herero (right) huts

The Himba share a common ancestry with the Herero and are, likewise, pastoralists and speak Herero. Herero settlements can be recognised immediately by their square or rectangular houses with upright walls and thatched roofs, while Himba huts are dome-shaped and constructed from flexible saplings. Another obvious difference is the dress of the women. The Herero women usually wear brightly-coloured long cloth dresses, a tradition inherited from the missionaries' wives almost a century ago. Himba women, on the other hand, wear leather aprons and their naked upper torsos, including their hair, are covered with a cream of butterfat, herbs and ochre powder to give it a rich glowing colour.

Although the Himba are nomadic, they do have semi-permanent settlements at Purros and at Orupembe. An important aspect of the proposed park is that the people already inhabiting the area will be allowed to continue their traditional way of life.

Vegetation

Bordering on the Namib Desert, the vegetation of the area is as fascinating as the animal life, but is often overlooked.

Rocky areas

A variety of *Commiphora* trees dot the rocky hills, but because they blend in so well with the rocks amongst which they grow, they are often overlooked. The occasional African star-chestnut (474) with its mottled purple bark, moringa (phantom) tree (137) and shepherd's tree (*Boscia* spp.) have also managed to established themselves amongst the rocks but are often so stunted that they resemble bonsais.

River valleys

In contrast the river valleys are relatively well vegetated with some impressive specimens of ana tree (159) and camel thorn (168), both of which often provide much sought-after shade for a midday break. Another obvious and widespread tree is the mopane (198) with its butterfly-wing leaves. All three are important sources of food for domestic stock and game.

Gravel and sand stretches

Gravel and sand expanses, like those in the Marienfluss and the Giribes Plains, as well as further westwards, are transformed into waving grasslands after a good rainy reason. Continuing its intermittent distribution from just north of the Kuiseb River into Angola, the *Welwitschia* (21.1) also grows here and can be seen on the flat gravel areas between the Hoarusib and Hoanib rivers and in the vicinity of the Sechomib River.

Mysterious barren circles

One of the most characteristic sights of Kaokoland are the dense clumps of *Euphorbia damarana* which dot the landscape. It has been suggested that the barren circles which are randomly distributed in the Marienfluss, the Hartmann's Valley and on the Giribes Plains were caused by poisons exuding from dead euphorbias. A more likely explanation, however, is that they are the result of harvester termites denuding patches of vegetation. In the absence of vegetation deflation hollows are created by the wind, inhibiting further plant growth. These intriguing circles have a diameter of up to five metres and appear to be completely sterile.

References

Malan, J.S. & Owen-Smith, G.L. (1974) 'The ethnobotany of Kaokoland'. *Cimbebasia* Ser B 2 (5).

Viljoen, P.J. (1982) 'The distribution and population status of the larger mammals in Kaokoland, South West Africa/Namibia'. *Cimbebasia* Ser A 7 (2).

Viljoen, P.J. (1988) 'The desert-dwelling elephant: hardy survivor'. *African Wildlife* 42 (2): 111 – 115.

Winterbottom, J.M. (1966) 'Results of the Percy FitzPatrick Institute – Windhoek State Museum joint ornithological expeditions: 5. Report on the birds of the Kaokoveld and Kunene River'. *Cimbebasia* 19.

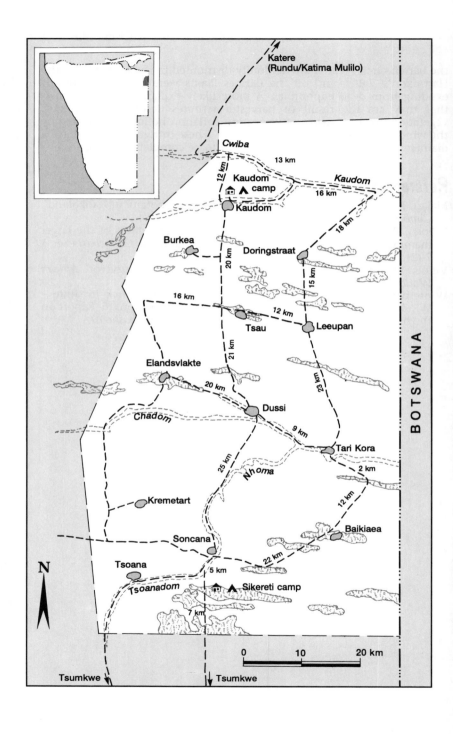

KAUDOM GAME PARK

Size: 384 162 ha   Proclaimed: 1989

Location

North-eastern Namibia.

What to do and see

Game-viewing, bird-watching, photography.

Climate

The climate of the Kavango consists of two seasons. There is a long dry season which can be sub-divided into a cool dry season (April to August), a hot dry season (September to November), and a short wet season (November to April). Humidity ranges from 30 per cent during the dry season to between 60 and 70 per cent during the hot rainy season. About 80 per cent of the area's rainfall, which averages between 550 and 600 mm per annum, falls between December and March.

Between October and April average daily maximum temperatures exceed 30 °C, sometimes reaching as high as 40 °C, while minimum temperatures range between 15 °C and 18,8 °C. During mid-winter daily minimum and maximum temperatures fluctuate between 5,7 °C and 26,1 °C.

When to visit

The park is open from sunrise to sunset throughout the year.

GAME-VIEWING: June to October.
BIRD-WATCHING: November to March.

Where to stay

Visitors are accommodated in two rustic bush camps. Sikereti camp, which is conveniently close to the southern border of the park, originally served as a base for prospectors. Facilities here include three rustic thatch-roofed timber huts, a communal open-air cooking area, a scullery, communal ablutions, fireplaces and three camp sites.

Further north, Kaudom camp on the northern banks of the Kaudom Omuramba affords visitors beautiful views of the wide floodplains. Facilities here are similar to those at Sikereti — three huts and a number of camp sites.

Each of the huts is equipped with a table, chairs and four beds with mattresses, but visitors must supply their own bedding, cooking and eating utensils, as well as lighting. The ablutions have flush toilets, and water for the showers is heated in a small wood-burning boiler — true luxury in the wilderness!

Visitor amenities

Since there are no facilities such as shops, restaurants and filling stations in the park it is essential to be completely self-sufficient.

Where to book

See page 13.

Because of the small number of people that can be accommodated, it is advisable to make reservations well in advance — especially for the winter school holidays in May.

How to get there

Access to the park can be gained either from the south via Tsumkwe or via Katere on the main road that links Rundu with Bagani in the north.

Approaching via Tsumkwe, turn north just beyond the school in Tsumkwe and continue for about 21 km to the Klein Dobe/Groot Dobe intersection. Ignore the turnoffs and continue in a northerly direction for about 13 km to reach a track that branches off to the right. From here there is a short 3 km detour to the historic Dorslandboom, an enormous baobab tree, where the Dorslandtrekkers camped for a while in the late 1870s and early 1880s during their epic journey to Angola. This a worthwhile deviation but if time is at a premium ignore it and continue in a north-easterly direction. The southern boundary of the park is reached about 17 km further on, while Sikereti camp is another 7,5 km.

The approach from the north is signposted at Katere on the B8, about 120 km east of Rundu. Turn south onto the track which is usually in a reasonable condition for the first 20 km, but is often very sandy further south. Turn left about 43 km from the turnoff to reach the Cwiba Omuramba 6 km away. Kaudom camp is another 12 km further on.

The park is traversed by a 300 km network of game-viewing tracks. These are mainly sandy and can only be negotiated by four-wheel drive vehicles. Travellers visiting the park in the rainy season should be prepared for the possibility of being bogged down whilst crossing the omiramba.

What you should know

☐ Because of the park's inaccessibility, there must be at least two four-wheel drive vehicles in the party.

☐ East Kavango lies within an endemic malaria area and appropriate precautions must be taken.

☐ As the camps are unfenced, visitors are advised to be careful to look out for wild animals which could pass through, especially at night.

☐ Petrol is only available at Tsumkwe in the south and at Mukwe or Divundu in the north. The sandy tracks often require constant use of four-wheel drive, increasing fuel consumption considerably. Allowing for travelling in the park, sufficient fuel should be carried to cover at least 500 km.

☐ Visitors must carry emergency water and food in case of a breakdown.

☐ Caravans are not permitted but one may tow a trailer with the same track width of the towing vehicle.

☐ After the summer rains, tall grass growing on the centre ridge of the tracks often collects under the protection plate and around the driving-shaft of the vehicle. As this could catch fire, it is essential that the grass is removed at regular intervals.

☐ It is also advisable to fix a fine wire mesh to the inside of the front grill to prevent grass seeds and insects from clogging the radiator. When travelling in long grass, remove grass seeds from the mesh regularly.

☐ Visitors may alight from their vehicles anywhere in the park, but extreme caution must be exercised as dangerous animals are present.

Situated in the remote north-eastern corner of Namibia, Kaudom is one of the few remaining wilderness areas in the country. It is the only conservation area in Namibia which gives protection to the Kalahari sandveld – a world of endless woodlands, a variety of big game and a bird-watcher's paradise. Unlike many of southern Africa's more popular game reserves, facilities for visitors are basic and as each camp accommodates only a small number of people you are unlikely to feel crowded.

Game

To be successful game-viewing will require you to put your skills to the test and to exercise patience. Because of the limited number of visitors passing through the park the animals are rather skittish, and the dense vegetation considerably reduces visibility, especially after the summer rains. As the park is unfenced, the animals are free to follow their natural migration routes. Thus game numbers vary considerably. As a general rule though game-viewing is most rewarding during the dry winter months when the animals concentrate in the vicinity of artificial waterholes and along the omiramba. However, the abundance of seasonally-inundated pans and natural waterholes that fill up after the summer rains encourage the animals to disperse more widely, and species such as elephant frequently leave the park.

At times more than 500 elephant congregrate in the park and, although it is not uncommon to encounter large herds, they can be incredibly elusive, despite their large size! Giraffe are also common, but as they are well-camouflaged by the trees, the best chances of seeing them are at waterholes. Vervet monkeys occur throughout the park.

Antelope

Kaudom is the stronghold of Namibia's roan population and visitors are almost assured of sightings of this antelope.

Kudu and steenbok are frequently seen throughout the park, while gemsbok and blue wildebeest are also common, but are seen less frequently. Keep an eye open in the central parts of the park for tsessebe, red hartebeest, eland and reedbuck. Although these antelope occur in smaller numbers than the other species, sightings are not unusual.

Predators

Predators include lion, leopard and spotted hyaena, as well as black-backed and side-striped jackal, while cheetah sightings have also been reported. A pack of wild dogs is often seen near Sikereti camp.

Birds

The diverse habitats in Kaudom attract an interesting variety of birds and to date about 320 species have been recorded. Birds favouring the woodlands account for almost two-thirds of the total number of species.

During summer the number of species is swollen by waterbirds attracted to the seasonally flooded pans and omiramba, as well as the arrival of more than seventy migrant species. Migrants to watch out for include dwarf bittern (79) (known as the rail heron in tropical Africa), openbilled stork (87), African crake (212), lesser gallinule (224), black coucal (388) and the African golden oriole (544).

Rare species

Species occurring in the area but with a fairly limited distribution in southern Africa include the copperytailed coucal (389), Senegal coucal (390), Bradfield's hornbill (461), rufousbellied tit (556), blackfaced babbler (561) and sharptailed starling (767).

Also look out for the yellowthroated sandgrouse (346) which reaches the southern limit of its distribution in north-western Transvaal.

Copperytailed coucal

Birds of prey

Compared to other parts of southern Africa the diversity of raptors is high and about fifty diurnal raptors and owls have been recorded in eastern Kavango. Noteworthy residents include western banded snake eagle (145), bateleur eagle (146), rednecked falcon (178) and Dickinson's kestrel (185), while summer visitors include Steppe eagle (133), lesser spotted eagle (134) and western redfooted kestrel (179). Of the three vulture species occurring within the park, the whitebacked vulture (123) is common, while lappetfaced (124) and whiteheaded (125) vultures are uncommon.

Colourful birds

Colourful species which could attract your attention include Meyer's parrot (364), a common resident of the tall dry woodlands and *Acacia* woodlands, the lilacbreasted roller (447), and the crimsonbreasted shrike (739). The northern race of the Cape parrot (362) is seen less frequently.

Winter viewing spots

If your visit is planned for winter because you are primarily interested in game-viewing, time spent at waterholes could also be very rewarding from a bird-watching point of view. Whitebacked and whiteheaded vultures often congregate around the waterholes and there is always the possibility of getting close-up views of bateleur eagle and African hobby falcon (174), as well as large flocks of sharptailed starlings.

Vegetation

The vegetation of the park is characterised by a mosaic of woodlands ranging from tall to short dry woodlands and *Acacia* belts.

Tall dry woodlands

The tall dry woodlands consist of trees that are ten metres or higher, and are dominated by wild teak (236), Zambezi teak (206), wild seringa (197) and copalwood (199). Characteristic species of the understorey, which is generally well-defined, include sand camwood (223) and *Bauhinia* species.

Short dry woodlands

These woodlands are generally less than five metres high and usually lack a canopy. The most common species include shepherd's tree (122), Kalahari apple-leaf (239), and silver cluster leaf (551), as well as several wild raisin (*Grewia*) and bushwillow (*Combretum*) species.

Acacia woodlands

Unlike the dry woodlands which favour the Kalahari sands, the *Acacia* woodlands are generally associated with soils that have a relatively high clay content and they usually occur along omiramba margins, pan edges and dune slacks. Dominant species include plate (165), camel (168), candle (170) and umbrella (188) thorns, as well as russet bushwillow (538) and leadwood (539).

Lowveld cluster-leaf — habitat specific

The close association between vegetation and soil types is well-illustrated by the clumps of Lowveld cluster-leaf (550) trees, known locally as the purple-pod terminalia, which are restricted to dolomitic and calcrete ridges in the south of the park – one such place being Sikereti Camp.

Teak species

The deciduous wild teak (*Pterocarpus angalensis*) can easily be identified in winter by its characteristic fissured bark and the distinctive dry brown disc-like fruit with a bristly centre. Although the common names of the wild teak and the Zambezi teak could give the impression that they are related, the wild teak belongs to the Pea family, while the Zambezi teak is a member of the Flamboyant family. Neither of the two species are related to the East Indian teak, but they owe their common names to the close resemblance of their timbers to that of the latter.

The leaves and fruit of the wild teak

Flowering species

The woodlands are particularly attractive shortly before the first summer rains. Especially eye-catching are the knob thorn (178) trees with their masses of creamy white flowers and the red dwarf combretum (*Combretum platypetalum*) with its conspicuous compact clusters of brilliant red flowers.

Omiramba habitat

Another distinctive habitat are the omiramba. The vegetation of the Kaudom and Nhoma omiramba systems consists of short to tall grassland while *Phragmites* reedbeds vary from isolated patches to extensive stretches of up to 30 km.

Geology

Sand sea

Kavango lies within the Kalahari sand sea which covers about two-thirds of Botswana, eastern Namibia, the north-western Cape and parts of Angola, Zambia and Zimbabwe. The origin of this vast sand sea stretches back some 100 million years to the time when the Kalahari Basin, a vast shallow depression, was formed as a result of continental uplift. Over countless aeons the basin gradually filled up with sediments to eventually form the beds of the Kalahari Sequence which is up to 350 metres deep in south-western Kavango but only about 50 metres deep in eastern Kavango. Then, some three million years ago, strong easterly winds shaped the sand into west-east orientated linear dunes which were subsequently stabilised by vegetation to form permanent dunes. These dunes are a dominant feature of central and southern Kavango and, in contrast with the light grey to yellow and pink colour of the sands over most of Kavango, the permanent dunes have a characteristic orange to red colour.

Isolated rocky outcrops

Except for a few isolated outcrops of Karoo basalts at Andara along the Kavango River and Nosib quartzites of the Damara Sequence along the Nhoma Omuramba and in the vicinity of Sikereti, the older formations underlying the Kalahari Sequence are completely covered by the sand sea.

Kimberlite

Of interest to geologists was the discovery in 1979 of four small kimberlite pipes 13 km south-west of Sikereti. Extensive geological surveys, however, failed to find any trace of diamonds. These pipes are probably of post-Karoo age and are thought to be at the north-eastern end of a line of alkaline intrusions and volcanics which extends from Cape Cross across Kalkfeld to the Paresis Mountains at Otjiwarongo.

Omiramba (fossil rivers)

The sand sea is dissected by several fossil drainage lines, locally known as omiramba (singular – omuramba), a Herero word meaning "poorly-defined drainage line". Except for the Omuramba Omatako which drains into the Kavango River from the south-west and a number of small ephemeral channels which drain into the Kavango River, the omiramba generally run parallel to the dunes towards the Okavango Delta.

The three major drainage lines traversing the park, the Omuramba Nhoma in the south, and the Kaudom and Cwiba omiramba in the north, fulfil an important ecological role. During the wet season the extensive peat beds act like sponges to gradually release the water during the dry months. Uncontrolled burning is, however, posing a serious threat to this natural process.

It seems likely that these fossil rivers once flowed into the Okavango Delta, but they are now fed entirely by local rainfall and even during exceptionally rainy years large areas are often not flooded. Indications are that subterranean water of the omiramba could seep towards the Okavango Delta during the rainy season. During the dry season, however, the process in the areas closest to the Delta, is reversed and the flood from the Delta helps to raise the water-table although this is unlikely to occur in the Kaudom/Cwiba system. Thus water is available for game long after the field water has dried up. In addition, the omiramba serve as natural migration routes.

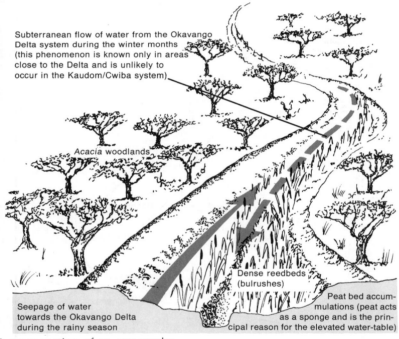

Subterranean flow of water from the Okavango Delta system during the winter months (this phenomenon is known only in areas close to the Delta and is unlikely to occur in the Kaudom/Cwiba system)

Acacia woodlands

Dense reedbeds (bulrushes)

Seepage of water towards the Okavango Delta during the rainy season

Peat bed accumulations (peat acts as a sponge and is the principal reason for the elevated water-table)

A cross-section of an omuramba

References

Correira, R.J. De Souza & Bredenkamp, G.J. (1987) 'A reconnaissance of the vegetation of the Kavango'. *SWA Scientific Society Journal:* XL/XLI 29 – 45.

Hegenberger, S. (1987) 'Stand der geologischen Kenntnisse uber das Kavangogebiet'. *SWA Scientific Society Journal* XL/XLI: 97 – 113.

Hines, C.J.H. (1987) 'The birds of eastern Kavango'. *SWA Scientific Society Journal* XL/XLI: 115 – 147.

Hines, C.J.H. (1989) 'The birds of North-eastern Namibia'. *Birding in Southern Africa* 41 (3): 89 – 92.

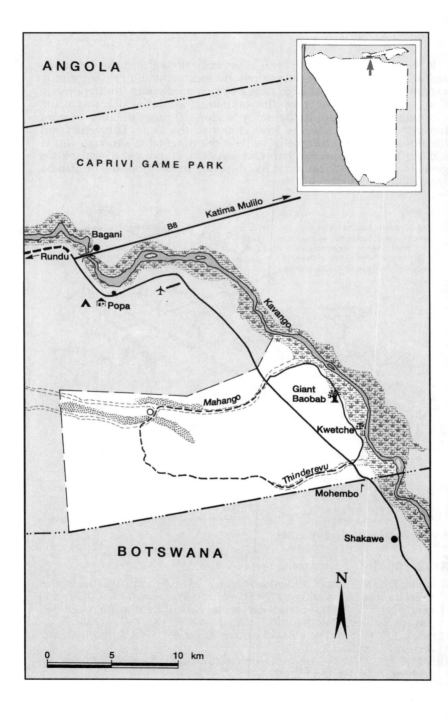

MAHANGO GAME PARK

Size: 24 462 ha   Proclaimed: 1989

Location

North-eastern Namibia.

What to do and see

Game-viewing, bird-watching, photography.

Climate

The climate of the region can be divided into two distinct seasons – a long dry season between April and November, and a short wet season which stretches from the end of November to late March/ early April.

October is the hottest month with an average maximum temperature of nearly 35 °C and, except for the months between May and August, the monthly average maximum temperature exceeds 30 °C. Daily average minimum temperatures range from 5,7 °C in July to 18,8 °C in January.

About 80 per cent of the region's rain (which varies between 550 and 600 mm a year) falls between October and April.

When to visit

The park is open from sunrise to sunset throughout the year.

GAME-VIEWING: June to October.
BIRD-WATCHING: November to March.

Where to stay

There is no accommodation in the park, but the rest camp at Popa Falls (see page 209) is a convenient base.

Visitor amenities

The only amenity in the park is a small picnic site on the banks of the Kavango River.

Where to book

Permits for entry to the park are obtainable at the northern park gate. Travellers using the main road through Mahango as a transit route between Namibia and Botswana do not require a permit, provided they do not deviate from the main road.

How to get there

The entrance gate to the Mahango Game Park is 15 km south-east of the Popa Falls Rest Camp on the road to Botswana.

What you should know

- ☐ Anti-malarial precautions must be taken throughout the year.
- ☐ Visitors are permitted to explore the Mahango Game Park on foot, at their own risk, but as there are dangerous animals present, caution must be exercised.
- ☐ Boating is prohibited in the park. The boundary on the Kavango River is clearly indicated by a large notice-board.
- ☐ Crocodiles and hippo abound in the Kavango River and swimming is therefore dangerous.

Sandwiched between the Botswana border and the Kavango River, the Mahango Game Park is a fascinating world of papyrus-lined channels, vast floodplains, dense riverine forests and woodlands.

The park was declared a conservation area by the former Kavango Executive Committee in 1983 and was opened to the public three years later. Access was initially restricted to four-wheel drive vehicles, but part of the park can now be explored in sedan cars.

Scenic drive

About 1 km from the park entrance on the Popa Falls side, a hard-surface road negotiable by sedan cars turns off to the left. This road follows the Mahango Omuramba for a short while before continuing along the edge of the Kavango floodplains. There are several good vantage points along this route where you can alight from your vehicle to take a closer view of the extensive floodplains. Caution must be exercised.

The highlights of this route are the cluster of giant baobabs (467) and the nearby picnic site at Kwetche. Shaded by large riverine trees the picnic site overlooks a papyrus-fringed channel of the Kavango River and is an excellent place for bird-watching. From Kwetche the road passes through dry savanna woodland to reach the main road nearly 10 km from the start of the loop.

Circular route

The more adventurous with four-wheel drive vehicles can explore a 19 km long circular route west of the main road. After following the course of the Thinderevu Omuramba for a few kilometres the track crosses the forested dunes into the Mahango Omuramba before winding back to the main road along the river course.

Birds

One of the main attractions of Mahango is its prolific birdlife, and the reserve boasts over 350 species, including 42 Palaearctic and 27 intra-African species. Birds recorded here but generally nowhere else in Namibia include western banded snake eagle (145), Dickinson's kestrel (185), African finfoot (229), lesser blue-eared starling (766) and yellow white-eye (797).

Distribution per habitat

On the basis of their habitat preferences, the birds of Mahango can be divided into three broad groups – species of the aquatic (river) environment, species of the semi-aquatic (omiramba and pans) environment and species attracted to the woodland habitats. The river habitat can be sub-divided into the open river, the backswamps and floodplains and the riverine fringe.

Aquatic (river) habitat

Open river

Boating is prohibited in the Mahango Game Park, but if you take a boating trip on the Kavango River (upstream of the park boundary), you are likely to see whitefronted (246) and whitecrowned (259) plovers, African skimmer (343), as well as whitefronted (443) and little (444) bee-eaters.

African skimmer

The African skimmer is a tern-like bird deriving its name from the characteristic way in which it catches food. Small fish are snapped up as it skims the water with its lower mandible just below the surface. Noticeably different from most other birds is the way in which the lower half of the bill extends beyond the top half of the bill.

In 1986 it was estimated that the world breeding population did not exceed 5 000 pairs. The African skimmer is extinct in South Africa and, because of its small population in Namibia and elsewhere in southern Africa, it is listed as threatened in the *Namibian Red Data Book for Birds*.

African skimmers breed on bare sandbanks when the level of the Kavango is low, usually between July and October. Nests consist of a mere scrape in the sand and eggs hatch after about three weeks. While breeding, African skimmers are particularly vulnerable, and the major natural threats to their survival are unintentional crushing of eggs and chicks by crocodile and hippo, unseasonal floods inundating sandbanks, and predators including snakes and birds.

African skimmer

Human disturbances are, however, a cause for concern. Waves caused by boats speeding up and down a river can destroy nesting sites. Breeding areas are best avoided! If you are unaware of nesting sites, bear the following in mind: When approaching a sandbank in a motorised boat, switch off the engine a fair distance away and allow the boat to drift up to the sandbank. Similarly, when leaving, pull away slowly to reduce the wake. Timing is also important – outings should be carried out in the late afternoon as parents will abandon their nests when disturbed, exposing their eggs or chicks to intolerable heat and eventual death.

Backswamps and floodplains

The backswamps and floodplains attract slaty egret (70) and squacco heron (72), as well as black (388), coppertailed (389) and Burchell's (391) coucals. Also keep an eye out for rufousbellied heron (75), openbilled stork (87), longtoed plover (261) and whiterumped babbler (562). Greater swamp warbler (636) and chirping cisticola (676) are confined to the papyrus swamps, while pinkthroated longclaw (730) have been recorded on the margins of the main floodplain. If you are fortunate you might also see wattled crane (207).

Riverine fringe
The riverine fringe is the most rewarding habitat, and among the interesting species which are common here are mourning dove (353), Meyer's parrot (364), swamp boubou (738) and longtailed starling (763), while African golden oriole (544) occurs between August and April. Less frequently seen are yellow white-eye and brown firefinch (843), while western banded snake eagle and Cape parrot (362) also occur, but are rare.

Semi-aquatic habitat
Omiramba and pans
Many of the birds attracted to the river habitat also occur in the omiramba and pan systems. During the dry winter months, however, the number of species to be seen in this habitat type is considerably reduced as about 40 per cent of the 150 species recorded in the omiramba and pans are confined to the open water.

Woodland habitat
In the tall dry woodlands you might see yellowthroated sandgrouse (346), Bradfield's hornbill (461), rufousbellied tit (556) and sharptailed starling (767). Look out here for arrowmarked (560) and blackfaced (561) babblers, which also occur in the *Acacia* woodlands.

The woodland habitats also harbour a rich diversity of raptors, including Dickinson's kestrel (185). Whitebacked vultures (123) are common, while lappetfaced (124) and whiteheaded (125) vultures are seen less frequently. Summer migrants include Steppe eagle (133), lesser spotted eagle (134), booted eagle (136), Steppe buzzard (149), hobby falcon (173), western redfooted kestrel (179) and lesser kestrel (183).

Game
Antelope
Your best chances of getting good views of red lechwe are during the early mornings and late afternoons when fairly large numbers can be seen grazing on the floodplains. However, they usually lie up during the heat of the day and are quite inconspicuous. Reedbuck also inhabit the floodplains, but in much smaller numbers. Consider yourself extremely fortunate if you manage to catch a glimpse of the rare sitatunga which favours the deep swamps. Elsewhere in southern Africa they are restricted to the northern part of the Okavango Delta.

Keep a close watch for Chobe bushbuck which favour the dense riverine fringe and which are usually active during the early mornings and late afternoons.

Two rare antelope species you might chance upon in the dry woodlands are roan and sable, both of which have a limited distribution in Namibia. Tsessebe, blue wildebeest, impala and gemsbok are less frequently seen, while buffalo are known to occasionally move into the park from the adjoining Caprivi Game Park. Kudu are common.

Elephant

Opportunities for spotting elephant are especially good during the dry season, when the elephants move into Mahango from Angola, Zambia and western Caprivi.

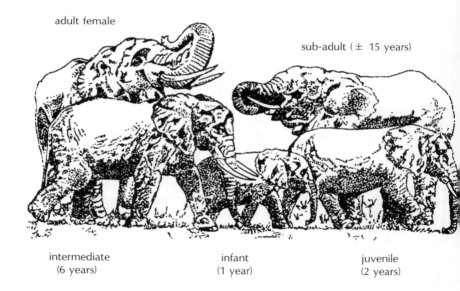

The sizes of elephants relative to age

Predators

Leopard are resident in the park, while packs of wild dog pass through from time to time. Lion occasionally cross the river from the Caprivi Game Park.

Small mammals

Smaller mammal species that might reveal their presence are warthog, common duiker, steenbok, chacma baboon, vervet monkey, tree squirrel, dwarf mongoose and scrub hare.

Crocodile and hippo

Crocodiles occur in fairly large numbers in the Kavango River, and as recently as 1989 a local fisherman was taken from his mokoro (dugout canoe) near the Kwetche picnic site. Hippo are common and, although you are unlikely to see them from the river-bank, their pig-like grunts are often heard. However, if you plan to take a boat trip on the Kavango River you are almost assured of seeing hippo at close range!

Vegetation

Although the vegetation of the reserve is dominated by extensive dry woodlands, the riparian vegetation is of particular importance. In Namibia it forms less than 0,01 per cent of all habitats, and 70 per cent of it has already been destroyed. Kalahari apple-leaf (239), Lowveld mangosteen (486), water pear (557) and jackal-berry (606) are the dominant species of the riverine fringe, while common false-thorn (155), knob thorn (178), umbrella thorn (188), Transvaal saffron (416), buffalo-thorn (447) and wild raisin bush (*Grewia* spp.) also occur. A conspicious species along the edge of the floodplain is the wild date palm (22) which is restricted elsewhere in Namibia to the Kwando/Linyanti and Zambezi rivers. Also prominent is a clump of large baobabs near Kwetche picnic site.

The vegetation of the dunes is dominated by mixed wild teak (236) and wild seringa (197) woodlands and dense stands of Zambezi teak (206). Other tree species occurring commonly are copalwood (199), manketti tree (337) and Rhodesian bushwillow (541), while coffee neat's foot (208.3) and sand camwood (223) are characteristic shrubs.

Grasslands are confined to the Mahango and the Thinderevu omiramba, which are fringed by extensive tall dry woodland dominated by *Acacia* and bushwillow (*Combretum*) species.

References

Butchard, D., Stannard, K. & Bell, C. (1989) 'Skimming on thin ice'. *Quagga* 26: 6 – 8.

Hines, C.J.H. (1987) 'The birds of eastern Kavango, SWA/Namibia'. *SWA Scientific Society Journal* XL/XLI: 115 – 147.

Hines, C.J.H. (1989) 'The birds of north-eastern Namibia'. *Birding in Southern Africa* 41 (3): 89 – 92.

Williams, A.J. (1986) 'African skimmers breeding in the Okavango River'. *Lanioturdus* 22 (3): 53.

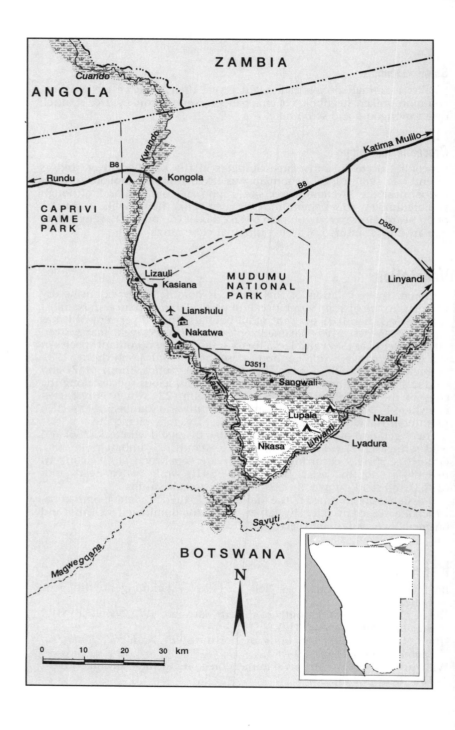

MAMILI NATIONAL PARK

Size: 31 992 ha   Proclaimed: 1990

Location

Eastern Caprivi.

What to do and see

Bird-watching, game drives, game walks, boating, angling, photography.

Climate

Eastern Caprivi has a subtropical climate with two distinct seasons — a long, dry season stretching from April to September and a short, wet season from October to March.

Summer days are generally hot and temperatures higher than 35 °C are not uncommon, while the humidity can reach 70 per cent. Summer is the rainy season and usually starts in October and lasts until April. However, more than 80 per cent of the area's average rainfall of 740 mm occurs between December and March.

Winter days are pleasant, but average minimum temperatures drop to below 10 °C between May and August.

When to visit

Mamili is open throughout the year between sunrise and sunset, but much of the park is flooded between May and August.

BIRD-WATCHING: November to March.
GAME-VIEWING: Variable.

Where to stay

Facilities are limited to basic camp sites without any facilities at Nzalu and Lyadura in the east and south-east of the park. Hutted accommodation is, however, available in the nearby Mudumu National Park.

Where to book

The necessary entry and camping permits must be obtained in advance from the Chief Conservation Officer at Katima Mulilo, telephone (067352) 27.

How to get there

Access to the park is gained via Sangwali or Malengalenga. Since the tracks in the park are not marked a map is essential and can be obtained from the Chief Conservation Officer at Katima Mulilo. Alternatively, visitors can join a tour conducted by one of the safari companies operating in eastern Caprivi.

What you should know

☐ The park is only accessible by four-wheel drive vehicle and the tracks can be extremely difficult to negotiate, especially when much of the area is flooded.

☐ Groups should consist of at least two vehicles and must be well-equipped to deal with possible emergencies.

☐ Visitors are cautioned to be wary of potentially dangerous animals when camping out in the open.

☐ Hippo pose a constant threat in the waterways which are best explored under the guidance of someone who knows the river.

☐ Because there are crocodiles and hippos in the river, swimming is dangerous.

☐ A licence is required if you wish to angle in the Kwando River where it passes through the park. Licences can be obtained from the Popa Falls Rest Camp or from the Chief Conservation Officer at Katima Mulilo.

☐ Eastern Caprivi lies within an endemic malaria area and the necessary precautions must be taken before entering the region. Also remember to carry a mosquito repellant and wear long-sleeved shirts and trousers.

☐ Remember to pack clothing in dull, inconspicuous colours such as green, brown or khaki for game-viewing walks.

☐ Since there are no shops or filling stations in the park, visitors must be self-sufficient.

The Mamili National Park is situated in the south-western corner of eastern Caprivi and is the largest wetland with conservation status in Namibia. The unrivalled scenery of the park is characterised by a mosaic of channels, vast reedbeds, ox-bow lakes and tree-covered islands, and it is a photographer's dream.

The nucleus of the park is formed by two large islands in the Kwando/ Linyanti River, Nkasa and Lupala. During the dry season the two islands are accessible by road, but after high floods up to 80 per cent of the area is flooded, cutting the two islands off from the mainland to the north.

Birds

Eastern Caprivi is a bird-watcher's paradise and to date some 430 species, or nearly 70 per cent of Namibia's total number of species, have been recorded in this water-rich region.

Species likely to be of particular interest to bird-watchers are slaty egret (70), whiterumped babbler (562), greater swamp warbler (636) – a species confined to papyrus swamps – chirping cisticola (676) and swamp boubou (738). Other noteworthy species include black coucal (388) – an intra-African migrant occurring between November and April – and coppery-tailed (389) and Senegal (390) coucals, both of which are resident.

Floodplains

Two exciting species to be seen in the floodplains are wattled crane (207), which are known to breed here, and pinkthroated longclaw (730).

Back swamps and islands

Pygmy goose (114) are common on the back swamps and flocks of knobbilled duck (115) are much in evidence between September and April on islands in the swamps. On quiet backwaters with floating vegetation there is a possibility of spotting lesser gallinule (224) between December and April, while African (240) and lesser (241) jacanas are resident.

Reedbeds

The reedbeds attract a variety of warblers, cisticolas and weavers, including the brownthroated weaver (818), which has a limited distribution elsewhere in southern Africa. Redfaced (674) and blackbacked (675) cisticolas, as well as thickbilled (807) and masked (814) weavers have been recorded.

Woodlands and thickets

Longtailed (763) and greater blue-eared (765) starlings are common residents of the woodlands on Nkasa Island, while tinkling cisticola (671) occur in the thickets.

Game

The river provides a habitat for aquatic species such as hippopotamus, crocodile and spotted-necked otter, while the extensive wetlands are a refuge for floodplain and swamp antelope species such as waterbuck, red lechwe and sitatunga. The park is also a sanctuary to a small population of puku – a species which elsewhere in southern Africa is restricted to the southern bank of the Chobe River. Other species that visitors might spot are elephant, buffalo, giraffe and warthog, while lion and leopard also occur.

Puku

Red lechwe

Effects of poaching

Unfortunately, many of the large herds of game which used to roam the area have been decimated by poachers. The dramatic decline in game numbers is perhaps best illustrated by the following statistics: between 1980 and 1986 the number of red lechwe in eastern Caprivi decreased from 12 928 to 2 679, while the sitatunga population crashed from 270 to a mere 26. As a result of anti-poaching patrols, environmental education programmes by local rangers, and the proclamation of two conservation areas, game numbers are again on the increase. In years to come the area will, hopefully, regain its former glory as a wildlife paradise.

Angling

Those interested in angling should refer to the information given for Mudumu National Park and the regulations included in the box on page 98.

Kwando/Linyanti/Chobe river system

Except for a 90 km strip in the north, the eastern Caprivi is surrounded entirely by rivers – the Zambezi in the north-east and the Kwando/Linyanti/Chobe in the west, south and east.

Here, these rivers give rise to a landscape dominated by floodplains, reed-lined channels, ox-bow lakes and extensive reedbed swamps. It is a complex system which is interlinked and forever changing.

A river of many names

The complexities of the Kwando/Linyanti/Chobe system are not limited to its hydrography, but also to its name which changes no less than five times along its course. In Angola, where it originates, it is named the Cuando, but where it cuts through the Caprivi Strip it becomes known as the Kwando, while further downstream the western bank which forms the border with Botswana is named the Mashi. At Nkasa Island the river swings sharply north-east and the stretch up to Lake Liambezi is known as the Linyanti. For the final stretch of its journey to the Zambezi River it is named the Chobe.

Linked to Okavango Delta

The Kwando River is linked to the Okavango Delta via the Magwegqana Channel, also known as the Selinda Spillway. In wet years water flows from the delta to the Kwando system and along the Savuti Channel to the Mababe Depression. Occasionally, water from the Kwando flows up the Magwegqana for a few kilometres, but the differences in levels are too high to reverse the flow further.

Tributary of the Zambezi

During years of average flooding the Kwando acts as a tributary of the Zambezi River – water flows through the Kwando River and the Linyanti Swamp into Lake Liambezi and from there into the Chobe River which joins the Zambezi River near Kazangula. When the level of the Zambezi is exceptionally high though, the flow of the Chobe River is reversed and water is discharged into the lake. In addition, water spilling over the banks of the Zambezi River flows into Lake Liambezi via the Bukalo Channel.

Lake Liambezi

When full, Lake Liambezi covers an area of 100 km^2, with depths ranging from two to five metres. It provides an ideal habitat for thousands of waterbirds, and at times more than a thousand pelicans converge on the

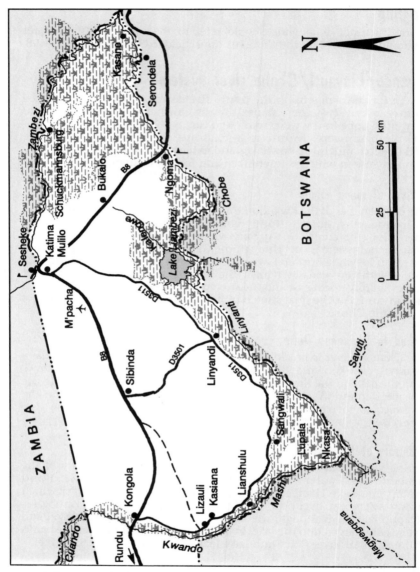

Kwando/Linyanti/Chobe river system

rich feeding grounds. Local fishermen also benefit and up to a tonne of fish is caught each day during these times of abundance.

The water in the lake evaporates at a rate of about two metres per year, but a constant inflow from the Kwando/Linyanti and occasional overflows from the Zambezi are sufficient to compensate for this loss.

Spontaneous fires on a dry lake

As a result of low rainfall in the catchment areas of the Kwando and the Zambezi rivers during the early 1980s, Liambezi received no inflow and by May 1985 the lake had dried up completely. A few months later spontaneous internal combustion of the rotting material caused fires which raged for almost two years over most of the lake bed.

The drying-up of Lake Liambezi was not entirely natural. The hunting of hippo resulted in the encroachment of reedbeds into the river course, restricting even further the already limited flow of the Kwando/Linyanti.

References

Branfield, A. (1989) 'A birding experience in the eastern Caprivi'. *Bokmakierie* 41 (2): 38 – 40.

Branfield, A. (1990) 'New bird records for the East Caprivi'. *Lanioturdus* 25 (1/2): 4 – 21.

Grobler, M. & Ferreira, J. (1990) 'The dying of Lake Liambezi'. *Custos* 19 (6): 40 – 44.

Koen, J.H. (1988) 'Birds of the eastern Caprivi'. *Southern Birds* 15.

Maclean, G.L. (1992) 'Eastern Caprivi revisited'. *Birding in Southern Africa* 41 (1): 8 – 11.

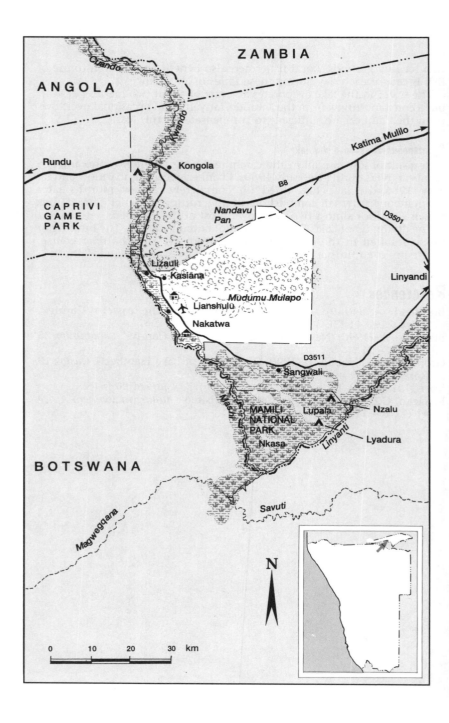

MUDUMU NATIONAL PARK

Size: 100 959 ha   Proclaimed: 1990

Location

Eastern Caprivi.

What to do and see

Bird-watching, game drives, game walks, boating, angling, photography, cruises on a double-decker barge.

Climate

See Mamili National Park, page 129.

When to visit

Open throughout the year between sunrise and sunset.

BIRD-WATCHING: November to March.
GAME-VIEWING: May to September.

Where to stay

State-owned facilities are limited to a hut at Nakatwa on the banks of the Kwando River. The hut, which can accommodate eight people, is equipped with beds, crockery and cutlery. Visitors must supply their own bedding and prepare their own meals. There are plans to establish camp sites for those who prefer less sophisticated accommodation. .

Accommodation at Lianshulu Lodge, a privately-run camp, on the banks of the Kwando consists of ten reed and thatch twin-bedded bungalows with *en-suite* facilities.

Visitor amenities

Lianshulu has a dining room and bar overlooking the Kwando River. Guided game-viewing drives and game walks, as well as boating and barge trips on the Kwando River, are conducted from the lodge.

Where to book

The necessary permits must be obtained in advance from the Chief Conservation Officer at Katima Mulilo, telephone (067352) 27.

Nakatwa camp: Chief Conservation Officer at Katima Mulilo, telephone (067352) 27.

Lianshulu Lodge: Namib Wilderness Safaris, P O Box 6850, Windhoek, telephone (061) 225178, fax (061) 33332.

How to get there

To reach the park, turn off the B8 onto the D3511 a short distance east of the Kongola Bridge over the Kwando River. The turnoff to Lianshulu is reached about 40 km along the D3511, while Nakatwa is a few kilometres on.

What you should know

☐ The tracks in the park can be negotiated only by four-wheel drive vehicle and tour groups must consist of at least two vehicles equipped to deal with any emergency.

☐ Since none of the bush tracks are signposted, getting around can be difficult if you are unfamiliar with the area. Be sure to get directions or a map of the area from the Chief Conservation Officer at Katima Mulilo.

☐ Crocodile and hippo make the Kwando/Linyanti River unsafe for swimming, and at least one incident of a hippo overturning a canoe has been reported. For the same reason anglers are advised to be cautious when fishing on the Kwando River.

☐ A licence is required if you wish to angle in the Kwando River in the park. Licences can be obtained from the Popa Falls Rest Camp or the Chief Conservation Officer at Katima Mulilo.

☐ Eastern Caprivi lies within an endemic malaria area and the necessary precautions must be taken before entering the region. Also remember to take a mosquito repellant, long-sleeved shirts and trousers.

☐ Pack clothing in dull, inconspicuous colours such as green, brown or khaki for game-viewing walks.

☐ Heavy rains during the summer months can make roads in the north-east of country extremely slippery and motorists are advised to drive carefully.

☐ Visitors (except guests of Lianshulu) must be self-sufficient in respect of food and fuel.

The Mudumu National Park has the Kwando River as its western border for more than 15 km, and the park extends eastwards for up to 40 km. To the north of the Mudumu Mulapo the river follows a well-defined valley that is up to 5 km wide, but a few kilometres south of Lianshulu the river breaks up into a labyrinth of channels to form the Linyanti Swamp.

Vegetation

The vegetation of Mudumu is dominated by extensive mopane (198) woodlands, while the camel thorn (168) is a conspicuous species of the relict floodplains to the south-east. The Kwando River, the western boundary of the park, is characterised by extensive stands of *Phragmites* reedbeds, while forests dominated by *Ficus* spp., Natal mahogany (301), Lowveld mangosteen (486) and forest waterwood (556) occur on islands and along the river.

Game

During a game drive visitors might be lucky enough to see elephant, buffalo, roan, sable, kudu, impala, oribi and Burchell's zebra, while wild dog are also spotted from time to time. The park is a sanctuary for small populations of red lechwe and sitatunga, while spotted-necked otter, hippo and crocodile inhabit the waterways.

Birds

Several rare species

North-eastern Namibia attracts several species of birds which have a limited distribution elsewhere in southern Africa and bird-watching is therefore one of the main attractions of this area. Species to watch out for in the backswamps and floodplains include slaty egret (70), rufousbellied heron (75), wattled crane (207), wattled (260) and longtoed (261) plovers, redwinged pratincole (304) and copperytailed coucal (389). The brownthroated weaver (818) is abundant in the reedbeds fringing the Kwando.

The western banded snake eagle (145), a species confined to the Okavango, Zambezi and Kwando/Linyanti/Chobe river systems, is a rare resident of the riverine woodlands where there is also the possibility of spotting Dickinson's kestrel (185), the most common small diurnal raptor in Caprivi. Other uncommon species you might see in the riverine woodlands include yellow white-eye (797) and brown firefinch (843). A species likely to be of considerable interest to bird-watchers is the coppery sunbird (778), an intra-African migrant which, in Namibia, has only been recorded at Lianshulu and M'Pacha, a few kilometres west of Katima Mulilo. It reaches the southernmost limit of its distribution in northern and north-eastern Zimbabwe and the Zambezi Valley and favours the edge of riverine forests. The purplebanded sunbird (780) has also been recorded at Lianshulu.

Bradfield's hornbill

Mourning dove (353) and whiterumped babbler (562) are common in thickets along the Kwando River, while the bearded robin (617) is less frequently seen.

In the mopane woodlands you might see several species which have a limited distribution elsewhere in southern Africa. These include Bradfield's hornbill (461), mosque swallow (525) and Arnot's chat (594), as well as longtailed (763) and lesser blue-eared (766) starlings, while broadbilled roller (450) is a possibility between September and April.

The most likely area to spot yellowbilled oxpecker (771) is in the transition zone between mopane woodland and grassland, while the more abundant redbilled oxpecker (772) favours open, grassy areas between mopane woodlands and grasslands. Research has shown that both species are more active during the afternoon than during the morning and at midday. Since the game tends to be skittish you are, however, more likely to come across both of these oxpeckers on cattle when passing through communal farming areas.

Angling

Since the Kwando River provides a habitat for no less than 56 of the 76 fish species recorded in Caprivi, angling is another popular pastime. For the regulations governing freshwater angling see the box on page 98. Green-headed (*Oreochromis macrochir*) and banded (*Tilapia sparrmanii*) tilapia are abundant in the Kwando River, as are sungwa (*Tilapia rendalli rendalli*), green happy (*Serranochromis codringtoni*), nembwe (*Serranochromis robustus jallae*) and thinfaced largemouth (*Serranochromis angusticeps*). Although tiger fish (*Hydrocynus vittatus*) is not common, it occurs regularly in the Kwando as it favours flowing water with a sandy or rocky substrate.

References

Branfield, A. (1989) 'A birding experience in the eastern Caprivi'. *Bokmakierie* 41 (2): 38 – 40.

Branfield, A. (1990) 'New bird records for the East Caprivi'. *Lanioturdus* 25 (1/2): 4 – 21.

Brown, C.J. & Brown, S.E. 'Some observations on oxpeckers in eastern Caprivi, SWA/Namibia'. *Lanioturdus* 22 (4): 74 – 79.

Koen, J.H. (1988) 'Birds of the eastern Caprivi'. *Southern Birds* 15.

Maclean, G.L. (1992) 'Eastern Caprivi revisited'. *Birding in Southern Africa* 44 (1): 8 – 10.

Van der Waal, B.C.W. & Skelton, P.H. (1984) 'Checklist of fishes of Caprivi'. *Madoqua* 13 (4): 303 – 320.

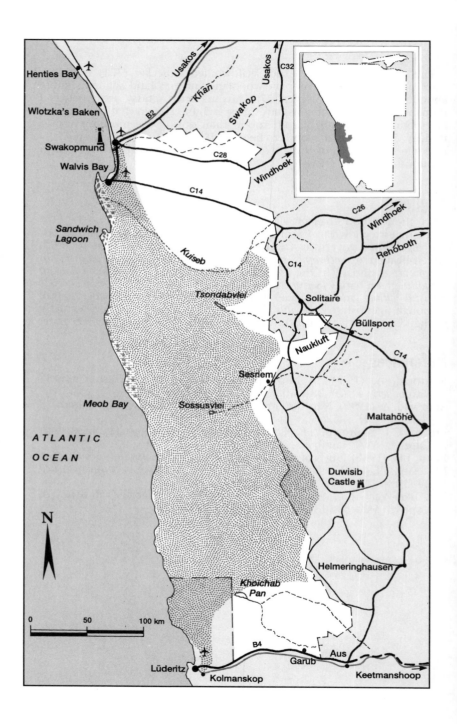

NAMIB-NAUKLUFT PARK

Size: 4 976 800 ha   Proclaimed: 1907

The Namib-Naukluft Park is not only Namibia's largest park, but it is also the largest in Africa and the fourth largest conservation area in the world.

The Namib is considered to be one of the oldest deserts in the world and to visitors it presents an ever-changing kaleidoscope of scenery that ranges from the shifting sand-dunes of the sand sea to expansive gravel plains and the scenic lagoon at Sandwich.

From a tourist perspective, the park can be divided into four areas: the Namib section between the Swakop and Kuiseb rivers, Sandwich, the Naukluft section and the central Namib sand sea, including Sesriem and Sossusvlei. Each of these areas has distinctive flora and fauna and offers visitors entirely different experiences and scenery. Consequently, they will be dealt with in this book as though they are separate entities.

The central area of the Namib section of the park was proclaimed a conservation area, originally named Game Reserve No. 3, by the German colonial administration in 1907. Following a request by Fisons Fertilizers, which held a concession to exploit guano at Sandwich in 1937, the Sandwich area was incorporated into Game Reserve No. 3 in 1941.

In 1956 the reserve was enlarged by the inclusion of the Kuiseb Canyon, the Swakop River Valley, and the Welwitschia Plains, and its name was changed from Game Reserve No. 3 to the Namib Desert Park.

The first steps to conserve part of the Naukluft Mountains were taken in 1966 when the farm "Naukluft" was purchased and two years later the Naukluft Mountain Zebra Park became a reality.

In response to repeated representations from farmers about the damage caused to their grazing by gemsbok migrating onto their farms from the adjoining Diamond Area II during the winter months, and the destruction caused to fences and grazing by mountain zebra, an ecological survey was carried out in 1970. In the following year it was decided to enlarge the park by gradually acquiring adjoining farms. A number of farms west of the Naukluft complex were also acquired to create a corridor, enabling gemsbok to migrate between the Namib dunes and the mountains.

Following negotiations with Consolidated Diamond Mines – the concessionaire of Diamond Area II – the Namib Desert Park, the Naukluft Complex, part of the diamond area and unoccupied state land were consolidated and in 1979 the 2 283 600 ha Namib-Naukluft Park, one of the largest conservation areas in Africa, came into being.

The park was enlarged to its existing size in 1986 when the remainder of Diamond Area II was added, except for a small area near Lüderitz.

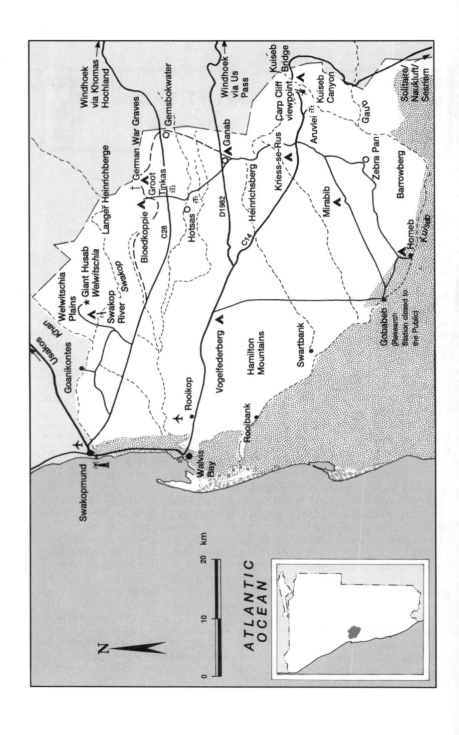

NAMIB-NAUKLUFT PARK:
NAMIB SECTION

Location

Central Namib Desert.

What to do and see

Game-viewing, sightseeing, photography.

Climate

Average temperatures along the coast vary from a minimum of 15 °C in September to a maximum of 20,7 °C in February, compared with 11 °C in July and 32,4 °C in March at Ganab, 110 km inland.

Rain is a rare phenomenon along the coast and seldom exceeds 10 mm a year, but further inland the annual average rainfall increases to around 87 mm. It is, however, extremely unpredictable.

Fog is common along the coast between April and August and between September and December further inland. It contributes significantly to the total precipitation.

When to visit

This section of the park is open between sunrise and sunset throughout the year.

Where to stay

Small camp sites have been established at Kuiseb Bridge and Homeb along the Kuiseb River and at Kriess-se-Rus, Mirabib and Vogelfederberg in the southern half of the park. Other camp sites include Ganab, Groot Tinkas and Bloedkoppie, as well as the Swakop River camp site near the Welwitschia Plains.

Visitor amenities

Facilities at camp sites are limited to fireplaces, refuse bins and toilets, and visitors must ensure that they have sufficient water, firewood, fuel and all other supplies for the duration of their stay.

Aruvlei boasts a picnic site shaded by dense buffalo-thorn trees, while picnic sites shaded by slatted wood are provided at the Ganab turnoff on the C28 between Windhoek and Swakopmund and alongside the road that links the C28 with the D1982. Similar facilities are planned for the Hotsas waterhole and the Kuiseb Canyon Lookout near Carp Cliff.

Where to book

A permit is required if you plan to deviate onto any of the signposted tourist roads in the park. Entry permits can be obtained at Hardap and Sesriem, as well as at the tourist offices in Lüderitz and Swakopmund and the reservation office in Windhoek. During weekends, permits are obtainable from Hans Kriess Motors in Swakopmund and from Suidwes and CWB service stations in Walvis Bay. Camping permits are also obtainable at these offices and service stations. Motorists travelling on the proclaimed roads THROUGH the park do not require permits.

How to get there

From the coast this section of the park is easily accessible from both Swakopmund and Walvis Bay along the C28 and the C14.

Visitors travelling from Windhoek have a choice of three gravel surface roads through the Khomas Hochland, but at least five or six hours are needed if you are coming from Windhoek, and motorists must ensure that they have sufficient fuel.

The C28 is the most direct gravel surface route between Windhoek and Swakopmund, but caravans are not permitted because of the steep gradient of the Bosua Pass (1:5) which is best travelled from east to west.

Most of the route linking Windhoek and Walvis Bay via the Us Pass (1:10) is a district road and corrugated sections are quite common. The road winds through several dry river courses which are sometimes impassable to sedan cars after heavy rains.

The southernmost route, the Gamsberg Pass, links Windhoek with Walvis Bay. It is the most spectacular of the three routes and is referred to as the Garden Route of Namibia. Travellers are afforded dramatic views of the rugged Kuiseb Canyon on entering the park.

What you should know

- [ ] Although it seems unlikely that an emergency situation could arise, motorists have occasionally been stranded on quiet back roads for a few days. It is, therefore, advisable to carry a second spare tyre, basic spares such as plugs, points, condenser and a fan-belt, at least ten litres of water, sufficient fuel and a two day food supply when travelling through the Namib.
- [ ] Do not forget to pack a sun-hat, sunscreen cream and lip balm.
- [ ] Mosquitoes can be a nuisance after the summer rains, even if no open water is apparent. So, if you stop overnight in the Namib, remember to use mosquito repellant.
- [ ] Even during summer you could be surprised by cold landward winds and fog which make it essential to include warm clothing – irrespective of the season.
- [ ] A daypack, water-bottle and stout walking shoes are essential if you intend undertaking short rambles.
- [ ] If you plan to make a fire during your visit to the Namib take your own firewood. Not only is it a criminal offence to collect wood in the park, but trees in the desert often appear dead, only to sprout after rain. Dead trees should be left to play their role in the ecosystem.

Despite the Namib Desert's reputation of being an inhospitable region, large areas of the Central Namib are surprisingly accessible even in a sedan vehicle. At first sight the desert appears to be barren, lifeless and uninteresting, but on closer inspection visitors will discover a fascinating variety of life forms uniquely adapted to desert life. Bordered in the north by the Swakop River and in the south by the Kuiseb River, the Namib section of the park stretches eastwards to the edge of the escarpment. The area is characterised by flat gravel plains which are occasionally broken by isolated remnant granite outcrops or *inselbergen*.

Welwitschia Drive

One of the best ways of discovering the carefully guarded treasures of the Namib is to follow the Welwitschia Drive which is easily accessible from Swakopmund. The drive is reached by turning off the B2 about 2,5 km east of Swakopmund onto the C28 which is followed for 15 km to the signposted turnoff.

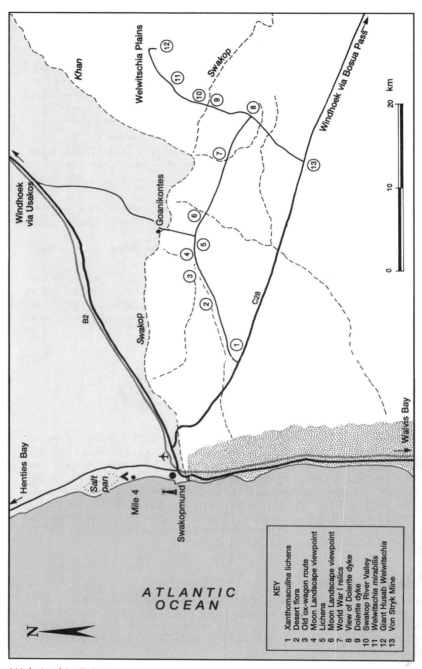

Welwitschia Drive

KEY

1 Xanthomaculina lichens
2 Desert flora
3 Old ox-wagon route
4 Moon Landscape viewpoint
5 Lichens
6 Moon Landscape viewpoint
7 World War I relics
8 View of Dolerite dyke
9 Dolerite dyke
10 Swakop River Valley
11 Welwitschia mirabilis
12 Giant Husab Welwitschia
13 Von Stryk Mine

Permits

Before setting off from Swakopmund visitors must obtain a permit from the offices of the Directorate of Wildlife, Conservation and Research at the corner of Kaiser Wilhelm and Bismarck streets. Outside office hours, permits are obtainable from Hans Kriess Motors in Swakopmund. Also remember to pack a picnic basket and to set aside time for a break under the shady camel thorn trees (168) on the banks of the Swakop River.

Thirteen beaconed places of interest

1. Wind-blown lichen species

The first of thirteen stone beacons marking places of botanical, geological and historical interest is reached a short distance from the start of the drive. Here visitors can see good examples of *Xanthomaculina convoluta*, a wind-blown lichen species which can easily be mistaken for dead plant material. In the heat of the day the lichens are often overlooked as they shrivel up. Fog rolling off the sea provides the moisture the lichens need to survive. Once the plants have absorbed moisture, they take on brilliant colours, depending on their species. If you are visiting the Namib on a hot day you can observe this colour transformation by pouring a little water on a few specimens and watching the seemingly dead "plants" uncurling within a matter of seconds. Stones encrusted with lichens should not be viewed as curiosities to be taken home.

2. Dollar bush and ink bush

Two plant species which are common on the Namib plains, the dollar bush (*Zygophyllum stapfii*) and the ink bush (*Arthraerua leubnitziae*), can both be seen at the second beacon.

3. Ox-wagon route

The third beacon marks the spot where the old ox-wagon route, Baaiweg (Bay Road), which linked the interior with the coast decades ago, crosses the drive.

4. Moon Landscape

A short way further on you can enjoy a magnificent view of the Moon Landscape with its multitude of eroded valleys. The softer overlying strata which were deposited about 450 million years ago were eroded to create scenery reminiscent of a lunar landscape.

5. More lichen species

At the fifth stone beacon nearby several more lichen species, including the orange *Telochistes capensis* with its characteristic tufts, can be seen.

Goanikontes farm — an oasis

The turnoff to "Goanikontes" with its tall eucalyptus and palm trees is signposted about 1 km on. Although the old farm is not part of the drive, the oasis is well worth a visit and is only 5 km from the turnoff. Situated on the banks of the Swakop River, the farm was established as long ago as 1848 and following the establishment of Swakopmund in 1892 Goanikontes provided fresh produce for the coastal town.

6. More views of Moon Landscape

More splendid views of the Moon Landscape can be enjoyed from the viewpoint at the sixth beacon.

7. World War I camp site

About 9 km further on a collection of rusted tins and metal tracks on the right-hand side of the road marks the spot where South African troops camped for a few days during World War I. Although the objects have historical value, they provide positive proof of the slow decomposition rate of metal in desert conditions. Please do not remove anything from the site.

8. & 9. Dolerite dykes

At the eighth beacon turn left and after a short distance you will notice a black band which forms the backbone of the ridge to the right. About 3 km on you will pass one of these dolerite dykes (ninth beacon) which was formed millions of years ago when molten lava intruded into the granite. The dyke was exposed through subsequent erosion.

10. Swakop River Valley

The road to the Swakop River now descends through primordial scenery created by a maze of dissected side canyons. On reaching the river, tall camel thorns along its northern banks provide a welcome retreat from the plains. From here the road winds out of the Swakop River Valley and soon the landscape is dotted with numerous welwitschias (21.1).

11. Male and female welwitschias

About 5,8 km beyond the river the tenth beacon indicates another point of interest — two good examples of the separate male and female welwitschia plants. Female plants can be identified by their "flowers" which resemble cones. Surprisingly this botanical curiosity has been classified as a cone-bearing tree of the genus to which pine trees and yellowwoods belong. However, more recent research has shown that it is not closely related to any present-day cone-bearing or flowering plants.

Although the welwitschia appears to have a multitude of leaves, closer inspection will confirm that only two leaves grow from the gnarled central stem.

They are endemic to the gravel Namib, with their distribution, although scattered, stretching northwards from the Kuiseb River to Namibe in Angola in a roughly 100 km wide belt from the coast. Moisture is obtained through the roots which reach down to a depth of three metres, as well as through the leaves which absorb condensation from the coastal fogs. Pollination between the separate plants is probably by insects which carry the pollen from the male plants to the female plants.

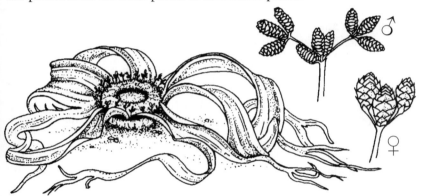

A welwitschia tree. The male and female cones are detailed on the right

12. Giant Husab *Welwitschia*
About 6,5 km further the road ends at the giant Husab *Welwitschia* which has an estimated age of about 1 500 years.

13. Von Stryk Mine
Retrace your tracks to the eighth beacon and continue south until you reach the main road to Swakopmund. At the T-junction turn right and soon you will notice the last beacon on your left. A short way off the road the disused Von Stryk Mine, where iron ore was mined during the 1950s, can be seen. From here you can either return to Swakopmund or continue along the C28 to Windhoek via the Bosua Pass.

Camp sites
If you are prepared to camp with only very basic facilities, you will find that one or more nights in the desert will reveal many more facets of the Namib to you. Don't forget, permits are required!

Kuiseb Bridge camp site
Conveniently situated along the C14 when entering the park from the south, or via the Gamsberg Pass, is the camp site at Kuiseb Bridge. This popular camp site is characterised by large ana trees (159) which provide

shade throughout the day. Unfortunately it can only comfortably accommodate two groups. The camp site affords easy access to the Kuiseb Canyon, so do take the opportunity to view the impressive cliffs by taking a short ramble down the canyon. Vehicles are not permitted in the river-bed! Although you are unlikely to experience rain at Kuiseb Bridge, the camp site is occasionally flooded when heavy summer rain in the highlands causes the river to come down in flood.

Homeb camp site

Campers are given another opportunity to stop overnight alongside the Kuiseb River at Homeb further downstream. Set amongst a clump of camel thorn and ebony trees (598), the fairly large camp site can accommodate several groups. Unlike anywhere else in the Namib, you could meet domestic stock here as the Topnaars living near the camp site graze their goats on the riverine vegetation. The Topnaars are one of the original Nama-speaking groups of central Namibia, but during the 1830s they were subjugated by the more powerful Oorlams Nama group. A small group, however, continued to live in the lower reaches of Kuiseb River. Not more than 2 000 Topnaars inhabit the lower reaches of the Kuiseb Valley at present, although most of the younger generation work in Walvis Bay and Swakopmund, returning "home" at weekends.

The Dutch name *Topnaar* contains a reference to the nara plant (*naar*). It is also said to mean "people of the point" or "the first people".

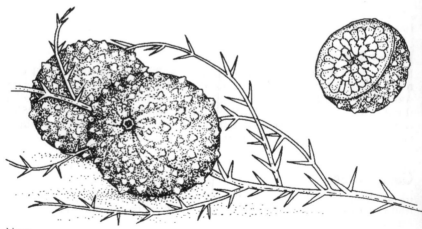

Nara

The nara (*Acanthosicyos horrida*) bushes along the southern bank of the river play an important role in the Topnaars' livelihood. The bushes are traditionally owned by particular Topnaar families and the rights to these bushes are hereditary. The spiny melon-like fruit is much in demand and is either eaten raw like a melon, cooked like pumpkin or boiled and preserved dry in thin, flat strips. The dried pips are also an important commodity which is sold in Walvis Bay from where it is exported as far as Cape Town – hence the economic value.

The river is not as deeply incised at Homeb as it is further upstream, giving quite a different perspective from that at Kuiseb Bridge. From Homeb it is recommended that you take an early morning or late afternoon stroll along the river-bed, where you are likely to be impressed by the dense riverine forest, to the southern bank. Depending on the time available and how energetic you are, it is worthwhile climbing the fairly steep river bank to gain access to the vast sand sea, as well an excellent view across the wide river. The effect of the Kuiseb River in preventing the sand sea from encroaching onto the gravel plains is clearly illustrated from this vantage point.

Swakop River camp site

The camp site on the banks of the Swakop River further north is conveniently close to Swakopmund and is *en route* to the Welwitschia Plains. Each of the camp sites is under a large camel thorn tree and the bright green clumps of real mustard trees (622) are unlikely to escape your attention. Bird-watching is usually surprisingly rewarding in the confines of the well-vegetated river-bed.

Mirabib camp site

Mirabib, a granite *inselberg* resembling a beached whale, is situated on the road between Gobabeb and the C14. Only two groups can be accommodated in the well-positioned camp sites under overhangs offering a fair degree of protection from the sun during the day. Zebra Pan, an artificial waterhole about 35 km to the south-east, can make an interesting deviation if you are camping at Mirabib. Hartmann's mountain zebra, gemsbok and ostrich are regularly seen here.

Radiocarbon dating of charcoal found at Mirabib has provided evidence of the presence of early inhabitants about 8 500 years ago. The shelter was also used by early pastoralists 1 600 years ago (a date obtained from a radiocarbon analysis of dung), while hair resembling that of fat-tailed or Persian-type sheep was also identified.

Bloedkoppie camp site

One of the most popular areas for overnighting in the Namib is Bloedkoppie, another granite dome which is substantially larger than Mirabib. Several camp sites are located here, while those on the western side of the *inselberg* are best left to visitors who have four-wheel drive vehicles because of sandy patches which have to be negotiated. Many interesting hours can be spent exploring the outcrop and you are bound to be amazed by the way in which shrubs and even trees grow in what seem to be the most awkward places. Take care though when rambling about the slopes of the *inselberg* as it is scattered with numerous flakes of loose rock as a result of the continual exfoliation of the granite. It is also well worth taking a ramble amongst the rocky outcrops to the west of Bloedkoppie where your attention will be attracted not only by the flora, but also by many fascinating rock formations – the result of weathering.

Groot Tinkas camp site

Groot Tinkas camp site is only accessible to those with four-wheel drive vehicles and is consequently more often than not deserted. Not only do the surroundings at Tinkas lend themselves to interesting rambles, but the 12 km drive between Bloedkoppie and Tinkas should be undertaken at a leisurely pace. About 4 km east of Bloedkoppie the graves of two German policemen dating back to 1895 are passed at Klein Tinkas, where the ruins of an old German police station can still be seen. Bear in mind that exploring the Tinkas area is best reserved for early mornings and late afternoons as it is often unbearably hot. The camp sites at Groot Tinkas are shaded by camel thorns and ebony trees.

After good summer rains the nearby dam holds water for several months, and the relatively large expanse of water in the desert is a rather unusual sight. Originally built as a weir to measure the runoff of the Tinkas Plains, it was converted into a dam during the 1970s with private funds to serve as a drinking place for animals. Unfortunately the water is too brackish for animals, but small numbers of water-birds are attracted to the dam.

Ganab camp site

Ganab is a camp site where you will be truly aware of the wide open expanses of the Namib. Situated in a wide, almost undefined river-course lined with well-established camel thorn trees, the camp site has the added attraction of being situated near a windmill which attracts springbok and gemsbok. Although they are much appreciated for their shade, the camel thorns do not provide much protection against the wind which can be quite gusty at times.

Kriess-se-Rus camp site

Kriess-se-Rus is, likewise, situated in a river-course and is conveniently close to the C14 linking Windhoek with Walvis Bay via the Gamsberg Pass.

Game

Elephant and rhinoceros

The Namib Desert seems a most unlikely habitat for elephant and black rhinoceros, but historical records provide positive proof of the presence of these animals in the Namib. The traveller Sir James Alexander recorded a discovery of the remains of a rhinoceros in the Kuiseb River in 1837, while Charles Andersson found ample evidence of rhinoceros in the Swakop River during his expedition in 1850. In more recent times a well-preserved rhinoceros horn and an elephant tusk were uncovered near the Tinkas waterhole.

In 1975 an attempt was made to re-establish black rhino along the Kuiseb River, but this project was unsuccessful. A mature bull died shortly after his release when he plunged from a cliff in the Kuiseb Canyon, and a cow also died soon after she was released. A calf, released subsequently, wandered off in a north-easterly direction and was later recaptured near Otjimbingwe, some 150 km from where it had been released.

A family of chacma baboon

Zebra, klipspringer and baboon

The rugged canyons of the Kuiseb and Swakop rivers provide an ideal sanctuary for herds of Hartmann's mountain zebra, small family groups of klipspringer and troops of chacma baboon.

Three small troops of baboon have been identified in the upper, middle and lower reaches of the Kuiseb River. Although the troop inhabiting the lower canyon has a relative abundance of food, there are no permanent waterholes and, unlike baboons elsewhere which usually drink daily, they have been observed going without water for up to two weeks. Another interesting behavioural characteristic of these baboons is that, in an apparent attempt to cool down, they throw sand over their bodies while resting under the shady trees of the canyon.

Springbok

Springbok can be seen throughout the year in the Namib section of the park, especially near the artificial waterholes. Herds of these antelope are especially common after good rains. They are, however, known to leave the gravel plains in search of fresh grazing in the dune streets after localised rain.

Gemsbok

Although gemsbok favour the plains they occur in a wide variety of habitats that range from rocky slopes to the coastal dunes and even deep into the sand sea. During periods of drought, however, they tend to gather in the Kuiseb river-bed where they dig holes of up to one metre deep in search of water. Numbers are especially high in the upper narrow reaches of the canyon where surface water is retained for longer periods.

Hyaena

A piercing "whoop" heard at night betrays the presence of one of the few large predators resident in the central Namib, the spotted hyaena. Three clans were monitored in the central Namib by scientists who noted that spotted hyaena favour preying on gemsbok, which make up nearly 80 per cent of their diet. Some of these hyaena venture up to 30 km into the dunefields or gravel plains at night but usually return to their shady lairs in the Kuiseb Canyon to lie up during the day. Other carnivores favouring the Kuiseb Canyon are leopard and African wild cat.

Small predators

Smaller predators of the Namib include black-backed jackal, which is widespread, and Cape fox which favours the central and western areas. Aardwolf and bat-eared fox occur mainly in the east.

Birds

Because of the smaller number of habitats, the birdlife of the central Namib is not as prolific as that of the Naukluft complex where 204 species have been recorded.

From a bird-watching point of view the riverine forest of the Kuiseb and Swakop rivers is the most rewarding. Bird species likely to be seen here include swallowtailed bee-eater (445), scimitarbilled woodhoopoe (454), cardinal woodpecker (486) and brubru (741).

Lappetfaced vulture

The Namib is an important breeding area for the lappetfaced vulture (124), and you are likely to see these large raptors perched at the top of the camel thorns lining the river washes during the breeding season (May to

September). They are extremely sensitive to human disturbance and visitors should not venture too close.

To obtain a better understanding of the population dynamics of this species, a ringing project was launched in 1975 when sixteen juveniles were ringed in the Namib-Naukluft Park. Birds have subsequently been re-sighted or recovered at locations ranging from 5 to 700 km from the ringing site.

Gray's lark

Gray's lark (514), one of only two endemic Namib birds, is confined to the gravel plains between Lüderitz and south-western Angola. The cryptic, pale colour of this species, which was first spotted by the Swedish explorer Johan Wahlberg between the Kuiseb and Swakop rivers in 1855, closely matches that of the gravel plains and, unless it moves, it is difficult to see.

Ostrich

Ostrich

Flocks of ostrich (1) are often seen on the plains after good rains. If you travel through the Namib, black specks in the distance often reveal themselves as male ostriches.

Other birds

A Namibian "special" which is often encountered on the gravel plains is Rüppell's korhaan (236) while the tractrac chat (590) is another common resident of this habitat type. Keep a watch out for longbilled lark (500), Herero chat (618) and palewinged starling (770) in rocky areas, while black stork (84) and rosyfaced lovebird (367) are associated with the cliffs of the Kuiseb Canyon.

Small creatures

The numerous smaller creatures for which the Namib is justifiably famous should not be overlooked.

Tenebrionid beetles

Look out for the tenebrionid beetles, many of which occur only in the Namib Desert and nowhere else in the world. While some species are confined to the sand sea south of the Kuiseb River, several species are restricted to the gravel plains.

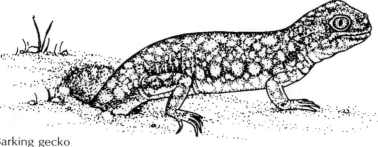

Barking gecko

Barking gecko

A characteristic sound of summer evenings is the call of the barking gecko (*Ptenopus* spp.). These reptiles are most vocal just after sunset when they take up their positions at the entrance to their burrows. After surveying their surroundings, a series of clicks is uttered in quick succession, and they then retreat into their burrow with only their heads showing. Each of the three species inhabiting the Namib plains has a different call, with the average number of clicks per call varying from as few as six to up to sixteen. Your efforts to obtain a glimpse of these vocal geckos are unlikely to be rewarded as they quickly take cover in their burrows at the slightest movement.

Other species

A wide variety of other small animals are to be seen. These include lizards and spiders. If you are lucky enough, you might come across another true inhabitant of the Namib, the Namaqua chameleon (*Chamaeleo namaquensis*).

Geology

Another fascinating aspect of the Namib is its geology. One of the best geological viewpoints is at Carp Cliff which overlooks the rugged Kuiseb Canyon. Millions of years ago a Proto-Kuiseb valley was cut into the underlying Namib Unconformity Surface. Then, some 20 to 40 million years ago arid conditions prevailed and sandstone deposits were laid down over a wide area. About 15 to 18 million years ago improved climatic conditions promoted the formation of a vast alluvial fan west of the escarpment which was characterised by gravel and conglomerate. During the next phase (5 to 7 million years ago) the conglomerate and the underlying sandstones were capped with calcrete. At this time there was no deeply incised canyon.

Formation of the Kuiseb Canyon

Some 2 to 4 million years ago, uplift of the southern African subcontinent initiated the incision of the Kuiseb River through the calcretes, conglomerates and sandstone into the Precambrian bedrock, and the river-course was incised to almost its present level. The extensive gramadoelas (badlands) of the Kuiseb Canyon were formed by the numerous tributaries which drain into the river.

The subsequent development of the Kuiseb River is characterised by several aggradational and degradational cycles. Between 1 and 1½ million years ago the river built up its bed with 30 to 40 metres of gravel conglomerate which subsequently became cemented with carbonate. During later re-incision, the river cut through the Oswater Conglomerate to its present level. At Homeb the remains of the Oswater Conglomerate, which was named after a Topnaar settlement in the middle reaches of the Kuiseb River, can be seen about 30 metres above the valley floor on the southern bank of the river.

During the second aggradational phase which took place some 20 000 years ago, fine silts were deposited away from the river-course. Horizontal layers of these purple-grey silts are preserved in the side canyons along the northern bank of the Kuiseb River.

Ecological role of the Kuiseb River

The Kuiseb River plays a vital role in the ecology of the central Namib and has been studied intensively. Research has shown that the dense riverine vegetation in the lower reaches of the river forms an effective barrier against wind-blown sand. Sand which does manage to make its way into the river-bed is washed away by periodic floods.

In the Kuiseb Delta vast subterranean reservoirs of fresh water have accumulated over millions of years. The expansion of Walvis Bay and Swakopmund, as well as the establishment of the Rössing Mine at Arandis has, however, resulted in the increasing exploitation of this water resource. Fears that the ecology of the river could be adversely affected have led to the establishment of a multi-disciplinary study of the Kuiseb River, which is being continually monitored.

In addition, the riverine vegetation is an important source of nutrition for several species of game, especially during droughts.

Desert Ecological Research Unit

Situated about 112 km south-east of Walvis Bay, the Desert Ecological Research Unit at Gobabeb is internationally renowned for its research into various aspects of the Namib ecology. The centre was established in 1963 under the direction of Dr Charles Koch of the Transvaal Museum. As Gobabeb lies at the convergence of three major ecosystems of the Namib – the sand sea south of the Kuiseb River, the Kuiseb River itself, and the gravel plains, a more suitable place for such a research centre is hard to imagine.

In addition to research into such diverse fields as zoology, botany and archaeology, the unit has also established a valuable databank on aspects such as climate.

As visitors are unlikely to benefit from casual visits the unit is closed to the public. However, to provide the public with an insight into the research conducted at Gobabeb, open weekends are held twice yearly. Activities include guided walks, illustrated lectures, film shows and poster exhibitions.

The Sheltering Desert

The Sheltering Desert is an appropriate book to read while touring the Namib. The author, Henno Martin, tells the story of how, in 1940, he and his friend Hermann Korn, as Germans, were faced with the prospect of being interned. Determined to maintain their neutrality, they put into action a plan they had previously joked about – to take refuge in the Namib. Fortunately they were both geologists and were familiar with the surroundings so they had a very good idea of the hardships this would entail.

After only four days of preparation they set off in a lorry with their dog Otto, and headed for the Kuiseb Valley. Their first "home" was established under an overhang at Carp Cliff. The site is easily accessible and well worth a visit. Sitting in the shelter one can easily picture the trials and tribulations related so vividly by Henno Martin, and one is amazed that the two Germans managed to eke out an existence in these hostile surroundings for 2½ years. Martin tells of unsuccessful attempts at collecting honey, growing vegetables in the river-bed and filling tooth cavities.

Although they were quite comfortable at Carp Cliff, the two were forced to search for another home when the pools in the Kuiseb River dried up. During their stay in the Namib they had three different homes.

Eventually the adventure ended when Hermann Korn became so ill that he was unable to walk and the men decided that they had no option but to get to a doctor. After treatment for a deficiency of vitamin B, Hermann soon recovered. Fortunately, the authorities were lenient to the two men and they were employed as geologists by the government for the remainder of the war.

References

Alexander, J.E. (1838) *An Expedition of Discovery into the Interior of Africa Through the Hitherto Undescribed Countries of the Great Namaquas, Boschmans and Hill Damaras.* London: Henry Colburn, 55.

Andersson, C.J. (1987) *Lake Ngami or Explorations and Discovery during Four Years of Wanderings in the Wilds of South-Western Africa.* Reprint from 1967; first edition 1856. Cape Town: Struik, 35 & 59 – 61.

Bornman, C. (1978) *Welwitschia: Paradox of a Parched Paradise.* Cape Town: Struik.

Craven, P. & Marais, C. (1986) *Namib Flora: Swakopmund to the Giant Welwitschia via Goanikontes.* Windhoek: Gamsberg.

Department of Agriculture and Nature Conservation, SWA/Namibia (undated). *The Welwitschia Plains – A Scenic Drive.* Windhoek.

Desert Ecological Research Unit. (1990) *Homeb Natural History.*

Hamilton, W.J., Buskirk, R. & Buskirk, W.H. (1977) 'Intersexual dominance and differential mortality of gemsbok *Oryx gazella* at Namib Desert waterholes'. *Madoqua* 10 (1): 5 – 19.

Huntley, B.J. (ed.) (1985) *The Kuiseb Environment: the Development of a Monitoring Baseline.* South African National Scientific Programmes Report No 106, Pretoria: CSIR.

Martin, H. (1991) *The Sheltering Desert: Robinson Crusoes in the Namib.* Johannesburg: A.D. Donker.

Marker, M.E. (1977) 'Aspects of the geomorphology of the Kuiseb River, South West Africa'. *Madoqua* 10 (3): 199 – 206.

Ollier, C.D. & Seely, M.K. (1977) 'Outline of the geological and geomorphic history of the Central Namib Desert'. *Madoqua* 10 (3): 207 – 214.

Seely, M. (1987) *The Namib: Natural History of an Ancient Desert.* Windhoek: Shell Oil.

Stuart, C.T. (1975) 'Preliminary notes on the mammals of the Namib Desert Park'. *Madoqua* Ser II (4): 5 – 68.

Tilson, R. & Henschel, J. (1985) 'The spotted hyaena – predator of the Namib night'. *African Wildlife* 39 (2): 50 – 55.

Tilson, R., Von Blottnitz, F. & Henschel, J. (1980) 'Prey selection by spotted hyaena (*Crocuta crocuta*) in the Namib Desert'. *Madoqua* 12 (1): 41 – 49.

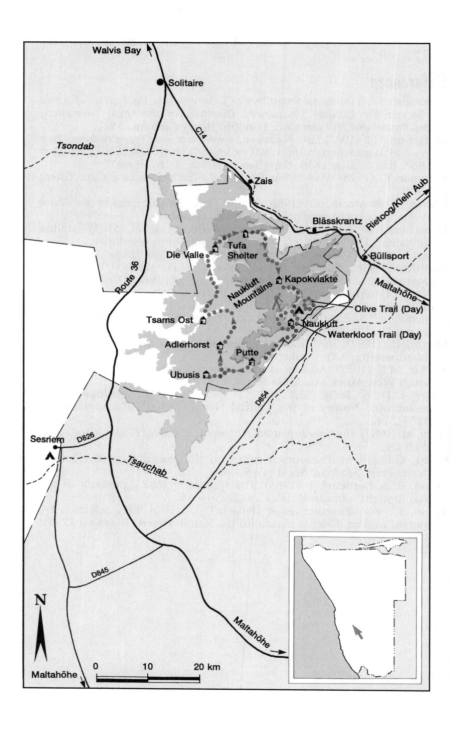

NAMIB-NAUKLUFT PARK:
NAUKLUFT SECTION

Location

Pro-Namib, central Namibia.

What to do and see

Hiking, day walks, bird-watching.

Climate

The average annual rainfall for the complex is 195 mm, but it is extremely unpredictable and ranges between 50 and 531 mm per year. Most of the rainfall occurs between December and April as localised thunderstorms, decreasing with altitude and from east to west.

During summer daily temperatures range between 35 °C and 40 °C in the valleys and average 30 °C on the plateau. In the afternoon, however, the cool south-westerly wind provides welcome relief from the blazing sun. Winter days are invigorating (20 °C), but sub-zero temperatures are not uncommon at night, especially after snowfalls on the escarpment to the east. The east winds occasionally cause unpleasant dust-storms.

When to visit

Naukluft is open between sunrise and sunset throughout the year to visitors with confirmed reservations only. Owing to the limited facilities, day visitors are not allowed.

HIKING: On account of the excessively high summer temperatures, the Naukluft Hiking Trail is only open between 1 March and 31 October.

Where to stay

Accommodation at Naukluft camp is limited to four sites with picnic tables and benches, fireplaces and drinking water, as well as ablutions.

Visitor amenities

Since there is no shop, restaurant or filling station, visitors must be totally self-sufficient. Firewood or charcoal can, however, usually be bought at the office.

SERVICE HOURS:
Office: Sunrise to sunset.

Where to book

See page 13.
   As there are only a limited number of camp sites at Naukluft, reservations should be made well in advance.

How to get there

The best route from the south is the C14 which links Maltahöhe with Solitaire, while the recommended route from Windhoek, the C24, is joined about 3 km south of Rehoboth. At Rietoog, however, turn onto district road 1206 and follow it for 28 km to Büllsport where the C14 is joined. Turn onto the D854 signposted about 2 km south of Büllsport to reach the Naukluft entrance gate about 11 km further on. The park office is 12 km beyond the gate.

What you should know

☐ The camp sites at Naukluft are not suitable for caravans.
☐ Petrol can *only* be obtained at Büllsport farm from sunrise to sunset daily, including weekends.
☐ Ensure that your belongings are put away safely before leaving the camp site unattended as baboons raid the camp sites from time to time.

Situated on the edge of the Namib Desert, the Naukluft complex takes its name from the spectacular, narrow kloof on the eastern side of the massif. Its rugged mountains, deep ravines and crystal-clear pools come as a complete surprise to the unsuspecting visitor. The mountain is ideal hiking country.

Because of the rugged terrain, no vehicular traffic is permitted other than along the access road to the camp site, and the only way this magnificent mountain range can truly be appreciated is on foot. Visitors have a choice of two day walks, and the more adventurous can set off on the Naukluft Hiking Trail.

Day walks

If you plan to hike either of the two day trails ensure that you are fit and properly equipped. An early start is advisable and a stout pair of well-worn walking shoes, a sun-hat and at least two litres of water per person are absolutely essential. A daypack is useful for carrying trail snacks, your water-bottle and spare clothing.

Waterkloof Trail

The 17 km long Waterkloof Trail is especially demanding, and will take about seven hours to complete. A circular route is followed in an anti-clockwise direction from the Koedoesrus camp site, and highlights of the trail are the tufa formations and crystal clear pools upstream of the camp site. The highest point of the trail (1 910 metres) is reached shortly after the half-way mark and here trailists are rewarded with breathtaking views of the rugged mountains and the wide valley far below. Points of interest along the descent include an enormous tufa formation and a large pothole which is particularly attractive after rain. Part of the descent also follows a short stretch of the old German cannon road, which dates back to the 1894 campaign against Hendrik Witbooi, while the final 6 km of the trail follows an easy route along the Naukluft River.

Olive Trail

The 10 km long Olive Trail takes its name from the wild olive (617) trees which can be seen along the route. It is usually hiked in about four hours. From the starting point, a steep climb to the top of the plateau awaits you, but once the plateau has been reached the magnificent vistas will soon make you forget your aches and pains. The trail traverses easier terrain before it makes its way down along a river valley. As you continue downstream, the valley rapidly deepens until it is caught up between the sheer cliffs of the gorge where a small waterfall has to be negotiated. The traverse may appear daunting at first sight but fortunately chains have been anchored along the canyon sides and there are sufficient good footholds. Further along the trail crosses a jeep track which gives access to the plateau and after a short distance rejoins the jeep track which is followed back to the parking area. Black eagles (131) are common breeding residents at Naukluft and if you scan the sheer cliffs carefully, their huge nests are unlikely to escape your attention.

Short walks

If you are not confident enough to tackle either of the two day walks, there are ample opportunities for short walks in the vicinity of the camp site. Not to be missed are the crystal clear pools upstream. It takes about twenty minutes to walk there and, even if the water temperature does not permit swimming, the beautiful scenery and tranquility make the walk worthwhile.

Naukluft Hiking Trail

Although the Naukluft Hiking Trail is considered by many hikers to be one of the most difficult routes in southern Africa, it is also rated as one of the most spectacular. The route traverses undulating plains and follows deep ravines where chains assist hikers to overcome obstacles presented by the sheer cliffs.

Hikers have two options – a circular eight day hike covering 120 km or a four day hike over 58 km. Accommodation is in old farm houses on the first and third nights while basic stone shelters are provided at the six other overnight stops. Beds and mattresses are supplied only at the Naukluft hut and, as no fires are permitted on the trail, a lightweight stove is essential. Drinking water is available at each overnight stop, while at two of the overnight stops hikers can treat themselves to the luxury of a cold shower!

Be warned – under no circumstances should this trail be attempted by inexperienced or unfit hikers.

Game

The massif is a sanctuary for animals typical of the highlands of Namibia and the rugged mountains are an ideal habitat for Hartmann's mountain zebra which occurs in the undulating escarpment region between the Namib plains and the interior plateau. The mountains also provide an ideal habitat for several troops of baboons which are especially common near springs, where they are often heard.

Hartmann's mountain zebra

Except for a small population in the Richtersveld and relatively small numbers in south-western Angola, Hartmann's mountain zebra is restricted to Namibia, where they inhabit parts of the mountainous transitional zone between the Namib Desert in the west and the inland plateau in the east. From Kaokoland they range southwards to the

Brandberg and into the interior as far as the Outjo District. After a break in their distribution they re-occur along the escarpment south of the Swakop River to the Naukluft Mountains and eastwards into the Khomas Hochland. Because of a lack of suitable habitat there is another break in their distribution and they do not re-occur until the rugged Huns Mountains and the Fish River Canyon, some 400 km further south.

Hartmann's mountain zebra is not a separate species, but one of two mountain zebra sub-species – the other being the closely-related Cape mountain zebra.

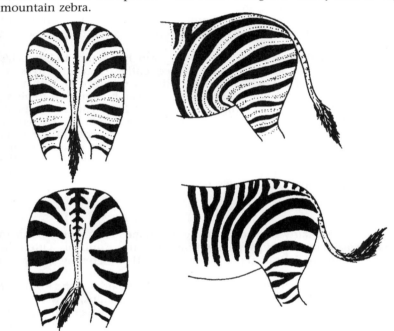

The difference in stripe patterns of Burchell's zebra (top) and Cape mountain zebra (bottom) – Hartmann's mountain zebra is closely related to the latter

The most significant difference between Hartmann's mountain zebra and the Cape mountain zebra is the body marking. Unlike the Cape mountain zebra where the dark stripes are considerably wider than the light stripes, those of Hartmann's mountain zebra are more or less equal in width.

With an average shoulder height of 150 cm, Hartmann's mountain zebra stands about 23 cm taller than the southern sub-species, the Cape mountain zebra, and about 14 cm taller than Burchell's zebra.

The South African sub-species of the mountain zebra, the Cape mountain zebra came close to extinction during the 1930s, but their numbers have increased to such an extent that they are no longer considered to be endangered. Except for small numbers which survived in the Gamka and the Kamanassie mountains, most of the animals were restocked from the Mountain Zebra National Park near Cradock in South Africa. Healthy populations have been re-established in the Karoo, Zuurberg and Bontebok national parks, as well as in several nature reserves since the mid–1970s.

Within their former distribution range, the Cape mountain zebra occurred widely in the mountainous areas of the Cape Province. The northern limit of their former distribution range was probably in the vicinity of the Kamies Mountains. From here they occurred southwards to the mountains in the south-western Cape and eastwards as far as the Zuurberg.

At first glance the mountain zebra is similar in appearance to Burchell's zebra, which inhabits savannas and is, consequently, also referred to as the plains zebra. One of the most significant differences, however, is that the body stripes of the mountain zebras are considerably narrower, totalling around 43 from head to tail compared to between 25 and 30 for Burchell's zebra. In addition, the stripes of the mountain zebras form a characteristic gridiron pattern, which is absent in Burchell's zebra, and do not meet under the belly. Another distinguishing feature is the absence of the distinctive yellow or grey shadow stripes of Burchell's zebra in the mountain zebra. Mountain zebra have a distinctive dewlap and their ears are larger than those of Burchell's zebra.

Antelope

Klipspringer are fairly numerous in the mountains and usually occur in pairs or small family groups ranging from three to six animals. Often the only indication of their presence is a sharp whistle which they emit when they are alarmed.

Kudu favour the densely wooded kloofs and are fairly abundant, while springbok roam the plains at the base of the mountains, as well as the plateau. Gemsbok occur mainly to the west of the massif, but are also found on the plateau. Small antelope include common duiker and steenbok.

Predators

Leopard are the most important predators in the area and, although they are rarely seen by visitors, a number of sightings have been reported by hikers. Other predators include black-backed jackal, Cape fox, bat-eared fox, African wild cat, small-spotted cat, small-spotted genet, caracal and aardwolf.

Small mammals

Not to be overlooked are the smaller mammals such as Cape hare, scrub hare, Cape ground squirrel, springhaas, badger, suricate and yellow mongoose.

Left: The Kuiseb Canyon at Homeb (see page 152)

Below: Namaqua chameleon

Bottom: A view across the Namib Desert from Ganab Mountain. A quiver tree (*Aloe dichotoma*) is in the foreground (see page 154)

Above: An early morning view of one of the basic camp sites at Ganab in the Namib section of the Namib-Naukluft Park (see page 154)

Below: The Naukluft Hiking Trail enables visitors to explore the beautiful Naukluft massif on foot (see page 166)

Left: A large tufa waterfall in the Naukluft section of the Namib-Naukluft Park (see page 165)

Below: A view of Sandwich Lagoon in 1990. Since this photograph was taken, the sea has encroached significantly on the lagoon (see page 175)

Above: The dramatic effects of light and shadow make scenes such as this sand-dune near Sossusvlei a photographer's dream

Below: Sossusvlei occasionally fills up with water (see page 185)

Birds

Since Naukluft lies at the limit of the distribution of several bird species, there is an interesting variety of birds to be found here. Not only is the complex the southernmost limit of distribution of several of the Namibian endemics, but it is also the northernmost limit of a number of Karoo species. In addition, the permanent pools with their associated riverine vegetation attract a variety of species which would otherwise not occur in this arid region, and to date 204 species have been recorded. The 98 resident species represent nearly half of the total, while 35 migrant and 19 vagrant species have also been recorded.

The number of species occurring in the complex is largely determined by the amount of rainfall, and varies from as few as 116 in dry years to 152 following good rains. February is usually the most rewarding month for bird-watching when there is a possibility of spotting up to 140 species in the Naukluft region.

Species reaching the southern limit of their distribution at Naukluft include Rüppell's korhaan (236), which is common on the plains, Monteiro's hornbill (462), Herero chat (618), rockrunner (662), white-tailed shrike (752) and chestnut weaver (812).

The complex also lies at the northernmost limit of the distribution of Karoo robin (614), cinnamonbreasted warbler (660), pintailed whydah (860) and African black duck (105) which are attracted to secluded pools in the riverine valleys.

Distribution per habitat

The mountainous complex is an important habitat for cliff breeding species. Rosyfaced lovebirds (367) are common, while several pairs of black eagle are known to breed in the complex. Other species to keep an eye out for include augur buzzard (153), lanner falcon (172) and Bradfield's swift (413).

Lesser honeyguide (476), goldentailed (483) and cardinal (486) woodpeckers, Layard's titbabbler (622) and longbilled crombec (651) are occasional possibilities in the well-vegetated valleys.

The bokmakierie (746), one of the six southern African species of green-and-yellow shrikes, is common throughout the mountains, and its characteristic call is frequently heard, while purple roller (449) are resident on the lower slopes and plains. A common species of the valleys and rocky outcrops is the familiar chat (589), while the shorttoed rock thrush (583) are confined to suitable rocky areas in the mountains.

Ostrich (1) occur on the plains surrounding the massif, and are particularly common on the plains to the west of the complex where you might also see whitebacked vulture (123), lappetfaced vulture (124), lanner falcon (172) and Stark's lark (511).

Other species to watch out for include black stork (84), a rare resident of the riverine valleys, and plumcoloured starling (761), an intra-African migrant which is common between October and April.

Geology

Another attraction of Naukluft is its interesting geological history which dates back one to two thousand million years to the time when the basement complex, which consists of metasedimentary and volcanic rocks, gneisses and granites, was formed. About 650 to 750 million years ago the entire south-western part of the southern African sub-continent was flooded by a shallow tropical sea. It was during this period that the Nama sediments, consisting mainly of black limestone, were deposited to overlie the basement complex.

Then, 500 to 550 million years ago, there followed a period of crustal movement and mountain building, and large sheets of sedimentary rocks were placed in their present positions. These rocks form the upper part of the mountain and are known as the Naukluft "nappes".

An interesting feature of the Naukluft Mountains are the numerous tufa formations. These porous limestone deposits usually occur on the faces of waterfalls, and the enormous size of some of these formations and their widespread distribution throughout the Naukluft Mountains provide evidence of a considerably wetter climate during the recent past. Also known as fountain stone or waterfall limestone formations, they were formed when calcium carbonate-rich water evaporated.

History
Early warfare

The lonely grave of a German soldier in the Naukluft Valley bears testimony to the conflict between the Germans and the Witbooi Namas during the early 1890s. Other reminders of this bloody period include sections of the route along which the Germans dragged their cannons onto the plateau, ramparts, trenches and cannon emplacements.

Following Hendrik Witbooi's defiance and refusal to submit to the supreme authority of the German emperor, a campaign under the leadership of Major Curt von Francois was launched against him on 12 April 1893. Although Von Francois succeeded in dislodging Witbooi from his settlement at Hoornkrans, he did not succeed in defeating him.

In January 1893 the *Schutztruppe* were deployed in the vicinity of the Oniab Valley north of the Naukluft Valley, and in one of the skirmishes with the Witboois a 25-year-old cavalryman, Richard Kramars, was killed on 31 March 1894. Kramars' grave can be seen near the Naukluft hut.

Von Francois was replaced by Theodor Leutwein as *Landeshauptman* in March 1894, and in the following month Leutwein launched a campaign against Witbooi in the Naukluft Mountains. After a series of failed negotiations, skirmishes and truces, Leutwein was joined by reinforcements from Germany.

Leutwein estimated that the Witboois could be defeated within three days, but several factors were against him. Not only was Witbooi a brilliant military strategist, but the Germans were unaccustomed to guerilla warfare and did not know the area as well as he did.

After the main Witbooi camp at the junction of the Naukluft and Oniabkloof had been captured on 27 August, Witbooi retreated into the interior of the Naukluft range. The Germans followed in pursuit, and he was tracked down at Gams nearly three days later. On 30 August after a battle of several hours he retreated to Garus where the two opposing sides engaged in battle for two days on 2 and 3 September.

Witbooi once again retreated into the mountains and, after resting his soldiers, Leutwein tracked Witbooi to his new camp at Tsams. By this time both sides had suffered heavy losses and endured dire hardships and Witbooi offered to negotiate a conditional surrender. Realising that an outright victory was unlikely, Leutwein accepted the offer and, after negotiations, a treaty was signed on 15 September. In terms of the treaty Witbooi accepted the paramouncy of the German empire and agreed to the stationing of a garrison at Gibeon, but he and his followers were to be allowed to retain their weapons and he retained his territory and control over his subjects and their land.

Hendrik Witbooi with some of his soldiers *circa* 1894

Vegetation

Naukluft lies in the transitional zone between the savanna and the desert and, based on the topography of the complex, five vegetation communities have been identified.

Gravel plain communities

On entering the park, the road traverses the gravel plains that surround the massif. Typical tree species of the gravel communities include blue-leaved (276) and white-stem (289) corkwoods, while the well-developed shrub stratum is dominated by pomegranates (*Rhigozum trichotomum*), wild raisin bushes (*Grewia tenax*) and trumpet thorn (*Catophractes alexandri*).

Mountain communities

A feature of the saddle which the road crosses later is the dense mass of resurrection bush (*Myrothamnus flabellifolia*) that covers the slopes. For most of the year the branches of this small erect plant curl inwards, creating the impression that it is a dead plant but shortly after rain the plant is transformed into a bright green bush that is very much alive.

The vegetation of the mountain slopes to the right of the access road has been classified as being part of the mountain communities. These communities encompass the mountainous parts of the complex, excluding the plateau and the kloof communities. The vegetation of the mountain communities on the northern and eastern slopes of the complex displays interesting differences from the vegetation of those on the cooler southern and western slopes. These differences can be attributed to the fact that the southern and western slopes lie in the rain shadow of the complex and the vegetation is consequently not only sparser, but also much hardier. Species of the northern slopes include shepherd's tree (122), mountain thorn (171) and the Namibian resin tree (369), while quiver trees (29), blue-leafed corkwood and paperbark milkbush (344) are conspicuous on the southern slopes. Moringa (phantom) trees (137) and white-stem corkwood grow on the talus slopes.

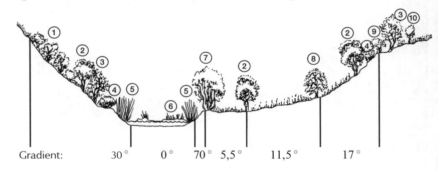

Gradient: 30°   0°   70° 5,5°   11,5°   17°

1. Blue-leaved corkwood (276)
2. Sweet thorn (172)
3. Buffalo-thorn (447)
4. *Grewia tenax*
5. *Phragmites australis*

6. *Cyperus*
7. Common cluster fig (66)
8. Ebony tree (598)
9. Black thorn (176)
10. Blue neat's foot (208)

Vegetation of the Naukluft Kloof about 500 metres above the camp site

Kloof communities

A walk to the pools upstream from the camp site gives one the opportunity of having a closer look at the trees and shrubs of the eleven kloof communities in the complex. The deep gorges with their perennial springs contain a variety of trees and shrubs and 157 species have been recorded in the Naukluft gorge. Large common cluster figs (66) are conspicuous on the river-banks, while sweet thorn (172) is also dominant. Stands of ebony trees (598) grow higher up the banks. Characteristic species of the rock-strewn slopes are *Euphorbia virosa*, blue-leaved corkwood, moringa (phantom) trees and quiver trees, while the Namaqua fig (51) is another species of the rocky cliffs. As a result of the steep gradients of the rivers, which are characterised by waterfalls, little material that would encourage the development of gallery forests is deposited.

Plateau communities

The plateau communities occupying the more even areas on the top of the Naukluft Mountains are dominated by typical Karoo species like kapokbos (*Eriocephalus ericoides*). The most conspicuous trees here are mountain thorn, Namibian resin tree and shepherd's tree while camel (168), black (176), umbrella (188), and buffalo-thorn (447) grow along the river washes.

Sandy plains transition communities

These communities occur to the west of the mountains at the eastern edge of the dunes. The soil is more sandy and less stony than the adjacent gravel plains and trees and shrubs are limited to camel thorns (168) and driedoring (three thorns, *Rhigozum trichotomum*) in river-courses and washes. The area is devoid of vegetation for most of the year, but after good summer rains the plains are transformed into expanses of waving grass.

References

Archeia 13. (1989) *The Hendrik Witbooi Papers*, translated by A. Heywood & E. Maasdorp. Windhoek: National Archives of Namibia.

Boyer, H.J. & Bridgeford, P.A. (1988) 'Birds of the Naukluft Mountains: an annotated checklist'. *Madoqua* 15 (4): 295 – 314.

Joubert, E. *Meesterplan: Namib-Naukluftpark – 'n Verslag met Beleid ten Opsigte van Doelstellings, Sonering en Benutting van die Naukluft-bergkompleks en Aangrensende Gruisvlaktes, Insluitende Sesriem en Sossusvlei.* Windhoek: Suidwes-Afrika Administrasie, Afdeling Natuurbewaring en Toerisme.

Olivier, W.A. & Olivier, S.W. (undated) *Naukluft Hiking Trail Map.* Windhoek: Directorate of Nature Conservation and Recreational Resorts.

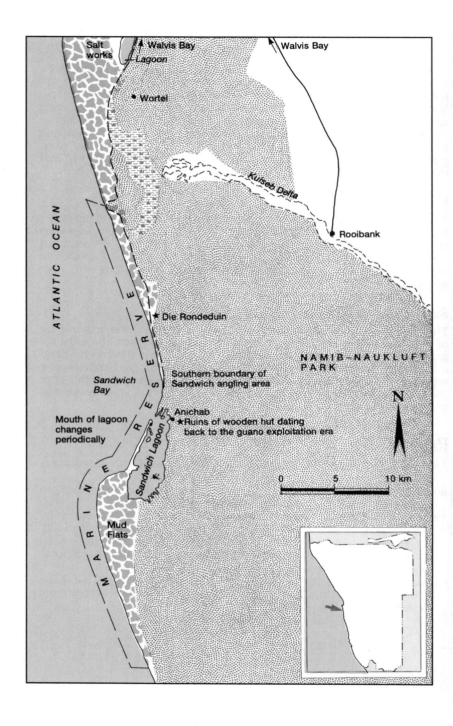

NAMIB-NAUKLUFT PARK: SANDWICH

Location

Central Namib coast.

What to do and see

Bird-watching, angling, photography, rambling.

Climate

Fog is common along the coast during the late afternoons and early mornings, especially between April and September when it can occur for more than half the month. By mid-morning the fog has usually dissipated but towards the late afternoon dense banks of fog start rolling inland once again.

During summer the dominant winds are southerly but between April and September the easterly berg winds can create unpleasant conditions along the coast.

When to visit

Open between 06:00 and 20:00 throughout the year.

BIRD-WATCHING: September to March.
ANGLING: Best time – November to 24 January.
Closed season – 25 January to 15 April.

Where to stay

Overnight camping at Sandwich is strictly prohibited.

Accommodation in Walvis Bay ranges from caravan and camp sites to hotels and fully-equipped bungalows (such as those at The Esplanade). In Swakopmund visitors have a choice of several hotels and pensions, while the Swakopmund Rest Camp offers a variety of accommodation types ranging from luxury flats to basic fisherman's cabins.

Visitor amenities

There are no amenities whatsoever at Sandwich.

Where to book

Permits to visit Sandwich are obtainable during office hours from the tourist office of the Directorate of Wildlife, Conservation and Research at Swakopmund. Outside office hours permits can be obtained from Hans Kriess Motors at Swakopmund and CWB and Suidwes service stations at Walvis Bay.

The Esplanade (self-contained bungalows): Private Bag 5017, Walvis Bay, telephone (0642) 6145.

Walvis Bay and Langstrand (camp sites): P O Box 86, Walvis Bay, telephone (0642) 5981.

Swakopmund Rest Camp: Private Bag 5017, Swakopmund, telephone (0641) 2807/8.

How to get there

Sandwich is accessible by four-wheel drive only.

From the traffic circle at the entrance to Walvis Bay continue along Union Street to its junction with The Esplanade. Turn left here (south) and continue with this road to the turnoff signposted Paaltjies where you take the left-hand fork. A short way further on the road forks once more and here you keep to the left. The road now winds through the salt works and the Kuiseb Delta along a well-defined track which soon splits into several tracks. Keep to the well-defined tracks closest to the sand-dunes along the edge of the salt pan. Shortly before reaching the park fence the tracks veer off onto the beach. From here it is roughly 20 km to the northern boundary of Sandwich through loose sand. There is a choice of two routes – a direct route along the beach or a more inland route. If you choose the latter option continue around the fence for a few hundred metres before the tracks continue southwards. Langduin (Long Dune) is reached after about 7 km and, depending on local conditions, is usually best crossed along its ridge. If there are no fresh tracks to follow, work your way around the base, but be extremely careful not to get bogged down in the salt flats. After traversing the dune the route once again passes through a salt pan until Rondeduin (Round Dune) where you reach the beach. The southern boundary of the angling area is about 9 km further on.

What you should know

- [ ] Vehicles are not permitted beyond the southern boundary of the angling area.
- [ ] Angling is not permitted south of the signposted fence at the northern end of the lagoon.
- [ ] The entire Sandwich area is closed to anglers from 25 January to 15 April.
- [ ] Consult a tide table and, if at all possible, plan the outward and return journey to coincide with low tide.
- [ ] Do not risk the chance of being bogged down by driving on the beach. Remain above the high water mark and deflate your vehicle's tyres if necessary.
- [ ] A pair of comfortable walking shoes or open sandals is essential when exploring Sandwich, while a daypack, water-bottle and snacks are useful.

Bounded by high dunes on its landward side, Sandwich is one of the most scenic sites along the Namibian coast. Here the sand-dunes, the lagoon, and the flocks of pink flamingoes seen against the yellow dunes present an ever-changing kaleidoscope of colour.

The lagoon area may only be explored on foot and from the northern boundary it is about 4 km to the nature conservation hut at Anichab. Since the sandbanks and channels in the lagoon are constantly changing, it is advisable to follow the edge of the dunes on the outward journey, rather than risking the possibility of having your way blocked by a deep channel.

Although tiring, a climb to the crest of the dunes flanking the lagoon is not to be missed. Those prepared to exert themselves will be rewarded with spectacular views of the lagoon and the dunes further inland.

Sandwich is one of only four large promontories along the Namibian coast which offers suitable conditions for large concentrations of shore birds. Sheltered from the continuous buffeting of the waves and with a temperature that is between 5° and 6°C warmer than that of the ocean during the summer months, the nutrient-rich water of the lagoon is the habitat of a wide variety of marine life and a nursery for young fish. The rich microscopic flora and the abundance of organic matter provide a constant source of food for a host of invertebrates and small fish which, in turn, are preyed upon by larger species and sea- and shore birds.

Stretching for about 11 km from north to south and with a width of up to 3,5 km, Sandwich is the country's most important coastal wetland for waders.

Birds

From a bird-watching point of view, September is usually the best month, as it is then that large numbers of Palaearctic waders, as well as inland water-birds, converge on Sandwich. To date more than 113 bird species, including 35 vagrant species, have been recorded here.

Internationally renowned wetland

The significance of Sandwich is, however, not its diversity of birds, but its international importance as a wetland. It has been estimated that the wetlands at Sandwich attract more than 195 000 wetland birds and, with a density of 7 791 waders/km² at low tide, the area boasts one of the highest wader densities in the world.

In terms of sheer numbers the southern mudflats, which cover an area of approximately 16 km², is the most productive. Extrapolations of subsample counts conducted during a bird count in February 1991 put the total number of birds attracted to this habitat at between 23 000 wading birds at high tide and a maximum of 141 000, or 73 per cent of the total count, at low tide. The western sand-spit and dry mudflats accounted for 24 per cent of the total count, while the lagoonside wetlands and the northern freshwater wetlands held one and two per cent respectively.

Arctic tern

Waders

Up to 179 000 Palearctic and intra-African waders are attracted to Sandwich with common (327) and Arctic (328) terns making up almost 30 per cent of this number, while curlew sandpiper (272) accounts for a further 25 per cent. Significant numbers of little stint (274) (31 000) and sanderling (281) (14 000) are attracted, while grey plover (254), turnstone (262), knot (271) and bartailed godwit (288) also occur. Sandwich terns (326) occur in relatively small numbers and, although it is often assumed that the name is derived from Sandwich Harbour, the species takes its name from Sandwich in Kent, England, where it was first discovered.

Inland water-birds

Flamingoes constitute the largest percentage of the inland water-birds and up to 12 000 greater (96) and 13 000 lesser (97) flamingoes, have been counted. During dry years they remain at Sandwich, but when there have been good rains in the interior most of them migrate there to breed. The lagoon also supports up to 2 400, or nearly a quarter, of the world population of the chestnutbanded plover (247), a Namibian Red Data species. Other Red Data species to watch out for are blacknecked grebe (7) and white pelican (49), as well as greyheaded (315) and Hartlaub's (316) gulls.

Northern wetland species

The Cape teal (106) is the most abundant species to inhabit the reed-lined pools of the northern wetlands. Other species recorded here include great crested grebe (6), dabchick (8), grey heron (62), Egyptian goose (102), South African shelduck (103) and Cape shoveller (112).

Decreasing numbers of freshwater wetland birds

From old maps of Sandwich Harbour and the reports of early mariners it is clear that Sandwich has always been a dynamic system – not only did the mouth of the lagoon shift intermittently, but it also periodically became sanded in. However, during the past twenty years the mouth has remained open and with the deposition of sand in the southern part of the lagoon, the northern sand-spit has been "starved" of sediments. As a result, the sea encroached 400 metres landward between 1979 and 1989, but the metamorphosis of the lagoon has been especially rapid since 1988. The vegetated salt marshes and the freshwater pools at the northernmost end of the lagoon have been smothered by sand, and the diversity and numbers of freshwater wetland birds have, consequently, decreased significantly.

Angling

Despite the importance of the lagoon as a wetland of international significance, more than 80 per cent of the visitors attracted to Sandwich are anglers. Angling is restricted to a 20 km section of the coast north of the lagoon, and each year thousands of anglers flock to the coast to try their hand and their luck at fishing.

Marine reserve

Since the lagoon and the surrounding bay is thought to be an important breeding ground for fish, a 45 km stretch of coastline extending 1,6 km into the sea from the low tide mark was incorporated into the Namib-Naukluft Park in 1979. The proclamation effectively gave Sandwich the status of a marine reserve – the only one of its kind in Namibia.

Angling season

The main season stretches from November to March but, in 1992, it was decided to close the area from 25 January to 15 April for a number of reasons. Not only was the fish that was caught from mid-December to mid-April found to be heavily in roe but, during a survey, it was also found that commercial fishing was increasing at Sandwich. During a monitoring programme undertaken between December 1989 and April 1990 it became apparent that while 15 tonnes of fish was caught during the December/January holiday season, 75 tonnes was caught after the season. Another concern was the impact of large numbers of vehicles on sensitive habitats like the intertidal and littoral zones, while pollution also posed a serious threat to the environment. In April 1990, for example, 518 kg of litter was collected, including 16 km of discarded fishing line.

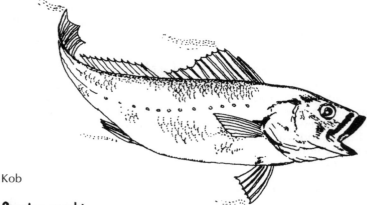

Kob

Species caught

Kob, steenbras, galjoen and blacktail are the most commonly caught species. The average-size kob caught at Sandwich weighs in at 3,2 kg, while steenbras, galjoen and blacktail pull the scales at an average of 1,6; 1,5 and 1,0 kg respectively.

Restrictions

No bait may be collected in the area and anglers should familiarise themselves with the regulations in respect of minimum sizes – see the box on pages 203 and 204.

Game

Small numbers of black-backed jackal and brown hyaena patrol the coastline in search of beached seals and whatever else they might find. You might also see the spoor of the few gemsbok which are resident in the area.

History

Origin of the name

The early pastoralists named the freshwater spring which seeps through the dunes at the nature conservation hut *Anichab*, a Nama word meaning "spring water". During the Portuguese explorations along the west coast of Africa the lagoon was named Port d'Ilheo, or "point of the island" and the name Sandwich Harbour first appeared on a map published in 1791 by a geographer of the British East India Company, Alexander Dalrymple. It appears that Dalrymple obtained the sketch map of the harbour from Samuel Enderby Jnr who ran a London-based whaling company towards the end of the 18th century. Between 1785 and 1786 one of Samuel Enderby Jnr's ships, the *Sandwich*, sailed for the south-east Atlantic. Although the ship's log-book has been lost, it has been established that the whaler did hunt along the Namibian coast and it has been suggested that the map published by Dalrymple was drawn by the captain of the *Sandwich*, James Shield.

Harbour

Although Sandwich seems a most unlikely site for a harbour, the lagoon once served as an anchorage for sailing vessels, and hence the reference to the harbour on old maps. When the lagoon was surveyed by Lieut. C.F. Oldham of the *HMS Sylvia* in 1880, the mouth was five fathoms deep, while the centre measured 3,5 fathoms.

The natural harbour is believed to have been used by pirates as a careening base, and it also offered safe anchorage to whalers operating along the coast. Legend has it that an East Indiaman with a cargo of gold, ivory and precious stones from the Great Mogul of Delhi ran aground here in 1770 while *en route* from India to England.

Towards the end of the 1800s the De Pass Company established a base at Sandwich, which was considered to be safer than Walvis Bay. From here cured fish and shark liver oil processed at Sandwich, as well as sealskins and guano from the offshore islands, were exported to Cape Town and Mauritius.

Meat canning factory

The South West Africa Company established a meat canning factory at the southern end of the lagoon in 1890, despite an unfavourable report about the route used for herding cattle to the coast. The enterprise consisted of an abattoir with a cooling room, a machine house equipped with an ice machine, three large houses, shops, store-rooms and a shed for building material, coal and wood chips. In 1895 the mouth of the lagoon became sanded in, the project was abandoned, and all that remains are the weathered beams of two old houses.

Guano industry

Undeterred by the failures of earlier projects, the Deutsche Kolonialgesselschaft began to exploit vast quantities of guano from the six natural islands at Sandwich in 1910. In 1923 the rights to the guano deposits were sold to a syndicate and, after changing hands several times, the concession was taken over by Fisons Fertilizers in 1937.

Towards the end of the same year the company embarked on an extensive reclamation scheme which involved pumping sand from the bed of the lagoon onto the islands. By December 1938 about 4 ha of land had been reclaimed and production rose from a total of 163 tonnes of guano in 1937 to 707 tonnes in 1938 from Long Island alone.

Transporting the guano overland to Walvis Bay was no easy feat. The Studebaker trucks followed a route between the high and low water marks and each truck was equipped with an anchor to prevent the vehicle from being washed out to sea in the event of a break-down.

Studebaker trucks were used to transport guano to Walvis Bay in the late 1930s

War interrupted further reclamation, but between August and December 1942 a further 4 ha of land was reclaimed. In 1943 the islands along the western arm of the lagoon became part of the mainland when the mouth of the lagoon was sanded in. As a result, jackal were free to move in and the sea-birds abandoned the colony. In April the following year the mouth was washed open by the autumn spring tide and conditions returned to normal. In 1945, however, disaster struck once again when the mouth was sanded in until the spring tide of 1946. A good amount of guano was obtained in 1947 but, at the end of the year the mouth was sanded in once more and in 1956 the concession lapsed as the concessionaire had not been exploiting its rights.

Relics from the past

Although nature has reclaimed much of the evidence of this era the remains of an old hut, partially buried by the advancing sand-dunes, and the nearby palm trees which mark the site of an old garden, can still be seen near the nature conservation hut. Other evidence includes a small graveyard and the rusting hulk of the barge used during the land reclamation operations.

References

Berry, H.H. & Berry, C.U. (1975) 'A check list and notes on the birds of Sandvis, South West Africa'. *Madoqua* 10 (2): 5 – 18.

Gebhardt, L. (1973) 'Sandwich Harbour: a sanctuary in the dunes'. *SWA Annual*: 97 – 103.

Kensley, B. & Penrith, M.J. (1977) 'Biological survey of Sandvis 1, introduction and faunal list'. *Madoqua* 10 (3): 181 – 190.

Kinahan, J. (1989) 'Hoe Sandwich-Hawe sy naam gekry het'. *Flamingo* 1 (3): 19 – 23.

Lenssen, J., Tarr, P. & Berry, H. (1991) 'An assessment of visitor statistics and linefishing along the Sandwich shoreline, Namib-Naukluft Park, Namibia'. *Madoqua* 18 (1): 33 – 36.

Simmons, R. (1991) 'Wading birds of the Sandwich Harbour wetlands, February 1991: preliminary estimates and alternative counting methods'. *Lanioturdus* 26 (1): 4 – 14.

Terblanche, D.J. (1980) 'The man-made island of Sandwich Harbour'. *SWA Annual*: 89 – 95.

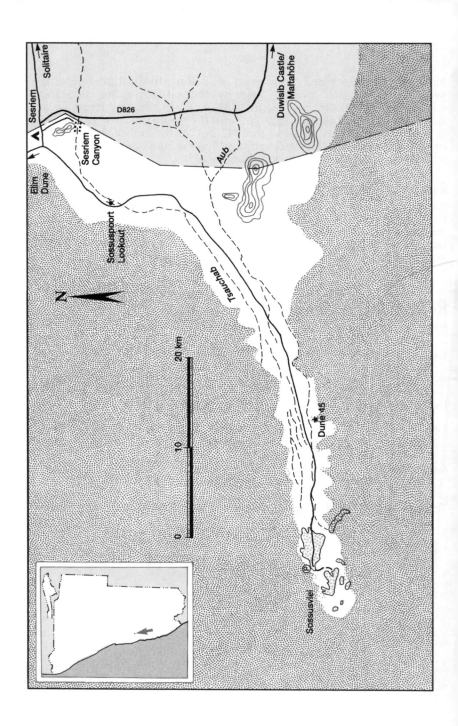

NAMIB-NAUKLUFT PARK:
SESRIEM AND SOSSUSVLEI

Location

Eastern edge of the central Namib sand sea.

What to do and see

Sightseeing, photography.

Climate

Be prepared for scorching temperatures in both summer and winter, especially when the east wind blows. Winter days are usually pleasant, but very cold spells do occasionally occur during the winter months. Rain is very rare and water at Sossusvlei and Sesriem Canyon is not from localised run-off.

When to visit

This section of the park is open from sunrise to sunset throughout the year.

Where to stay

Facilities at Sesriem consist of a number of shady camp sites laid out under huge camel thorn trees. Each camp site has its own fireplace and tap, while some camp sites are encircled by a stone wall. Two small ablution blocks, as well as scullery facilities, are provided.

Visitor amenities

Petrol, diesel, firewood and cooldrinks can be obtained at Sesriem, but there are no other amenities and visitors must, therefore, be self-sufficient.

SERVICE HOURS:
Office: Sunrise to 13:00 and 14:00 to sunset.

Where to book

See page 13.

How to get there

There are various approach routes but from Windhoek the best way to travel is along the B1 to just south of Rehoboth and then to turn onto the C24 (signposted Klein Aub). Take the D1261 about 36 km further on, and then the D1275 via the Spreetshoogte Pass to the junction with the C14. Turn left to reach Solitaire after 9 km and continue along Route 36 to the signposted turnoff to Sesriem some 70 km further south. Motorists are warned that the Spreetshoogte Pass is too steep for towing caravans.

What you should know

☐   Book well in advance because the camp is popular and there are only a limited number of sites.

☐   Take along sufficient beverages on your excursion to the pan – cooldrinks are much appreciated after a long, hot walk! In addition it is a 60 km drive back to the camp site.

☐   A really early start is advisable if you plan to climb one of the dunes at the vlei.

☐   The desert ecology is extremely fragile and vehicles should not deviate from the road. Drivers of four-wheel drive vehicles proceeding beyond the parking area for sedan vehicles should take special care to keep the vehicle on the marked route.

☐   Protection against the sun is essential if you plan to explore the dunes or have to walk the last few kilometres to the pan.

☐   Electricity in the ablutions is supplied by a generator which is switched off at around 22:00, so make sure that you are not caught in the dark.

Sesriem is a delightful camp site on the edge of the vast sand sea of the Namib, and it is the only place which affords visitors the rare opportunity to travel into the sand-dune desert in a sedan vehicle.

Since the sand-dunes are seen at their best immediately after sunrise when the rich orange dunes contrast sharply with the black shadows, it is advisable to spend at least two nights at Sesriem in order to fully appreciate the area. Departure and return times when visiting Sossusvlei must be confirmed with the office at Sesriem as they vary with the seasons, but be sure to make an early start.

Sesriem Canyon

About 4 km south of the camp site is one of the most amazing features of the Namib – the Sesriem Canyon where the Tsauchab River has carved a gorge that is up to 30 metres deep and about 1 km long.

From the parking area a track leads to the canyon floor and a walk into Sesriem is like descending through the layers of time.

Geological formation of the canyon

The deposition of alternating layers of sand, gravel and heavy pebbles began some 15 to 18 million years ago during a wetter phase in the history of the Namib.

The layers of large pebbles indicate periods of fast river flow, while the layers of finer gravel and sand provide evidence of reduced flow. Calcium carbonate dust blown in by the wind and washed westwards from the limestone-rich escarpment subsequently cemented the layers into calcrete conglomerate.

Then, 2 to 4 million years ago, continental uplift caused the incision of the Tsauchab River, and of most of the other westward-flowing rivers in the Namib.

The canyon is usually dry, enabling visitors to explore this interesting geological feature. As you walk towards the head of the canyon it becomes gradually narrower until it is a mere two metres wide in places.

After good rains the canyon holds water for several months and it is possible to swim in the deep pool where the track from the parking area reaches the canyon floor.

West of the parking area the canyon gradually becomes shallower until the river broadens out into a valley which it follows for about 60 km to Sossusvlei.

Origin of the name

The name "Sesriem" is said to be derived from the fact that early travellers had to join six (*ses*) ox thongs, or *rieme* in Afrikaans, to lower a bucket to the pools.

Elim Dune

Another feature which is easily accessible from the Sesriem camp site is the well-known Elim Dune on the farm which was named "Elim" until it was incorporated into the park. Situated about 4,5 km from the camp site, the dune can be reached in a sedan car and a visit is especially rewarding during the early morning hours or late afternoon. A closer look at the seemingly lifeless dune will reveal a wide variety of fascinating tracks left by the numerous creatures inhabiting the dune. If you are a keen bird-watcher, you stand a good chance of spotting the dune lark (503), an endemic Namib species, here.

Sossuspoort Lookout

About 24 km after leaving the camp, you reach the Sossuspoort Lookout shortly before crossing the Tsauchab River. The viewpoint offers excellent views of the wide river valley, the dunes and the escarpment. If it is too early to stop here on the outward journey, remember to stop here on your return.

Tsauchab River

After crossing the Tsauchab River, the road continues along the broad river valley. Looking north, numerous dead camel thorn (168) trees provide evidence that the Tsauchab River once followed a more southerly course, while the course of the Aub River is hardly visible to the south of the road.

Dune 45

About 21 km beyond Sossuspoort Lookout you reach Dune 45 which takes its name from its distance (45 km) from Sesriem. Although it is not the highest dune in this area, it is one of the most photographed dunes because of its convenient proximity to the road. Dune 45 is a typical star dune and rises to over 170 metres above the valley floor.

Sossusvlei

About 15 km further on the parking area for sedan cars is reached. The remaining 5 km to Sossusvlei is negotiable by four-wheel drive only, so if you are travelling in a sedan car you will have to continue to the vlei on foot.

Sossusvlei, a large clay pan, is a spectacular sight when filled with water and, after strong floods, it can hold water for up to eighteen months. When the pan is dry the white, cracked mud surface formed by silts deposited here by the Tsauchab River contrasts sharply with the surrounding orange dunes. The dense clumps of nara (*Acanthosicyos horrida*) along the edge of the vlei are conspicuous, while the ancient camel thorns at the parking area provide welcome shade.

Pans to the west of Sossusvlei suggest that the Tsauchab River once flowed into the Atlantic Ocean, but the encroaching sand-dunes, combined with a decreased water flow, smothered its course thousands of years ago. The Tsondab River, 75 km to the north, suffered a similar fate and research has shown that the course of the river was blocked about 60 000 years ago.

Central Namib sand sea

Extending for 300 km along the coast between the Koichab and the Kuiseb rivers and up to 140 km inland, the central Namib sand sea covers an area of 32 500 km².

Most of the present central Namib sand sea is underlain by ancient dunes which were active between 20 and 40 million years ago. These dunes became solidified during a wetter period and are known as the Tsondab Sandstone Formation. An excellent example of these reddish-purple ancient dune deposits can be seen about 50 km north of Sesriem on the farm "Dieprivier", where the river of that name has exposed sections of the sandstone formation.

Geological history of the sand sea

The sand of the present Namib sand sea began to accumulate on the Tsondab Sandstone between 3 and 5 million years ago. It seems likely that this sand was washed down the Orange River and then swept northwards by the ocean currents to be deposited onshore south of Lüderitz. From here the prevailing winds transported the sand into the main sand sea – a process which is continuing.

Awesome dune height

Most visitors are under the impression that Sossusvlei boasts the highest dunes in the world. Although they are probably the highest in the Namib Desert and definitely the most impressive, they are not the highest in the world.

Some of the dunes on the northern side on the Tsauchab River valley reach heights of up to 325 metres, but it has to be realised that they do not rise from the valley floor, but from the elevated Tsondab Sandstone Formation. The highest free-standing dunes, on the other hand, rise to about 200 metres above the valley floor.

Undoubtedly the best way to get an idea of how high these dunes actually are, is to climb to the crest of one of the many dunes surrounding the vlei. The loose sand and the deceptively close crests of the dunes exact a heavy toll but the view from high up makes the effort worthwhile. Exploring the dunes is best accomplished during the cool early morning hours, as sand temperatures often become unbearably hot by mid-morning.

Characteristic dune formations

Dwarfed by the dunes, visitors can easily gain the impression that the dunes are arranged haphazardly. Although they are certainly complex, satellite photographs of the Namib sand sea show that they are clearly arranged into three distinct zones.

Reticulate and star dunes

The low reticulate or network dunes along the eastern edge of the sand sea are formed by multi-directional winds and are modified by vegetation. The impressive star dunes at Sossusvlei are characteristic along the eastern margin of the central Namib sand sea. These dunes are formed by complex, multi-directional winds and are characterised by three or more arms extending from their peaks.

Linear dunes

West of the star dunes is a 60 km wide belt of north to south trending linear dunes. These complex dunes lie parallel to the southerly winds which blow between September and April, but are also influenced by the strong easterly winds which are dominant during the winter months. The dunes are between 60 and 100 metres high, up to 50 km long and are separated by interdune plains that are up to 1,5 km wide.

Crescentic dunes

Adjacent to the coast is a belt of crescentic dunes which are perpendicularly aligned to the strong southerly wind. This wind prevails throughout the year. The belt extends up to 20 km inland and includes barchan and transverse dune types. Covering about 15 per cent of the central sand sea, the crescentic dune belt is best developed between Conception Bay and Sandwich.

Dune movement

The movement of the dunes is generally northwards and barchans have been measured as moving up to 75 metres a year in the southern and northern Namib. In the central Namib, however, northward movement averages about ten metres a year. Linear dunes, on the other hand, extend northwards at a rate not exceeding two metres a year.

Variation in sand colour

An interesting feature of the Namib sand sea is the colour transformation of the sand from west to east. Along the coast, the sand is a pale yellowy-brown, but further inland it progressively changes to deep brown in the central areas and to a yellow- or orangey-red at its eastern margin. The colour of the sand depends on the extent of oxidation, and the lighter colours along the coast and in the central areas have been attributed to the bleaching effect of the ever-present fog.

Small fauna

Although it does become very hot walking around in the dunes during the day, many hours can be spent examining fascinating aspects of the dunes which at first seem so insignificant that they are often ignored. Many small animals have adapted to survive in this extremely harsh environment and often the only signs of their presence are their tracks in the loose sand.

Distinctive fig-leaf-like tracks will reveal the presence of the elusive nocturnal *Palmatogecko*, a gecko which is almost transparent. A large spider-like spoor will betray the presence of one of the species of dancing white lady spiders. These conspicuous tracks are made by large adult males which drum the sand with their legs and bodies. Also keep an eye out for the distinctive rounded, paired impressions of the hairy-footed gerbil which inhabits the dunes. A semi-circular raised track provides tell-tale clues of Grant's golden mole, which is often also referred to as the Namib Desert golden mole.

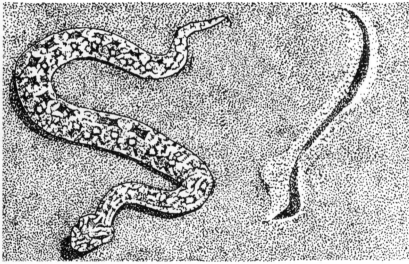

Side-winding adder

Desert snakes

Regular "S" shaped patterns will indicate that a side-winding adder (*Bitis peringueyi*) has been active on a dune. Consider yourself fortunate if you happen to see this snake as it lies submerged in the sand with only its eyes and the tip of its tail just protruding, waiting to surprise an unsuspecting gecko or other small reptile. This species, which has an average length of 20 to 25 cm, has developed an ingenious way of moving across the soft, loose sand – by lifting the curves of its body and moving them sideways in a series of continuous contortions.

Another snake that inhabits the dunes is the whip snake (*Psammophus leightoni*) which can easily be mistaken for a shoot amongst a clump of dune grass. Both species of snake are poisonous but their bites are not dangerous.

Anchieta's dune lizard

Anchieta's dune lizard (*Aporosaura anchieta*), also known as the shovel-snouted or sand-diving lizard, is commonly seen foraging for seeds on the slip faces of dunes. When surface temperatures rise above 40 °C, it engages in a thermoregulatory dance. It dashes across the hot sand and stops abruptly to lift a fore and a hind leg into the air. Then it alternates with the other two legs while supporting itself with its tail.

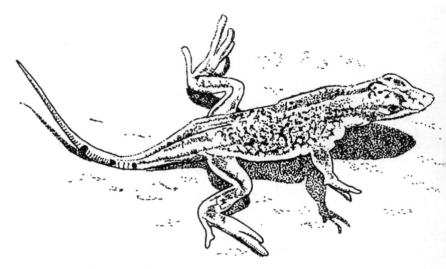

Anchieta's dune lizard engaging in a thermoregulatory dance

Tok-tokkies

The numerous tenebrionid or tok-tokkie beetles of the Namib are unlikely to escape your attention. Of the more than 200 species recorded in the Namib to date, some 22 species have become adapted to the practically vegetationless dunes.

Ants

Although there are 36 ant species occurring in the central Namib, you are most likely to see only the large red and white honeydew ant (*Camponotus detritus*). This species is restricted to the dunes where it feeds on honeydew secretions of aphids and scale insects.

Spiders

The Namib is the habitat of no less than 160 spider species and, if you keep a close watch on the dune slopes, you might notice the trapdoor to the burrow of a cartwheel spider (*Carparachne aureoflava*). This spider uses a very effective technique to escape from its enemies – when threatened, it folds in its legs and rolls down the dune slope at an incredible speed.

The dancing white lady spiders of the Namib hunt mainly at night and are, therefore, unlikely to be seen. One of the interesting characteristics of these spiders is the way that they line their burrows in the sand with cobwebs to prevent them from collapsing.

Mammals

Grant's golden mole, a Namib Desert endemic, is a nocturnal predator which spends its day underground, usually at the base of a clump of grass. At night it emerges to forage on the surface, intermittently making shallow burrows. Living as it does in the loose sand, it is unable to construct a tunnel, but "swims" just below the surface of the sand. The golden mole feeds on insect larvae and small reptiles and, in turn, is preyed upon by owls and black-backed jackal.

Also endemic to the Namib are the dune hairy-footed gerbil and Setzer's hairy-footed gerbil. The former inhabits the sand-dunes south of the Kuiseb River, while the latter species is confined to the gravel plains and sand-dunes from the Kuiseb River northwards into south-western Angola. The hairy feet of these two species are adapted to enable them to live on the loose sand.

Other mammals inhabiting the central Namib sand sea include black-backed jackal, while gemsbok and springbok venture into the dunes after good rains.

Adaptation of animals to desert conditions

To survive in this inhospitable environment where surface temperatures can reach up to 60 °C, the inhabitants of the Namib are adapted either physiologically, morphologically or behaviourally.

Thermoregulation

The gemsbok is an excellent example of an animal which has adapted physiologically. To most mammals a body temperature of 42 °C is usually lethal, but a network of fine blood vessels at the base of the gemsbok's brain facilitates the cooling of blood to the brain, enabling the gemsbok to survive with its body temperature as high as 45 °C.

Behavioural adaptations range from the thermoregulatory dance of the sand-diving lizard to "stilting" – a technique employed by several beetle species. By extending their legs fully the beetles utilise the air which is cooler away from the ground. Larger animals also exhibit thermoregulatory behaviour; springbok have been observed to orientate the long axis of their bodies towards the sun during the heat of the day. Gemsbok are also known to stand on dune crests to make full use of a cool breeze.

Movement across loose sand

To enable the animals to move easily across the loose sand, many species have specially-adapted feet. The *Palmatogecko* has broad, webbed feet which enables it to dig a burrow beneath the sand, while the nocturnal *Comicus* cricket has lobed feet.

Water procurement and conservation

It seems incredible that such a diverse variety of life forms can exist in the arid Namib Desert where the average rainfall is as low as 15 mm a year. For many animals and plants, fog sustains their existence and they have developed ingenious ways of obtaining water. The head-standing beetle (*Onomacris unquicularis*) takes advantage of fog by facing into the wind at the crest of a dune and extending its back legs to tilt its body forwards. When it adopts this pose, the precipitating fog trickles down to its mouth. Research has shown that these beetles can drink as much as 40 per cent of their body weight in one foggy spell.

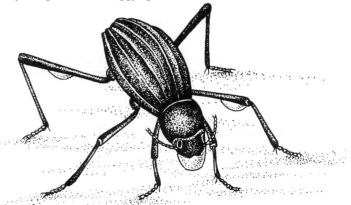

Head-standing beetle

The disc-shaped *Lepidochora* tenebrionid beetles construct shallow trenches perpendicular to the fog-bearing wind. Fog-water is trapped between the parallel ridges and is extracted from the sand when they return along the trench. In this way the beetles can take in water that will make up 14 per cent of their body weight.

Many of the tenebrionid beetles of the Namib have also undergone physiological adaptation and secrete a waxy material to reduce water loss. Research has shown that beetles with a waxy bloom are more abundant in the interior where temperatures are higher and the humidity lower than along the cool coast which is often shrouded in fog. However, when humidity is high, the bloom quickly disappears.

The side-winding adder obtains water by licking precipitating fog from its back, while black-backed jackal have been observed to lick condensed fog or dew from rocks along the Namib Coast.

Compared with other antelope species, the water intake of gemsbok is considerably less even when water is abundant. During prolonged droughts when no surface water is available they can survive by obtaining moisture from subterranean roots and bulbs, tsammas (a desert melon) and naras.

Detritus

Another key to the survival of many of the Namib's animals is the wind-blown detritus which is a major source of food for a number of beetle species, termites and fish moths. Detritus consists mainly of plant material – leaves, flowers, seeds – but it also comprises animal faeces and dead insects. These primary consumers, in turn, provide a ready source of food for the secondary feeders.

Birds

Birds are poorly represented in the central Namib sand sea because of the harsh conditions and the low diversity of habitats. However, two Namib endemics are particularly interesting to bird-watchers: the dune and Gray's lark (514). Elim Dune is a good spot for seeing the dune lark – a species restricted to sand-dunes and sandy flats between northern Namaqualand and Walvis Bay. Gray's lark occurs from Lüderitz to south-western Angola and favours gravel plains along the coastal strip and the eastern edge of the desert. Ostrich (1) are common on the gravel plains west of the Naukluft Mountains, while the tall acacias lining the course of the Tsauchab provide ideal nesting sites for lappetfaced vulture (124).

Birdlife is far more prolific along the well-vegetated Kuiseb River where over 70 species have been recorded in a year. Among the commonly observed species are scimitarbilled woodhoopoe (454), pied barbet (465), titbabbler (621), longbilled crombec (651) and brubru (741). At night you might hear the mellow hoot of the spotted eagle owl (401) or the thin screeching call of the barn owl (392). As the Kuiseb River is used as a migratory corridor you might also see species which usually occur further inland, but not in the Namib.

Feral horses

Although not true desert dwellers, the feral horses of the Namib have long fascinated visitors travelling between Aus and Lüderitz. The origin of these horses is still the subject of much debate, but the most likely explanation of their origin is that they are the descendants of horses abandoned by the

Germans when German South West Africa was invaded by the South African forces in 1915.

The horses are also romantically linked with Baron von Wolf of Duwisib Castle. It has been suggested that they are the offspring of Von Wolf's stud which ran wild after the nobleman was killed in France during World War I.

Whatever their origin, the physical appearance of the wild horses of the Namib suggests that they are derived from Arab, Hackney, Trakehner and English Thoroughbred stock. Although they are built like horses that stand 15 to 16 hands high, they are about 15 to 20 cm smaller at shoulder height and it has been suggested that their smaller size could be attributed to inbreeding and their harsh surroundings.

Life on the Garub Plains centres around the watering point where water is available all year round. During dry years, however, the horses are forced to graze up to 20 km from Garub and may only visit the watering point every second day. Stallions form "harem bands" varying in size from three to fourteen mares and foals – the average herd size being five, while bachelor herds are made up of up to six adult stallions and colts.

Estimates on the number of horses vary considerably, the average population being about 150 animals. Following good rains, however, their numbers increase rapidly and by the end of 1991 the population stood at between 300 and 320. As a result, the Garub Plains were severely overgrazed and during 1992 some of the horses were captured and sold to interested buyers to reduce their numbers.

Vegetation

The plants of the central Namib sand sea are no less interesting than the animal life and are, likewise, adapted to survive in their harsh environment. At least five perennial and one ephemeral grass species, as well as a geophyte, a leaf succulent and a cucurbit, the nara (*Acanthosicyos horrida*), exist in the sand sea of the central Namib.

The tall dune grass *Stipagrostis sabulicola* has developed an extensive, shallow root system which can absorb fog-water precipitating on the dune surface, while the succulent, *Trianthema hereroensis*, can absorb water through its leaves. To reduce water loss the nara does not have any leaves, and photosynthesis takes place through the thorns and the stem, while its tap root grows to a depth of 30 metres in the search for water.

References

Barnard, W.S. (1972) *Fisiografie van die Sentrale Duinsee van die Namib.* South African Geographical Association. Unpublished lecture.

Barnard, W.S. *Die Ordelike Woestyn: 'n Vergelykende Verkenning van die Duinsee van die Namib.* Serton Memorial Lecture delivered at the Academy, Windhoek.

Desert Ecological Research Unit. (1990) *Homeb Natural History.*

Desert Ecological Research Unit. (1990) *Natural History of Sossusvlei and the Sesriem Canyon.*

Directorate of Nature Conservation, SWA/Namibia. (1985) *Assessment of the Physical Condition of the Namib Feral Horses.* Unpublished internal report.

Louw, G.N. & Seely, M.K. (1982) *Ecology of Desert Organisms.* London: Longman.

Seely, M. (1987) *The Namib: Natural History of an Ancient Desert.* Windhoek: Shell Oil.

Van der Merwe, F.J. (undated) *Notes on a Herd of Wild Horses in the Namib Desert of South West Africa.* Pretoria: Department of Agriculture. Unpublished report.

Ward, J. & Seely, M. (1989) 'Namib dunes: patterns in space and time'. *Rössing Magazine*: April: 6 – 11.

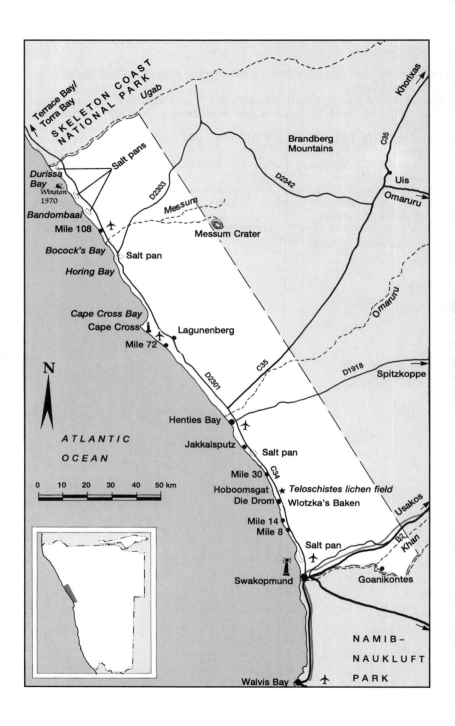

NATIONAL WEST COAST
RECREATION AREA

Size: 780 000 ha   Proclaimed: 1973

Location

Central Namibian coast.

What to do and see

Sightseeing, angling.

Climate

The coast enjoys a moderate climate. Average maximum daily temperatures vary from 15 °C in September to 20,7 °C in February, while minimum temperatures range between 9 °C from July to August and 16,4 °C in February.

On average fog occurs 113 days a year along the coast, with a mean frequency of up to 16 days in May and 14 days in June and August. Between October and March the average incidence of fog is below ten days a month.

Rain is a rare phenomenon along the coast and only averages 8 mm a year.

When to visit

The recreation area is open throughout the year, and there are no restrictions on hours of travel.

ANGLING: November to March.

Where to stay

Camp sites managed by the Directorate of Tourism are situated at Mile 14, Mile 72 and Jakkalsputz, as well as at Mile 108, although the latter is only open during the December/January school holidays.

The camp sites are basic, the only amenities being communal ablutions.

Swakopmund on the southern boundary of the National West Coast Recreation Area has a number of hotels and pensions, and is an ideal base for many day drives and fishing trips.

Accommodation at Mile 4 caravan park, 7 km north of Swakopmund, ranges from conventional camp sites (with or without power points) to luxury cluster units and rest houses. The camp sites are served by communal kitchens equipped with gas stoves and scullery facilities, covered eating areas and ablutions. The luxury clusters are each made up of four sites with their own fireplaces and communal ablutions.

The Hotel de Duine is the only hotel in the recreation area and is a privately-owned one star establishment at Henties Bay. Other accommodation at Henties Bay includes the Desert Rose, a timeshare development offering fully equipped six- and eight-bedded apartments, and Die Oord where fully equipped bungalows are available.

Visitor amenities

There are no shops at any of the state-owned camp sites, but a mobile kiosk visits the camp sites during the December/January school holidays. Fuel is available at Henties Bay, Mile 72 and at Mile 108 during the December/January school holidays.

Amenities at Mile 4 include a shop which stocks groceries and fishing tackle, coin-operated laundromats and freezing facilities.

Where to book

Entry permits are not required.

See page 13 for information on accommodation at state-owned camp sites.

Mile 4:   The Caretaker, P O Box 3452, Vineta,
                   telephone (0641) 61781.
Hotel de Duine: P O Box 1, Henties Bay, telephone (06442) 1.
Desert Rose: P O Box 124, Henties Bay, telephone (06442) 181.
Die Oord: P O Box 82, Henties Bay, telephone (06442) 239/165.

How to get there

From Swakopmund the main coastal road (C34) can be reached by either turning off Kaiser Wilhelm Street into Nordring Street near the eastern entrance to the town, or by following Molkte Street into Garnison and Mittel streets to the T-junction with Nordring Street. Turn left here and follow the road past Tamariskia and Vineta.

What you should know

- ☐ The salt surface of the main coastal road is extremely slippery during misty conditions and after rains, and caution should be exercised at these times.
- ☐ Although there are no restrictions on off-road driving, drivers should bear in mind that careless driving poses a serious threat to the unique lichen fields and the rare Damara tern. Follow existing tracks rather than make your own!
- ☐ Drivers of sedan cars should use the hard-surface roads which provide access to the beach at regular intervals and not deviate onto any of the sandy tracks.
- ☐ Water has to be carted to camp sites at Miles 14, 72 and 108, as well as at Jakkalsputz and is, consequently, sold by the litre. There is also a minimal charge for hot showers.
- ☐ Even on overcast days it is advisable to apply sunscreen cream when spending time outdoors.
- ☐ Remember to pack a warm jersey and either a waterproof windbreaker or a raincoat.
- ☐ The cold water temperatures usually experienced along this coast make it unsuitable for bathing.

The coast of Namibia is renowned for its excellent fishing, and every year thousands of visitors flock to the National West Coast Recreation Area – a roughly 50 km wide belt stretching between the Swakop and Ugab rivers over a distance of 200 km – in search of the "big ones".

Angling

The most popular angling season stretches from November to the end of March. April is generally quiet, but the May to June/July period is usually rewarding for galjoen and steenbras catches.

Galjoen is eagerly sought, while kob, steenbras and blacktail are also popular. Sea catfish, also known as sea barbel, is commonly caught and, although most anglers discard them, they are delicious when smoked.

Anglers unfamiliar with conditions along the coast will find the angling review in the Friday edition of the *Namib Times* to be a handy guide. Information is given on where you can expect to catch what, the tides and other useful tips. Anglers able to read Afrikaans should try to obtain a copy of Gert van Zyl's *Hengel- en Uitspan* as it contains valuable hints. The 88-page book is available from the author at P O Box 1766, Louis Trichardt, 0920, South Africa.

Angling spots

Many of the popular angling spots along the coast were named simply to indicate their distance from Swakopmund at a time when imperial measurements were still used. These names have persisted until today, while others like "Bennie se Rooi Lorrie" and "Dup se Gat" have been coined by the regular visitors.

Some of the popular angling spots, such as Mile 4, Mile 8, Mile 30, Horingbaai, Mile 98 and Mile 100, are connected to the main coastal road by hard-surface gravel roads, but many of the tracks are only negotiable by four-wheel drive vehicles.

Wlotzka's Baken

Wlotzka's Baken, a holiday fishing village 30 km north of Swakopmund, was named after a local fisherman who used to make a living from fishing. His favourite spot was in the vicinity of a trigonometrical beacon ("baken"). The site soon became a fisherman's paradise and Wlotzka's Baken became increasingly popular especially once the road to Cape Cross had been completed. The first fisherman's hut was erected in 1936 and others soon followed. A characteristic feature of this quaint village is the use of whale bones to demarcate properties.

Henties Bay

The only other resort along the coast, Henties Bay, was similarly named after an ardent fisherman, Hentie van der Merwe, who began visiting the freshwater spring near an old mouth of the Omaruru River in 1929. As the years went by the small bay grew in popularity until, in the early 1950s, the first permanent inhabitants came to settle. Over the past 40 years Henties Bay has grown into a town with more than a thousand houses, a hotel, several shops and garages, a post office and a police station. The town also boasts a fourteen hole golf course with grass greens and tees and sand fairways, as well as tennis courts and a squash court.

Bait

Red worm is a good all-purpose bait, while fresh pilchard is taken by all fish except galjoen. If you are after galjoen, use white mussels or red-bait. White mussel is also taken by kabeljou and steenbras, the latter being partial to shrimps.

Anglers must ensure that they are familiar with the regulations regarding the collection of bait and the minimum angling sizes. See the box below.

Rock and surf angling and rock lobster regulations

The following regulations currently apply in Namibia, but anglers must check with the nearest Directorate of Sea Fisheries office to inform themselves of the latest regulations.

Minimum sizes

(As measured side-on from the tip of the nose to the tip of the tail.)

blacktail	15 cm	shad	30 cm
gurnard	15 cm	white steenbras	30 cm
mullet	15 cm	garrick	38 cm
mackerel	15 cm	Cape salmon	40 cm
galjoen	20 cm	kob	40 cm
white stumpnose	20 cm	snoek	60 cm
hottentot	22 cm		

Undersized fish should be returned to the sea immediately.

Galjoen

Restrictions on galjoen

Bona fide anglers may not be in possession of more than thirty kob, white steenbras, blacktail and galjoen or 35 kg processed fish of these species. Anglers are limited to a maximum of eight galjoen (10 kg processed) per *bona fide* angler and may transport a maximum of sixteen (20 kg processed) galjoen provided that the *bona fide* anglers are travelling in the vehicle.

Bait

It should be noted that the only bait which may be purchased or sold is pilchards. The following limits in respect of bait collection apply at present:

barnacles	5	black mussels	50
limpets	15	periwinkles	25
white mussels	25	prawns	5
hermit crabs	5		

White mussels may only be collected by hand and their diameter must exceed 38 mm

Only red-bait washed up on the beach may be collected and no one may collect more than 2 kg of red-bait, excluding the pod, per day.

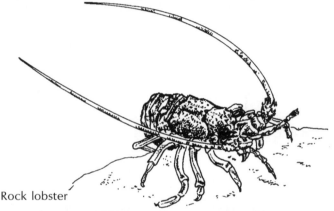

Rock lobster

Restrictions on the catching of rock lobster (crayfish)

Permit: Not required, unless in the Walvis Bay enclave where South African regulations apply.

Open season: 1 November to 30 April.

Times: Sunrise to sunset.

Number: Seven per *bona fide* diver per day, 21 per vehicle provided the *bona fide* divers are present.

Size: Minimum measurement of 6,5 cm from head to thorax. Rock lobster must be measured immediately after capture.

Equipment: Only a snorkel may be used. Traps and boats can only be used by commercial catchers who have the necessary permit.

General: Rock lobster with a soft shell and females in berry (carrying eggs) must be returned to the sea immediately. Only those with the necessary licence may sell rock lobster. Certain areas along the coast are designated as reserves and under no circumstances may fish or rock lobster be caught there.

More than meets the eye

Although angling is the main attraction for many visitors, an increasing number of tourists are becoming aware that the area offers much more than meets the eye. Not only does it boast an interesting variety of plants and small creatures, but the area is equally interesting from a historical point of view (see Cape Cross Seal Reserve, pages 39 to 43).

Vegetation

The vegetation is sparsely distributed along this part of the coastal strip, which falls within the central Namib vegetation type. Characteristic of the vegetation west of the main coastal road are the small dune hummocks which have formed around the dollar bush (*Zygophyllum stapfii*), *Z. clavatum, Psilocaulon* spp. and ganna (*Salsola* spp.) bushes. These plants play an important role in stabilising the dunes, which can be up to two metres high and three metres in diameter.

The vegetation of the gravel flats east of the main coastal road consists mainly of *Zygophyllum* spp. and ganna (*Salsola* spp.). These are largely confined to depressions and shallow river washes, while the hills provide a habitat for several other species, such as the Bushman's candle (*Sarcocaulon* spp.).

Lichen fields

The frequent occurrence of fog along the coast has resulted in the development of extensive lichen fields and more than a hundred species have been recorded along the coast. These can broadly be divided into four major communities, the *Combea mollusca* communities, rock lichen communities, *Paramelia hypomeleana/Teloschistes capensis* communities and fine gravel communities.

Lichens occur in a variety of growth forms. While some species grow on rocks, others have leaf-like thalli, while a third group resembles diminutive shrubs. One of the best examples of the shrub-like lichens is the *Teloschistes capensis* community which can be seen to the east of the road, about 4 km north of Wlotzka's Baken. A rather interesting species, the wandering lichen (*Xanthomaculina convulata*), resembles small dried out twigs and usually collects in shallow drainage lines.

Ecological role of lichens

Soil stabilization is one of the several important functions that lichens fulfil. Although the plains are seemingly barren, research has shown that the dry lichen biomass east of Swakopmund may be as high as 5,8 tonnes per ha.

In addition, they also reduce the impact of raindrops and water runoff and act as barriers that minimise the movement of sand by the wind. On the other hand, species growing on rocks contribute to the formation of soil by slowly breaking them down.

Another important function of lichens is soil enrichment, and studies have shown that the oxygen content of soil around lichen fields is as much as seven times that of areas where no lichens occur.

Since lichens grow in areas where other plants do not occur or are sparsely distributed, they form the basis of the food chain, supporting a wide variety of insects, reptiles, birds and mammals. During times of drought even larger mammals such as gemsbok and springbok have been observed eating lichens.

As they are frequently associated with the soft calcrete layer, lichens are extremely sensitive to disturbance and a vehicle's tracks over 1 km will destroy about 300 m^2 of lichens. Further, their growth rate is only 1 mm a year, and it can therefore take up to 200 years for damaged areas to become re-vegetated.

Birds

Because of the small number of habitats within the National West Coast Recreation Area, birdlife is not as prolific as it is in the Skeleton Coast National Park to the north or at Sandwich to the south.

Breeding area for Damara tern

Of far greater significance, though, is the fact that the coast is an important breeding ground for the Damara tern (334) – an intra-African migrant which, until the early 1990s, was estimated to have a world population of only 2 000 breeding pairs. More extensive counts have, however, shown that the Namibian population is between 10 000 and 14 000 birds strong, a significant percentage of which breeds along the coastal strip between Swakopmund and Terrace Bay.

Each year these small white birds migrate from as far north as the Gulf of Guinea to the Namibian coast where they arrive in September and October. Unfortunately, their breeding season coincides with the peak tourist season and off-road driving poses a severe threat to the future of this species.

The nest, a shallow scrape which is sometimes lined with bits of shell, is made on gravel plains and shell slacks between sand dunes. The nesting sites can be up to 5 km inland, but are usually about 2 to 3 km from the sea where they are protected against predators such as black-backed jackal, brown hyaena, kelp gulls (312) and crows. A single buff or fawn-coloured egg spotted with brown and purple blotches is laid. This hatches after eighteen to 22 days and the nestling remains on the nest for a further twenty days.

Game and small creatures

Except for the Cape fur seal colony at Cape Cross (see pages 41 to 43), mammals do not occur in large numbers and except for smaller mammals such as rodents you are unlikely to see anything more than black-backed jackal and brown hyaena. Marine mammals you might spot include dusky dolphin and pilot, humpback and killer whales.

Not to be forgotten, though, is the fascinating variety of insects, reptiles and other small creatures which inhabit the hummock dunes and the gravel plains.

Salt works

Prominent features of the coastal strip are the extensive salt pans that occur along the coast. The salt works at Panther Beacon, 11 km north of Swakopmund, is currently the largest in Namibia. Production here dates back to 1933 but, since 1955 when the bedded sea salt deposits were exhausted, sea water has been pumped into the evaporation ponds where the salts in the water crystalise.

Vast reserves also occur at the White Lady salt pan near Cape Cross, further north at Bocock's Bay, in the vicinity of Bandom Bay, at Durissa Bay, and in the Skeleton Coast National Park.

Shipwreck

Over the centuries numerous ships have met with tragedy along this section of the coast. One wreck still visible in her sandy grave on the beach is the *Winston* which ran aground in 1970. The turnoff is clearly signposted 12 km south of the Ugab River Gate and, except for the final kilometre which tends to be rather sandy, the site is easily accessible. Sedan cars are best parked when the road ahead becomes too sandy!

References

Tarr, J. (1986) 'Namibia's rare and endangered Damara tern'. *Rössing Magazine:* May: 1 – 5.
Van Zyl, G. (1988) *SWA Hengel- en Uitspan.* Louis Trichardt: G. van Zyl.

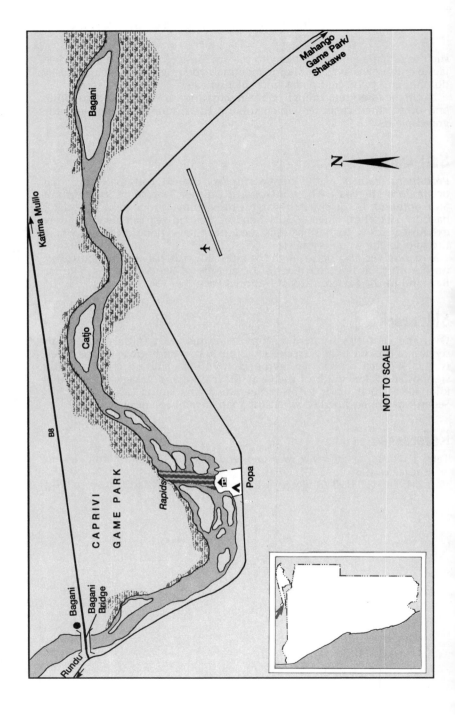

POPA GAME PARK

Size: 25 ha   Proclaimed: 1989

Location

North-eastern Namibia.

What to do and see

Bird-watching, boating, angling, photography.

Climate

See Mahango Game Park, page 121.

When to visit

The rest camp is open throughout the year.

GAME-VIEWING: June to October (Mahango Game Park).
BIRD-WATCHING: November to March.
ANGLING: August to December and February to April.

Where to stay

Visitors can choose between staying in rustic thatched-roofed huts and pitching a tent in the shady camp site. Each hut consists of two rooms with two beds in each, as well as a large balcony with a bench, table and chairs. Cooking is not permitted inside the huts, but there are outside fireplaces, as well as a communal field kitchen equipped with a fridge, freezer and scullery. The central boma is ideal for groups. The ablution facilities are, likewise, communal. Gas lighting, bedding, towels and soap are supplied, but visitors must bring their own cooking and eating utensils.

The camp site is served by a communal kitchen and ablutions.

Visitor amenities

Although non-perishables and cooldrinks are available from a kiosk adjacent to the reception office, you are well advised to be self-sufficient.

Petrol is not sold in the park, but is usually obtainable at Divundu near Bagani Bridge or at Mukwe 17 km further west.

SERVICE HOURS:

Office: Sunrise to sunset.

Kiosk: 08:00 – 12:30 and 14:00 to sunset (Monday to Friday)
             08:30 – 12:30 and 16:00 to sunset (Saturday and Sunday)

There is no restaurant at Popa, but visitors are welcome at the restaurant of Suclabo Lodge downstream from Popa. Other services offered by the lodge include game-viewing and photographic safaris to Mahango and Kaudom, and transfers from the nearby airstrip. Equipment such as boats, fishing rods and tackle can be hired. Enquiries can be made with Suclabo Lodge or at the tourist office at Popa Falls.

Grassed picnic sites shaded by tall trees are provided for day visitors.

Where to book

See page 13.

How to get there

The turnoff to Popa Falls Rest Camp is signposted 210 km east of Rundu on the B8 to Katima Mulilo. Turn right here and follow the road to Botswana for 5 km to reach the entrance gate of the rest camp.

What you should know

☐ Anti-malarial precautions must be taken throughout the year.
☐ The petrol supply in this part of the world is erratic at times, and it is advisable to carry sufficient fuel for your onward journey. Also remember to take cash to pay for fuel.

Popa Falls is a welcome stop-over for visitors travelling between Rundu and Katima Mulilo, and is a convenient base for those wishing to explore the nearby Mahango Game Park.

Rest camp

The rest camp on the banks of the Kavango River is dominated by mature stands of knob thorn (178) and dense bushwillow (*Combretum*) scrub. Much to the credit of Namibia's conservation authorities, the vegetation was disturbed as little as possible when the rest camp was being built and today the tall, shady trees are much appreciated after a long, hot drive.

Popa Falls

From the camp it is an easy ramble to the falls. A wooden bridge has been built across the channel that flows past the camp sites, and this gives day visitors access to an island, on which a short walk will bring them to the cascades.

Provided the level of the river is low, it is possible to boulder-hop across some of the smaller channels to get a better view of the falls. However, you must not expect to see a waterfall in the true sense of the word. The name is a misnomer as the falls are nothing more than a series of rapids created by a rocky quartzite ledge which obstructs the course of the Kavango River at this point. Although the rapids have a total drop of only about four metres, they extend across the full width of the river – about 1,2 km at Popa.

When the river is in flood, the rocky ledge is submerged – the cascades are, therefore, best viewed during the dry season when the fully-exposed ledge reveals a multitude of rushing channels and small islands.

Kavango River

With an approximate length of 1 450 km, the Kavango River is one of the longest rivers in southern Africa. Rising in the highlands of Angola, it loses some 600 metres in altitude during its 600 km journey through Angola (where it is known as the Cubango). At Katwitwi the river swings sharply to the east and runs for approximately 350 km along Namibia's northern border where it becomes known as the Kavango. During this part of its journey the Kavango meanders slowly through deep Kalahari sand, forming extensive floodplains that are up to 4 km wide. At Rundu it has an average annual volume of about 5 700 million m^3, but at Katere where it is joined by the Cuito River the volume increases to about 10 300 million m^3 – ten times as much as the combined average annual run-off of all of Namibia's other inland rivers.

In its lower middle reaches the Kavango River swings south-eastwards to form the border between Kavango and the western Caprivi. Below Mukwe the river breaches a 25 km long quartzite barrier to form a multitude of channels, rapids and islands, the longest of which – Tanhwe – is 2 km long. Downstream of Popa the Kavango again flows slowly across flat countryside, forming papyrus-fringed channels, ox-bow lakes and lagoons covered in waterlilies. In Botswana it forms the vast Okavango Delta – an 18 000 km² inland delta.

The average annual flow at Mukwe is 326 m³ per second, but it has been measured at a maximum of 1 473 m³ per second. The second half of October usually sees the flow at its minimum, and in 1991 an all-time minimum flow of 109,5 m³ per second was recorded. The river usually starts rising in December, following the onset of the summer rains in its catchment area. When the flood peaks, which normally occurs between February and April, the level of the Kavango can reach up to five metres, which is nearly double that of the dry season.

However, the first flood waters do not reach Maun on the eastern edge of the Delta until four months later, and do not reach their peak until the end of July or early August. Although the delta has an estimated capacity of 16 000 million m³, only three or four per cent of this eventually flows into the Thamalakane River. The remainder is lost through evaporation, transpiration of vegetation and seepage into the soil.

Birds

Bird-watchers visiting Popa are unlikely to be disappointed. A noteworthy bird species to watch out for during the dry season is the rock pratincole (306) which uses the exposed rocks of the cascades as perching and nesting sites. In southern Africa, this species is confined to the Zambezi River, the Save River in southern Mozambique, and the Caprivi Strip.

Among the species you are likely to see are pied (428) and malachite (431) kingfishers, whitefronted bee-eater (443), blackcollared barbet (464), arrowmarked babbler (560) and terrestrial bulbul (569), while Swainson's francolin (199) are frequently heard calling at dawn or dusk.

The riverine vegetation at Popa is alive with the song of numerous birds. Species recorded include Senegal coucal (390), Narina trogon (427), whiterumped babbler (562), swamp boubou (738) and yellow white-eye (797) (this is the western limit of its southern African distribution).

Other species which might be of interest are yellowbellied bulbul (574), Heuglin's robin (599) and golden weaver (816), as well as brownthroated weaver (818), which favours the reedbeds. Also keep a watch out for the plumcoloured starling (761), a non-breeding intra-African migrant over much of its range in southern Africa, but which is resident in northern Namibia, Botswana and Zimbabwe.

Game

Because of the small size of the park, game-viewing opportunities are extremely limited. Large four-toed tracks on the island adjacent to the facilities for day visitors provide evidence of hippo activity at night and crocodile have been observed above the rapids. The rest camp is, however, a mere 15 km from the Mahango Game Park where a variety of game can be seen and it therefore serves as an ideal base camp.

Angling

Visitors to Popa can also try their hand at angling. Licences are obtainable at the rest camp office, while boats and tackle can be hired from the nearby Suclabo Lodge. For details of freshwater angling regulations see the box on page 98. The river is the habitat of a large variety of fish including three-spot (*Oreochromis andersonii*) and greenhead (*Oreochromis macrochir*) tilapia, green happy (*Serranochromis codringtoni*), nembwe (*Serranochromis robustus jallae*) and sharptooth catfish (*Clarias gariepinus*), but the most sought-after species is undoubtably tiger fish (*Hydrocynus vittatus*). Angling for this species is generally most rewarding when the level of the river is low as the receding flood waters force the smaller species of the floodplains into the river where they are preyed upon by larger species such as tiger fish. Tiger fish are also common when flood levels are high, but are scarce at intermediate levels.

Rare species

The Popa rapids are an important habitat for two of southern Africa's rarer fish species. The dark brown to black broadhead catfish (*Clariallabes platyprosops*) reaches a length of about 28 cm and to date has been recorded at only four locations in the Kavango and Zambezi rivers. It favours crevices and holes in fast flowing water. Another rare species found in the rapids at Popa is the ocellated spinyeel (*Afromastacembelus vanderwaali*), which takes its name from the series of brown and yellow ocellations (eye-like spots) along the dorsal and anal fins. This dark brown, eel-like fish reaches a maximum length of 15 cm and is easily identified by the series of 22 to 26 spines along its back. Both species are listed in the *South African Red Data Book – Fishes* as being rare.

References

Fisch, M. (1987) 'Die Hydrographie des Kavangoflusses'. *SWA Scientific Society Journal* XL/XLI: 55 – 74.

Hegenberger, W. (1987) 'Stand der geologischen Kenntnisse über das Kavangogebiet'. *SWA Scientific Society Journal* XL/XLI: 97 – 113.

Hines, C.J.H. (1987) 'The birds of eastern Kavango, SWA/Namibia'. *SWA Scientific Society* XL/XLI: 115 – 147.

Hines, C.J.H. (1989) 'The birds of north-eastern Namibia'. *Birding in Southern Africa* 41(3): 89 – 92.

Skelton, P.H. (1987) *South African Red Data Book – Fishes*. South African Scientific Programmes Report No 137, Pretoria: CSIR, 124 – 126 & 136 – 138.

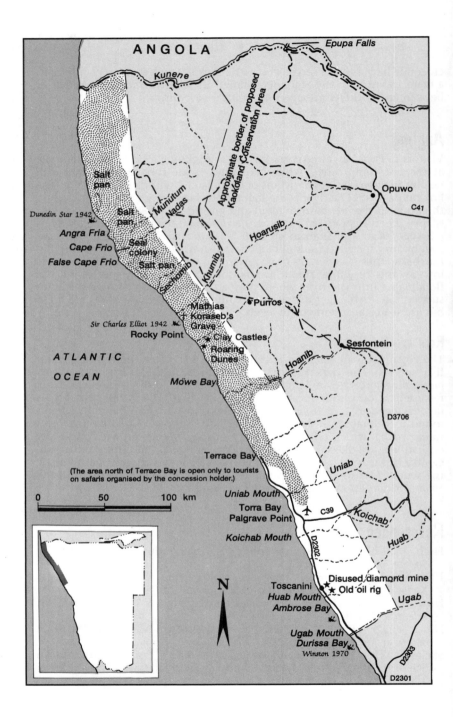

SKELETON COAST
NATIONAL PARK
Size: 1 600 000 ha   Proclaimed: 1967

Location

Northern Namibian coast.

What to do and see

Angling, sightseeing, photography, guided wilderness trail, guided safaris.

Climate

The park falls entirely within the fog zone, and this has a significant influence on the climate. Temperatures are generally moderate (the daily average is 16 °C) and the variation between minimum and maximum temperatures is only about 5 °C.

Between October and May the days are usually sunny with clear blue skies, but during the winter months the coast is often shrouded in mist from mid-afternoon until around 10:00 the following morning. During these months the strong westerly winds often create cold conditions.

When to visit

The park is open throughout the year.

ANGLING: November to March are the most popular months.
GUIDED WILDERNESS TRAILS: Second and fourth Tuesday of every month.

Overnight visitors must enter the park through the Ugab River Gate before 15:00 and the Springbokwasser Gate before 17:00 and must be in possession of a reservation advice issued by the reservations office in Windhoek.

Day visitors must enter through the Ugab River and Springbokwasser gates before 15:00 and are not permitted to visit Terrace Bay and Torra Bay.

Departures via Ugab River Gate are permitted between sunrise and 19:00 and via Springbokwasser Gate between sunrise and sunset.

Where to stay

Terrace Bay is open throughout the year. Visitors are accommodated on a fully-inclusive basis in bungalows containing two-bedded bedrooms, showers, wash basins and toilets. Bedding is provided, but as the tariff includes three meals a day, appliances such as kettles, stoves and fridges are not supplied, nor are there any outside fireplaces.

Torra Bay is open from 1 December to 31 January only. Facilities are limited to camp and caravan sites served by communal ablutions. A small fee is charged for the use of the showers as the water has to be carted in.

Visitor amenities

Amenities at Terrace Bay include a filling station and a shop which stocks a limited range of groceries, liquor, souvenirs and bait. Ample freezing facilities are available for anglers.

At Torra Bay fuel, firewood and water are sold during the Namibian December/January school holidays only, while a kiosk is also open during this period.

SERVICE HOURS:
Office: 07:00 — 13:00 and 14:00 to sunset

Shop: 07:30 — 09:00; 11:30 — 14:00 and 17:30 — 19:30
(Monday to Saturday)
08:00 — 09:00; 11:30 — 13:30 and 17:30 — 19:30
(Sunday and public holidays)

Restaurant (Terrace Bay only): Confirm meal times on arrival.

Where to book

See page 13.

Day permits to drive through the park are available from the reservations office in Windhoek and at the tourist offices at Swakopmund and Okaukuejo and can also be obtained at the gates.

How to get there

The park can be reached either along the C34 linking Swakopmund and Terrace Bay or from Khorixas via Springbokwasser along the C39.

Travelling from the south, the Ugab River Gate is about 200 km north of Swakopmund. Torra Bay is 117 km further north while Terrace Bay is another 48 km on.

Approaching from the west, the gate at Springbokwasser is reached 170 km west of Khorixas. From here it is a further 40 km to the junction with the C34, with Torra Bay and Terrace Bay being 10 and 58 km north respectively.

There are landing strips at Torra Bay and Terrace Bay, but no aviation fuel is available. If you fly in by plane you should circle the camp before landing to draw the attention of camp staff who will then collect you.

What you should know

☐ As the morning and evening temperatures are cool, warm clothing and windproof garments are essential.

☐ Even during overcast days it is advisable to take precautions against sunburn.

☐ In the past, large areas along the coast have been destroyed by indiscriminate off-road driving. Hard-surfaced roads provide access to fishing spots in the angling area and off-road driving is strictly prohibited.

Although the early mariners passing along the desolate coastline of Namibia centuries ago feared the Skeleton Coast, the park is today a popular tourist attraction. Many anglers are lured to the Skeleton Coast by its reputation for excellent catches, while other visitors are attracted by the name which evokes a sense of excitement. For some the appeal of the Skeleton Coast is simply the solitude.

Extent of the park

The park stretches over a distance of nearly 500 km from the Ugab River in the south to the Kunene River in the north, and extends about 40 km inland. It is divided into two zones, each covering about 800 000 ha. The southern section comprises the area between the Ugab and the Hoanib rivers, but visitors are not permitted beyond Seal Beach, 14 km north of Terrace Bay. The northern section lies between the Hoanib and Kunene rivers and access is limited to those who undertake safaris with the company which holds the tourist concession for the area (see page 227).

Origin of the name

The name of this inhospitable coastline conjures up visions of the bleached skeletons of hapless survivors of shipwrecks who died of hunger and thirst – a perception which is reinforced by the large sign of a skull and crossbones that adorns the Ugab River Gate. It has, however, been suggested that the coastline owes its descriptive name to its reputation for being a graveyard not only for people, but also for countless ships.

Another explanation attributes the name to the numerous skeletons of beached whales which were put to use by early coastal dwellers as frames for their rudimentary shelters as long as 600 years ago.

Angling

For many visitors the chief appeal of the Skeleton Coast is that it is one of the finest angling spots along the coastline of southern Africa. The most sought after species is galjoen, followed by kob (which weighs in at an average 2,5 kg, although specimens of up to 55 kg have been landed).

Steenbras and blacktail are other popular angling species, while white stumpnose and strepie are caught occasionally. Barbel are abundant, but as this species is detested by most anglers they are usually returned to the sea. Bronze and spotted sharks are the most commonly caught sharks along the Skeleton Coast.

Angling areas

Angling is only permitted in the two areas set aside for this purpose. The Torra Bay angling area stretches for about 32 km along the coast, while the Terrace Bay area stretches from Steenbrasrif, 10 km south of Terrace Bay, to Seal Beach, 14 km north of Terrace Bay.

Visitors to Torra Bay may not enter the Terrace Bay angling area unless the necessary permit has been obtained in advance.

All anglers must ensure that they are fully acquainted with the regulations in respect of minimum sizes and bait regulations (see the box on pages 203 and 204).

Walks and trails

Since vehicular traffic is restricted to demarcated roads, there is no better way to discover the fascinating desert life and scenery of the Skeleton Coast than on foot.

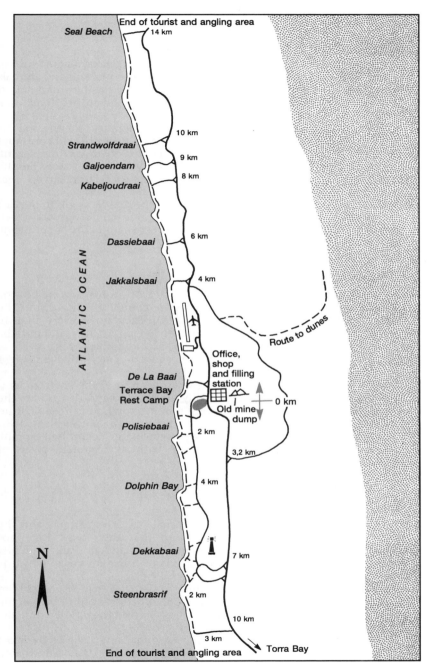

Terrace Bay

Uniab Delta and waterfall

A particularly rewarding area to explore is the Uniab Delta, 33 km south of Terrace Bay, where a series of springs creates a haven for birds and animals in an otherwise stark landscape. From the parking area at the pump station just west of the road it is a pleasant hour-and-a-half to two hour walk down to the sea and back to your vehicle.

About twenty minutes after setting off the highlight of the walk is reached. Here, crystal clear water cascades over a waterfall and continues down a narrow canyon which has been eroded to reveal bright pink sandstone. After a few hundred metres the canyon whittles away but, by continuing along the wide valley which the river has carved over thousands of years, you will soon reach the beach.

Do not neglect to explore the reedbeds and the shallow pools to the east of the parking area. Consider this as an alternative ramble on your return trip. Not only do the reed-fringed pools attract small herds of springbok and gemsbok, but also a variety of birds.

Wilderness trail

The more adventurous can join a three-day guided wilderness trail in the vicinity of the Ugab River Valley. Trails are conducted throughout the year, beginning on the second and fourth Tuesday of every month. Groups consist of at least six and no more than eight trailists, and must be self-sufficient in respect of all equipment, including backpacks, sleeping bags, clothing, water-bottles, eating and cooking utensils, lightweight stoves and food for three days.

The emphasis is on education and interpretation of the environment. The routes and distances covered daily are flexible and depend on the fitness of the group and the prevailing weather conditions. Although no set route is followed, the trail alternates between the gravel plains with their fascinating variety of lichens, spectacularly sculptured granite boulders, and the rugged Ugab Canyon with its contorted layers of schist, dolomite and marble.

Shipwrecks

The treacherous coastline was greatly feared by early mariners and the rusty relics of shipwrecks provide proof that their fears were not unfounded. On entering the Skeleton Coast National Park, the first evidence of this is the half-buried remains of a fishing vessel which is signposted some 16 km north of the Ugab River.

At Terrace Bay the cabin of the fishing vessel *Orca*, which sank 24 km north of Palgrave Point on 1 April 1978, now serves as a bar in the recreation hall. Only two of the crew of ten survived the ordeal, while the bodies of four crew members were never recovered.

Another interesting relic which can be seen at Terrace Bay is the mast of the *Dunedin Star* – the most famous of the Skeleton Coast shipwrecks.

The 13 000 tonne liner ran aground north of Angra Fria on the night of 29 November 1942 with 21 passengers and a crew of 85 on board. Fearing that the ship might break up, the captain decided to abandon her. After three trips to the shore the only motor boat was disabled and 63 people were stranded on the beach without any shelter and only a limited supply of food and water, while the rough surf prevented the remaining crew members from reaching the shore with the life-boats.

Three days later four rescue vessels arrived at the scene and the remaining 43 crew members were transferred to the *Manchester Division*.

At the same time another drama was developing a few kilometres north of Rocky Point. On her return journey to Walvis Bay, the rescue tug, *Sir Charles Elliot*, ran aground after a strong current forced her off course. Eighteen crew members eventually managed to get ashore safely while the first mate drowned. Another crew member, Mathias Koraseb, swam to the shore with two other crew members, but he died soon afterwards and his modest grave serves as a reminder of this episode.

The wreck of the *Dunedin Star* resting on a sandbank in 1942

A Ventura bomber was despatched from Cape Town to drop food, water and medical supplies to the castaways of the *Dunedin Star*. After dropping the supplies safely a suitable landing place from where the women and the children could be rescued was located, but disaster struck again when the Ventura became bogged down in loose sand while attempting take-off.

Another Ventura was flown up from Cape Town and, after dropping supplies to the crew of the *Sir Charles Elliot*, more supplies were dropped for the survivors of the *Dunedin Star*, as well as the four airmen.

An overland rescue operation was mounted by the police in Windhoek, but progress was slow and after four days the convoy was only halfway to the wreck.

The rescuers' trucks bogged down in the dry Hoanib River in December 1942

On 9 and 10 December the *Nerine*, anchoring as close inshore as possible, dramatically rescued 26 people with a life-boat and a surf-boat. This left 41 still stranded. Meanwhile, a second overland rescue team had set out from Windhoek and was spotted on 11 December at Rocky Point, six days after leaving Windhoek.

The first convoy came to within 3,5 km of the *Dunedin Star* on 12 December and had to complete the remaining distance on foot. The return journey, with both overland rescue teams, commenced on 14 December and it took another four days to reach Rocky Point from where eighteen castaways and five rescuers were evacuated by air. The remaining nineteen survivors were transported overland, arriving in Windhoek on 24 December, 26 days after their ordeal had begun.

Aircraft disasters

One of the mysteries of this treacherous coastline is the fate of Carl Nauer, a Swiss aviator, who took off in his aeroplane from Cape Town in August 1933 in an attempt to set a new record for the fastest solo flight between Cape Town and London. After refuelling at Walvis Bay, Nauer and his aeroplane were never seen again. Searches of both land and sea revealed nothing and it is believed that he crashed into the sea.

At Terrace Bay a simple stone monument has been erected next to the landing strip as a memorial to three members of the South African Police and two Consolidated Diamond Mining Company employees who were killed when their Alouette helicopter crashed into the sea on take-off on 21 April 1966.

Relics of attempted exploitation of resources

Rusty pieces of machinery and mine dumps serve as constant reminders of the numerous ill-conceived attempts to exploit diamonds, gemstones and even oil along the Skeleton Coast.

About 10 km south of Toscanini, a signpost indicates the turnoff to an old oil rig which was erected near the Huab River Mouth in the 1960s by the dashing entrepreneur Ben du Preez, despite warnings that it was highly unlikely that the venture would meet with any success. Today the rusty structure provides an ideal nesting site for a colony of Cape cormorants (56). Although breeding takes place throughout the year, the main breeding season stretches between September and March and visitors are requested not to venture beyond the parking area if the cormorants are breeding or roosting.

Toscanini was once the scene of a frantic search for diamonds, but all that remains today are numerous cement slabs where buildings once stood, and the remains of the diamond sorting plant close to the sea. At Terrace Bay the large mine dump behind the office complex provides further evidence of the feverish search for diamonds. Although diamonds were found they were not only small, but also widely scattered, and the mining company was eventually liquidated.

Vegetation

The vegetation of the Skeleton Coast National Park is predictably sparsely distributed. Amongst the most common species are dollarbush (*Zygophyllum stapfii*), brakspekbos (*Z . simplex*) and ganna (*Salsola* spp.) which favours river washes. Stands of this species are especially obvious west of the road shortly before you reach Torra Bay and east of the road a few kilometres south of Terrace Bay.

A large variety of lichens are also to be seen and you are unlikely to miss the bright orange lichens which cling to the rocks to the west of the road some 12 km north of Toscanini.

After good rains you might be fortunate enough to see clumps of *Mesembryanthemum cryptanthum* on the plains south of the Uniab River Delta. The leaves of this succulent resemble little puffed fingers and change gradually from green to red as they age, hence the local German name *Blutigefinger* (bloody finger).

Desert landscape

Covering some 4 200 km^2, the northern sand sea forms part of the Namib Desert which stretches between the Olifants River in South Africa and San Nicolau in southern Angola. The landscape in the southern section of the Skeleton Coast National Park alternates between flat gravel plains and low rocky hills occasionally interspersed with salt pans and small hummock dunes. Except for an isolated patch north of Toscanini, dunes are noticeably absent in the southern section of the park.

Dune fields traversed by rivers

Unlike the sand sea of the central Namib, the dune fields of the Skeleton Coast are traversed by several large seasonal rivers which act as barriers, resulting in the northern sand sea being far more discontinuous than the central one. Sand which accumulates in the river beds is periodically swept out to sea when the rivers come down in flood and it is carried north by the longshore drift and deposited further along the coast.

Barchan dunes

The first major dunes are encountered near Torra Bay where a sand-spit juts southwards from Terrace Bay. Keep a watch out here for the barchan dunes on the plains north of the Khorixas turnoff. These crescent-shaped dunes form where there is little sand, at right angles to the prevailing intermediate to high energy south-westerly winds, with their arms extending downwind. Depending on the size of the dune, it will move about ten metres a year northwards in the central sand sea, but movements of up to 75 metres a year have been recorded in the southern and northern sand seas.

High transverse dunes

Take the signposted turnoff 5 km south of Torra Bay to get a close-up view of the high transverse dunes which are formed by the prevailing strong southerly winds on the western edge of the sand sea. Closer inspection of the slip face here will reveal interesting abstract patterns which are formed by magnetite, a black iron mineral, in the sand. Equally fascinating patterns can also be seen on the hummock dunes.

More hummock dunes in the Uniab Delta

Continuing further north, good examples of hummock dunes can be seen in the Uniab Delta, where fairly large areas have been colonised by *Salsola nollothensis* and *Zygophyllum clavatum*. By extending their roots, these plants manage to prevent being covered by the windblown sand which accumulates on the small dunes, forming hummock dunes of up to three metres in diameter and more than two metres high.

Circular dune drive

At Terrace Bay those with four-wheel drive vehicles have the opportunity to drive into the dunes. Take the signposted turnoff 3,3 km south of the office complex and turn right again after 6 km. The circular route through the dunes is reached a short way on and is clearly marked with stakes. Although short, the drive is quite exhilarating. Return to the gravel surface tourist route and continue for 2 km in a north-westerly direction to join the main access route through the park north of the landing strip.

Game and small creatures

Although the larger mammals of the park are neither abundant nor varied, they are of special interest because of the harsh conditions to which they have adapted. The key to their survival is the occasional spring, and herds of springbok are usually to be seen at the Uniab Delta. Gemsbok too are resident in the Uniab Delta, but the population appears to have been isolated from those in western Damaraland. Not only is their colouring generally paler, but the mane of some animals is creamy instead of the usual black. Further inland the mountainous region supports herds of Hartmann's mountain zebra, while the more densely-vegetated upper reaches of the river valleys are inhabited by kudu.

Black-backed jackal

Black-backed jackal and brown hyaena are common along the coast where they scavenge for carrion and, until a few years ago, lion used to be rather unusual visitors to the coast. These so-called "coastal lions" did not permanently inhabit the coast, but moved between the interior and the coast along the river valleys where they came into conflict with herdsmen. Sadly they have all been hunted down. Although they were no different from other lions, their marine diet of beached seals and even whales made them unique.

Although unobtrusive, the numerous smaller creatures – lizards, beetles, chameleons – which have adapted to survive in this arid environment are of great interest to scientists. One such inhabitant of the dune fields is Skoog's lizard (*Angolosaurus skoogi*) which occurs only in the northern Namib and nowhere else in the world.

Birds

To date 224 bird species have been recorded, excluding 23 offshore and ten extra-limital species. Vagrants account for 56 species and are usually seen during winter when the strong easterly winds carry them out of their usual range, while 31 summer migrants have been recorded.

Coastal area

The most important habitat is the coast which supports more than 26 000 birds during the summer months. Sanderling (281) is the most common coastal visitor and can account for up to two-thirds of the total number of Palaearctic birds, while grey plover (254) and turnstone (262) are also well-represented. Whitefronted plover (246) is a common resident wader. Whitebreasted cormorant (55), as well as common (327) and Arctic (328) terns, are the most abundant non-waders along the coast.

Wetlands

The adjacent wetlands are another important habitat. Little stint (274) accounts for more than 50 per cent of the wetland Palaearctic migrants, while curlew sandpiper (272) is also common. The Cape cormorant (56) is the most abundant non-wader of the wetlands and can comprise up to two-thirds of the total number of non-waders.

Freshwater pools

Some of the most accessible and rewarding bird-watching places are the freshwater pools in the Uniab Delta. Species you could spot here include Cape teal (106), Cape shoveller (112), black crake (213), purple gallinule (223) and moorhen (226), while wood (266) and curlew sandpipers, and little stint (274) have been recorded during the summer months.

Ugab River wilderness trail

Trailists undertaking the Ugab River wilderness trail will be able to add several species that occur on the gravel plains, as well as those that favour cliffs, to their bird lists. Keep an eye out for Rüppell's korhaan (236), Namaqua sandgrouse (344) and Gray's lark (514) on the gravel plains and for tractrac chat (590) in rocky areas. Black eagle (131), augur buzzard (153), peregrine falcon (171) and rock kestrel (181) are four raptors you might spot on the trail. The reedbeds in the Ugab River are a habitat for a variety of warblers and weavers.

Northern section of Skeleton Coast National Park

The section of the park between the Hoanib and Kunene rivers (about 800 000 ha) has been set aside as a concession area and is, therefore, closed to do-it-yourself tourists.

Fly-in safaris

Visitors are flown into the area and are accommodated on a fully-inclusive basis at base camps from where trips are undertaken to places of interest by four-wheel drive vehicle. Tented accommodation is provided.

Although there is always a possibility of seeing game, including the desert-dwelling elephants, the safaris present an ideal opportunity to capture the exquisite scenery of the Skeleton Coast on film.

To join a fly-in safari contact: Skeleton Coast Fly-in Safaris, P O Box 2195, Windhoek, telephone (061) 224248, fax 225713. The after hours numbers are: telephone (061) 51269, fax 52125. As from 1 January 1994 Olympia Reisen Namibia will be the concessionaire for a ten-year period. The address of this company is: P O Box 5017, Windhoek, telephone (061) 225539.

Clay Castles, roaring dunes and seal colony

One of the highlights of this fascinating area is the Clay Castles of the Hoarusib Canyon, about 17 km upstream from the river mouth. These spectacular yellowish-white formations were sculptured when the river re-incised its course through silts, clays and fine-grained sands which had built up in the main river and its tributaries during a wetter phase in geologically recent times. Other attractions include the seal colony at Cape Frio and the roaring dunes south of the Hoarusib River. Although the phenomenon of "roaring" has not yet been fully explained, it has been suggested that it is caused by friction between sand grains when sand cascades down the slipface of a dune. The rumbling noise is especially common to barchan dunes and their crescentic shapes tend to intensify the sound.

"Roaring" occurs naturally, but can also be activated by a person sliding down the slipface and moving as much sand as possible with him or her.

References

Braine, S. (1988) 'Vagrants and range extensions found in and adjacent to the Skeleton Coast Park'. *Lanioturdus* 24 (1/2): 4 – 15.

Clinning, C.F. & Jensen, R.A.C. (1979) 'Additions to the bird check-list of Kaokoland and the Skeleton Coast'. *Madoqua* II (3): 247 – 253.

Davis, S. (1979) 'The naming of the Skeleton Coast'. *SWA Annual*: 141.

Penrith, M.J. & Loutit, R. (1982) 'Coastal anglers' catches at Terrace Bay during 1980'. *Madoqua* 13 (1): 35 – 43.

Ryan, P.G., Cooper, J. & Stutterheim, C.J. (1984) 'Waders (*Charadrii*) and other coastal birds of the Skeleton Coast'. *Madoqua* 14 (1): 71 – 78.

Ryan, P.G., Cooper, J. & Stutterheim, C.J. (1984) 'An annotated list of the birds of the Skeleton Coast Park'. *Madoqua* 14 (1): 79 – 90.

Schoeman, A. (1989) *Skeleton Coast*. Johannesburg: Southern.

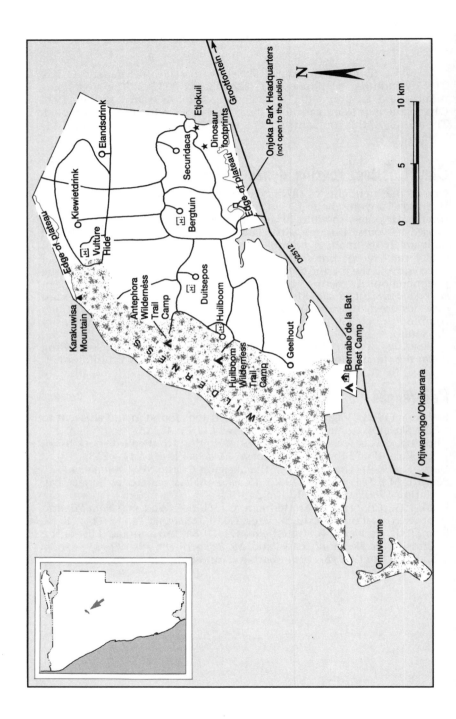

WATERBERG PLATEAU PARK

Size: 40 549 ha   Proclaimed: 1972

Location

Northern Namibia.

What to do and see

Guided game-viewing tours by vehicle, guided wilderness trails, self-guided wilderness trails and walks.

Climate

The summer months are hot, with temperatures of up to 40 °C, while daytime temperatures are pleasant during the winter months. Although winter nights are generally cool, sub-zero temperatures are not uncommon. About 85 per cent of the region's average annual rainfall of 500 mm is recorded between November and March.

When to visit

The park is open throughout the year. There is no restriction on entry and exit times for overnight visitors, provided entrance fees have been paid.

GUIDED WILDERNESS TRAILS: Second, third and fourth weekends from April to November.

Where to stay

Accommodation at the Bernabe de la Bat Rest Camp ranges from two-bedded tourisettes to one- and two-bedroomed bungalows sleeping three and five people respectively. Each bungalow has a kitchen equipped with a hot plate, kettle and fridge, but no crockery, cutlery or cooking utensils. There is also a shower, wash basin and toilet. Bedding, soap and towels are provided. Each bungalow has its own outside fireplace.

The grassy camp site laid out amongst tall *Acacia* trees will appeal to those who are seeking less sophisticated accommodation. Amenities include communal ablutions and a field kitchen.

Visitor amenities

Facilities at the Bernabe de la Bat Rest Camp include a restaurant, a kiosk which is open outside restaurant hours and a swimming pool at the *Rasthaus* complex. Adjacent to the reception office is a shop which stocks groceries, meat, liquor, wood and souvenirs.

SERVICE HOURS:
Office: 08:00 − 13:00 and 14:00 to sunset

Shop: 07:30 − 09:00; 11:30 − 14:00 and 17:30 − 19:30
(Monday to Saturday)
08:00 − 09:00; 11:30 − 13:30 and 17:30 − 19:30
(Sunday and public holidays)

Restaurant:
Breakfast: 07:00 − 08:30
Lunch: 12:00 − 13:30
Dinner: 19:00 − 21:00

Where to book

See page 13.

How to get there

Take the signposted turnoff to the park about 20 km south of Otjiwarongo on the B1 and continue for 19 km along the C22. Ignore the C30 which branches off to the right and continue for a further 22 km before turning onto the B2512. The turnoff to the park is reached after 18 km and the park office is 1 km further on. **Following heavy rains the last 18 km of the road to the park can become impassable and motorists are advised to telephone the park office [(0651) 3191] to check on the condition of the road before setting off.**

What you should know

☐ Although a filling station is planned for the rest camp, fuel is not currently available in the park. It is, however, obtainable at the farm "Okosongomingo", 25 km west of the rest camp during the following times only: Monday to Friday: 08:00 – 12:00 and 14:00 – 17:00 and on Saturday, Sunday and public holidays: 09:00 – 12:00 and 14:00 – 16:00. Alternatively you can obtain fuel at Otjiwarongo or Okakarara.

☐ Visitors may only enter the park via the gate to the Bernabe de la Bat Rest Camp, unless they are undertaking a guided wilderness trail, in which case they must report at the Onjoka Gate, 17 km further east. This gate is closed to all other visitors.

The Waterberg Plateau is one of the most spectacular features of the northern region. Towering some 200 metres above the surrounding landscape, the plateau with its sheer cliffs and fascinating rock formations is the habitat of several rare species of game and Namibia's only breeding colony of Cape vulture (122).

Although the park is a popular stopover for those travelling to the Etosha National Park or to the Caprivi Strip and Kaudom, visitors planning to spend a few days here will not be disappointed.

Guided tours

Because of the deep, soft sand on the plateau, visitors are not permitted to explore the area in their own vehicles, but guided tours in custom-built four-wheel drive vehicles are undertaken by conservation officials. Depending on demand, tours are conducted in the early morning or late afternoon, and a visit to the thoughtfully designed game-viewing hides is often a highlight of the tour. Remember to take warm clothing as it can be chilly on the open vehicles.

Guided wilderness trails

One of the best ways of exploring this fascinating park, however, is by joining a guided trail in the 18 000 ha wilderness area set aside on the plateau. Distances covered will depend on the fitness of the group but, as the emphasis is on education and interpretation, they generally do not exceed 15 km. Trailists meet at the Onjoka park headquarters at 16:00 on Thursdays, from where they are transported to the trails camp which serves as a base for the walks which are guided by an armed ranger. Trails end around midday on Sunday.

Self-guided trail

For the more adventurous a self-guided four-day (42 km) trail has been laid out on the plateau. Trailists follow a demarcated route, but as there is the possibility of an unexpected encounter with a rhino, this trail should only be attempted by experienced trailists. Overnight shelters with water are provided, but trailists must be self-sufficient in all other respects.

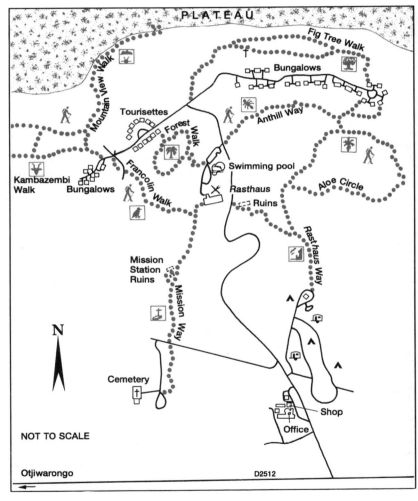

Bernabe de la Bat Rest Camp

Above: The Messum Crater, on the boundary of the National West Coast Recreation Area, is evidence of a volcano which was active 80 million years ago

Below: Cormorants roosting on the wreck of the *Winston* which ran aground in 1970 near the Ugab River Mouth, National West Coast Recreation Area (see page 207)

Above: The rapids at Popa Falls (see page 211)

Below: Rustic thatched huts provide comfortable accommodation at Popa Falls Rest Camp (see page 208)

Above: The formations beyond this dead tree are called the Clay Castles and are found in the Hoarusib River Canyon, Skeleton Coast National Park (see page 227)

Below: A fog bank approaches a pebble-strewn beach near Terrace Bay, Skeleton Coast National Park (see page 216)

Above: Hikers on the four-day self-guided trail in the Waterberg Plateau Park – eroded sandstone formations may be seen in the background (see page 232)

Below: A view of the sheer cliffs of the Waterberg Plateau from the Mountain View viewpoint (see page 233)

Easy walks

To encourage visitors to appreciate their surroundings and to reduce traffic, a number of easy walks have been laid out between the accommodation units, the *Rasthaus* complex and various places of interest in the Bernabe de la Bat Rest Camp. Each route is marked with a distinctive symbol and is indicated on a map obtainable from the park office.

Mountain View Walk

Not to be missed is the Mountain View Walk which winds up to the base of the perpendicular cliffs before making its way up to the plateau through a narrow kloof. The view is particularly impressive in the late afternoon when the lichen-clad cliffs are washed in shades of bright orange, ochre, yellow, luminous greenish-yellow and grey.

Kambazembi Walk

Do not be deterred by the fact that the Kambazembi Walk is the longest of the routes. Set aside two to three hours for this route which is mostly level along a well-defined path at the base of the cliffs.

Fig Tree Walk

The Fig Tree Walk is named after the large common cluster (66) or sycamore fig trees which are a highlight of this route. Set aside about an hour for this walk and if you walk quietly you might surprise a pack of banded mongoose scratching for food amongst the undergrowth.

Forest Walk

Instead of driving to the swimming pool you can take the short Forest Walk which links the swimming pool and the tourisettes, and which is an ideal activity on a hot summer afternoon. You pass under some magnificent weeping wattles (215) which are particularly attractive between September and December when they are covered with fragrant, bright yellow flowers. The enormous trees and lush undergrowth here are evidence of an abundance of water. Benches along the way invite you to spend some time in these tranquil surroundings.

Other walks

Visitors in the eastern group of bungalows can follow Anthill Way to the *Rasthaus* complex, while the Francolin Walk links the complex with the western bungalows.

Some of the trees along the walks have been marked with name plates and your experience will be further enhanced if you take a copy of the book *Waterberg Flora – Footpaths in and around the camp* (see page 239) on your walks.

Game

The main conservation objective of the park is the breeding of rare and endangered species with a view to restocking those areas where these species occurred historically. After the park had been proclaimed a wide variety of game was re-introduced. Roan were translocated from the Kavango, sable from western Caprivi, eland and giraffe from Mangetti, while blue wildebeest were transferred from the Daan Viljoen Game Park outside Windhoek. White rhino were obtained from the Natal Parks Board, common duiker came from Tsumeb and red hartebeest from a farm in the vicinity. The park also boasts the only herd of foot-and-mouth disease-free buffalo in Namibia, obtained from the Addo Elephant National Park in the Eastern Cape. Black rhino were re-introduced into the park from Etosha and Damaraland in 1989.

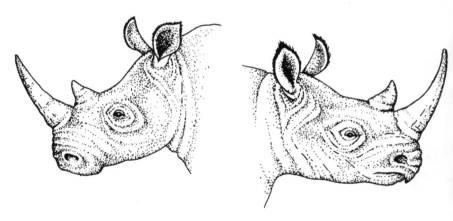

The heads of white (square-lipped) and black (hook-lipped) rhino

Other game species include tsessebe, black-faced impala, kudu, gemsbok, steenbok, klipspringer, warthog, chacma baboon and rock dassie. Predators include cheetah, leopard, black-backed jackal, side-striped jackal and caracal.

Pairs of the diminutive Damara dik-dik are regular visitors to the rest camp and you are almost sure to see them during the early mornings and late afternoons. At dawn or dusk you might also spot the agile South African lesser bushbaby amongst the dense vegetation in the rest camp.

Birds

Of the more than 200 bird species recorded in the park, seven Namibian endemics occurring here will be of particular interest to bird-watchers. Keep a watch out for Hartlaub's francolin (197), Rüppell's parrot (365), Bradfield's swift (413), Monteiro's hornbill (462), Carp's black tit (555), shorttoed rock thrush (583) and rockrunner (662).

The cliffs of the Okarukuwisa Mountain are the habitat of Namibia's only breeding colony of Cape vulture. Other species favouring this habitat include black eagle (131), booted eagle (136), augur buzzard (153), peregrine falcon (171), lanner falcon (172), rosyfaced lovebird (367), Alpine swift (418) and palewinged starling (770).

On the scree slopes you might be lucky enough to see Hartlaub's francolin, Monteiro's hornbill, shorttoed rock thrush, rockrunner, golden-breasted (884) and Cape (885) buntings, as well as whitetailed shrike (752). At night you might identify the yelping call of the freckled nightjar (408).

In the broadleafed woodlands on the plateau you might add Owambo sparrowhawk (156), Coqui francolin (188), Namaqua (344) and Burchell's (345) sandgrouse, Bennett's woodpecker (481), mousecoloured flycatcher (696) and white helmetshrike (753) to your list.

Cape vulture

One of the most important management objectives of the Waterberg Plateau Park is to ensure the survival of the only breeding colony of Cape vultures in Namibia.

Cape vulture

The Cape vulture is one of eight vulture species occurring in southern Africa, and it is endemic to the sub-region. This species used to occur widely throughout southern Africa, but the number of birds has declined alarmingly since the 1970s and there are probably less than 2 000 breeding pairs surviving worldwide. It favours open grasslands and can cover an area of up to 3 000 km² in search of food. The Cape vulture is a cliff-breeding species which nests in colonies of up to 300 pairs.

The Waterberg colony numbered about 500 birds in the late 1950s, but by 1970 their numbers were down to about 250 birds. Then, within ten years, the population crashed to about twenty birds and by 1987 the population had decreased to a mere fifteen birds.

Two main factors contributed to the rapid decline of the colony – bush encroachment and the indiscriminate use of poison such as strychnine by farmers to kill problem animals. The dense vegetation not only obscures carcasses, but also restricts access, as the high body mass to wing area ratio of the Cape vulture requires open ground of up to 100 metres for take-offs.

An extensive campaign to ensure the survival of this species in Namibia was launched by the Namibian conservation authorities. An intensive awareness campaign on the need to conserve the Cape vulture and the selective use of poison and alternative control methods was directed at farmers living in the area. This strategy has met with considerable success and "farmers' days" at Waterberg are highly successful.

Another strategy was to supplement the vultures' diet during the winter months, when food is naturally scarce, by placing carcasses of game species such as gemsbok and kudu near their breeding cliffs on a weekly basis. In addition, a long-term programme to revert bush-encroached land on the plateau to grassland by means of controlled fires was also initiated.

As a result of these strategies the population has increased to about 25 birds and there are currently five breeding pairs.

Vegetation

Waterberg Flora – Footpaths in and around the camp is recommended reading for those interested in the flora of the park (see page 239).

Trees of the mixed thornbush savanna at the foothills of the southern escarpment include worm-bark false-thorn (150), flame (160), blue (164), plate (165), camel (168), candle (170), sweet (172), false umbrella (174), black (176), red umbrella (181) and umbrella (188) thorns. Higher up the slopes enormous common cluster figs, weeping wattles and leadwood (539) have established themselves in the vicinity of the springs.

On the plateau silver cluster-leaf (551) is the most characteristic tree, covering more than half the area which is typically a tree and shrub mosaic. The centre of the plateau is dominated by the hairy red bushwillow (532.1) and shrubs like wild seringa (197) and gemsbok bean (*Tylosema esculentum*), interspersed by areas of open grassland. Characteristic species of the tree savanna community belt along the south-eastern edge of the plateau include wild seringa, weeping wattle, blue sourplum (102) and Kalahari apple-leaf (239).

Lichen-encrusted cliffs

The lichen-encrusted cliffs of the Waterberg are an often neglected feature of the Waterberg's flora. From a distance it looks as though a giant has splashed luminous green, bright orange and grey paint over the reddish-brown rock faces, but if you would like to get a closer look at this fascinating life form you should not neglect to do the Mountain View Walk.

Many of the more than 140 lichen species which have been recorded in the park are restricted to the cliffs where, together with wind, rain and temperature, they play an important role in shaping the rocks.

Flowering species and ferns

Eye-catching flowering plants include the flame lily (*Gloriosa superba*) and the white bauhinia (*Bauhinia petersiana*). Visitors are likely to be surprised to learn that ten fern species have been recorded in the park – one of which, *Cheilanthes dinteri*, is endemic to Namibia and Angola. While some of the hardy species are hardly noticeable during the dry winter months, others like *Microlepia speluncae* favour moist habitats and have fronds of over a metre long. They are especially prolific at the spring on the Forest Walk.

Geology

Another fascinating aspect of the Waterberg is its interesting geology and it is, therefore, not surprising that the conservation of a representative area of the geologically important Etjo Sandstone Formation is one of the management objectives of the park.

The Waterberg is an erosional relic of a sandstone casing which covered large parts of Namibia millions of years ago.

The lower Omingonde Formation was formed when sediments from the surrounding highlands were washed into a basin, which was then periodically partly covered by shallow water.

The upper Etjo Formation, on the other hand, was formed by wind-blown sand which filled the basin during drier climatic conditions. The cross-layered sandstone of this formation indicates that these winds blew mainly from the north-west and north-east.

Fossilised pre-historic reptile tracks

During this period, some 200 million years ago, some of the reptiles in the south-western part of the basin became extinct. However, in the north-eastern part of the basin some of the reptiles survived, leaving their tracks in the wet sand along the shores of scattered island lakes. These impressions became fossilised when they were covered by further sediments, and erosion has subsequently exposed evidence of these pre-historic reptiles on the Waterberg Plateau and near Kalkfeld.

Waterberg Plateau formation

During the closing stages of the Karoo Era, pressure in the earth's crust elevated the Karoo sediments south of an imaginary line that joins Grootfontein and Omaruru in a north-west/south-east direction, giving rise to a plateau stretching westwards for more than 300 km. Most of this plateau was carved up over countless aeons, but the resistant Etjo sandstone prevented the erosion of the Waterberg and a few other isolated mountains like the Omatako and Mount Etjo.

Springs

The sandy soils of the plateau have a low water retention capacity and consequently rainwater flows down the seams which formed in the Etjo sandstones during the earth's crustal activity. However, when the water reaches the impermeable mudstone band of the Omingonde Formation, it is forced to the surface at the base of the cliffs to emerge as springs.

History

The Waterberg region has a rich and interesting history.

Stone Age rock engravings

Rock engravings in the Karakuwisa Mountain provide evidence that Stone Age inhabitants were attracted to the plateau. The first whites to explore the region, Francis Galton and Charles Andersson, camped for a few days at one of the springs at the base of the mountain in 1851 and described it as

> ... a perfect paradise. We enjoyed it the more on account of the marked contrast it presented to the country we had previously traversed.

Here they found a few San people and the remains of a Hill-Damara settlement.

Pastoral tribes

Pastoralists, too, were attracted to the area and called it Otjozondjupa – "the Place of the Calabash". The legendary Herero chief, Kambazembi, was said to have kept 40 000 head of cattle in the Waterberg area and one of his kraals was situated within a kilometre of the modern rest camp.

Mission station

In 1873 a Rhenish mission station was established at Otjozondjupa, but during the 1880 Khoikhoi/Herero War the mission station was destroyed and it was only rebuilt in 1891. Five years later the German authorities established a police post at Waterberg. The ruins of the mission station can be seen a short way below the Rasthaus by taking a leisurely walk along Mission Way.

Graveyard

The graveyard below the rest camp is a reminder of Namibia's turbulent history during the late 1800s and the beginning of this century. Motivated by the fear of losing their land, the Hereros decided to take up arms against the Germans while the *Schutztruppe* were engaged in quelling a Bondelswarts uprising in the south of the country early in 1904. After several skirmishes, the deciding battle between the German *Schutztruppe* and the Herero took place at the Waterberg in August that year. The Herero were devastated and those who survived fled eastwards to the wastelands of the Omaheke sandveld, with some even seeking refuge in Botswana. The battle is commemorated every year on the weekend before or after 11 August by the Alte Kameraden, MOTHS, Pfadfinder, Boy Scouts and the Herero.

Rasthaus

Other reminders of this era include the foundations of the stables used by the *Schutztruppe* and the beautifully-restored *Rasthaus* which now serves as a restaurant. Built in 1908, the *Rasthaus* served as a police station until 1955 when it was converted into a guest house – a purpose it served until 1966, after which it fell into disrepair. Fortunately, however, it was restored to its former glory when the rest camp was built.

References

Andersson, C.J. (1987) *Lake Ngami or Explorations and Discovery during Four Years of Wanderings in the Wilds of South-Western Africa.* Reprint from 1967; first edition 1856. Cape Town: Struik, 153.

Craven, P. & Marais, C. (1989) *Waterberg Flora – Footpaths in and around the camp.* Windhoek: Gamsberg.

Directorate of Nature Conservation and Recreational Resorts (Namibia). (1989) *Waterberg Plateau Park – Birds.*

Mossolow, N. (undated) *Waterberg: Beitrag zur Geschichte der Missionstation Otjozondjupa, des Kambazembi-Stammes und des Hererolandes.* Windhoek: Mossolow.

SWA Department of Agriculture and Nature Conservation (undated) *Please Help Us Save the Cape Vulture.*

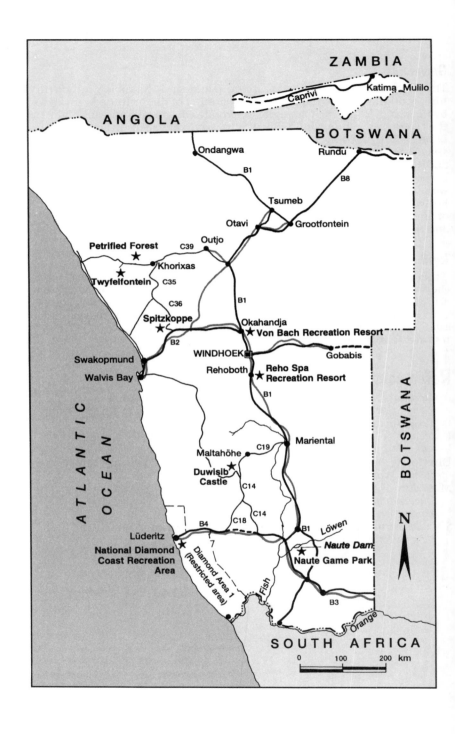

OTHER RESORTS AND PROPOSED CONSERVATION AREAS

Duwisib Castle

This imposing castle situated 72 km south-west of Maltahöhe dates back to 1908–9. Willi Sander designed the 22-room castle for the German nobleman Baron Hans-Heinrich von Wolf. It was restored in 1990 and much of the original funiture is displayed.

Facilities include picnic sites for day visitors and camp sites for overnight visitors.

National Diamond Coast Recreation Area

This area of approximately 5 000 ha is unique in the sense that it is Namibia's only conservation area which falls within the boundaries of a local authority. Surrounded by Diamond Area 1, it is centred mainly on the Lüderitz Peninsula and Agate Beach. The main attractions are sightseeing, crayfishing, angling, bird-watching, walking and picnicking.

Camping facilities are provided on Shark Island.

Naute Game Park

Proclaimed in 1989, this 23 000 ha game park is still undeveloped and appeals mainly to water sport enthusiasts and anglers. The focal point of the park is the Naute Dam, Namibia's third largest dam.

No overnight facilities are provided (1993).

Petrified Forest

(Proclamation under consideration in 1993)

Situated 42 km west of Khorixas, the Petrified Forest covers an area of approximately 65 ha. The site is exceptional because of the large number of petrified trees, but the combination of fossil trees and *Welwitschias*, which are often described as living fossils, makes the site even more remarkable.

Covered picnic facilities and a shaded parking area are provided.

Reho Spa Recreation Resort

The hot-water spring (39 °C) at Rehoboth has been developed as a recreation resort comprising a modern thermal hall, open-air swimming pool and cafeteria. Bungalows and camp or caravan sites are available.

Spitzkoppe

(Proclamation under consideration in 1993)

Also referred to as the Matterhorn of Namibia, the 1 728 metre high mountain is a typical pointed *inselberg* rising sharply from the surrounding flat plains. It is a familiar landmark seen on the northern side of the road when travelling between Usakos and the coast.

No facilities are available (1993), but there are several informal camp sites.

Twyfelfontein

(Proclamation under consideration in 1993)

Twyfelfontein, 105 km west of Khorixas, is without doubt the most significant rock engraving site in Namibia. Nearly 2 500 engravings have been recorded at seventeen main sites of which 32 per cent portray animals. Especially interesting are large images of elephant, rhino and a lion with spoor instead of paws!

Shady camp sites are available at the Aba-Huab River camp site, 9 km from Twyfelfontein.

Von Bach Recreation Resort

Von Bach Dam near Okahandja lends itself to a variety of water sports – water-skiing, windsurfing, yachting and canoeing, as well as angling. Visitors are free to explore the surrounding game park on foot.

Accommodation facilities include basic two-bedded huts (bedding not supplied) with communal ablutions, as well as a camp site.

BIBLIOGRAPHY

Where possible, references have been listed at the end of each conservation area. The following general references and field guides were, however, consulted throughout.

Berruti, A. & Sinclair, J.C. (1983) *Where to Watch Birds in Southern Africa*. Cape Town: C Struik.

Coates Palgrave, K. (1977) *Trees of Southern Africa*. Cape Town: Struik.

Giess, W. (1971) 'A preliminary vegetation map of South West Africa'. *Dinteria* 4.

Jankowitz, W.J. (1975) *Aloes of South West Africa*. Windhoek: Division of Nature Conservation and Tourism, Administration of South West Africa.

Louw, G.N. & Seely, M.K. (1982) *Ecology of Desert Organisms*. London: Longman.

Maclean, G.L. (1984) *Roberts' Birds of Southern Africa*. Cape Town: The Trustees of the John Voelcker Bird Book Fund.

Muller, M.A.N. (1984) *Grasses of South West Africa/Namibia*. Windhoek: Directorate of Agriculture and Forestry.

Newman, K. (1983) *Newman's Birds of Southern Africa*. Johannesburg: Southern.

Olivier, W.A. & Olivier, S.W. (1993) *Visitors' Guide to Namibia*. Johannesburg: Southern.

Raper, P.E. (1987) *Directory of Southern African Place Names*. Johannesburg: Lowry Publishers.

Skinner, J.D. & Smithers, R.H.N. (1990) *The Mammals of the Southern African Subregion*. Pretoria: University of Pretoria.

Smithers, R.H.N. (1986) *Land Mammals of Southern Africa – A Field Guide*. Johannesburg: Southern.

Von Breitenbach, F. (1986) *National List of Indigenous Trees*. Pretoria: Dendrological Foundation.

Weather Bureau, Department of Transport (1986) *Climate of South Africa: Climatic Statistics up to 1984*. Pretoria: Government Printer.

Williams, A.J. (1987) *Popular Checklist of the Birds of South West Africa/Namibia*. Windhoek: Department of Agriculture and Nature Conservation.

Further reading

The following books on Namibia were not consulted, but are recommended for further reading.

Bergot, S. & Robert, E. (1989) *Namib Dawn to Twilight.* Johannesburg: Southern.

Hall-Martin, A., Walker, C. & du P. Bothma, J. (1988) *Kaokoveld – The Last Wilderness.* Johannesburg: Southern.

Helbig, L. & Hillebrecht, W. (1992) *Growing to Nationhood: The Witbooi.* Windhoek: Longman Namibia.

Jacobsohn, M. & Pickford P. and B. (1990) *Himba – Nomads of Namibia.* Cape Town: Struik.

Kinahan, J. (1992) *Pastoral Nomads of the Central Namib Desert.* Windhoek: New Namibia Books.

Lambrechts, H.A. (1985) *Namibia – A Thirstland Wilderness.* Cape Town: C Struik.

Reardon, M. & Reardon, M. (1984) *Etosha – Life and Death on an African Plain.* Cape Town: C Struik.

Reardon, M. (1986) *The Besieged Desert – War, Drought, Poaching in the Namib Desert.* London: Collins.

INDEX